The Secret Scroll

Also by Andrew Sinclair

FICTION

The Breaking of Bumbo
My Friend Judas
Gog
Magog
King Ludd

NON-FICTION

Prohibition: the Era of Excess
The Better Half:
the Emancipation of the American Woman
Jack London
John Ford
The Other Victoria
Dylan the Bard
War like a Wasp: the Lost Decade of the Forties
Francis Bacon: His Life and Violent Times
The Sword and the Grail
Jerusalem: the Endless Crusade
The Discovery of the Grail

The Secret Scroll

ANDREW SINCLAIR

Birlinn

This edition published in 2002 by
Birlinn Limited
West Newington House
10 Newington Road
EH9 1QS

www.birlinn.co.uk

First published in the United Kingdom in 2001 by
Christopher Sinclair-Stevenson, London

Reprinted 2004 (twice)

ISBN 1 84158 219 0

British Library Cataloguing-in-Publication Data
A catalogue record for this book is available from the British Library

Printed and bound by
Antony Rowe Ltd, Chippenham

Contents

To the Clan Sinclair,
in which past and present and
future are all one

Prologue

FOR TEN YEARS, I have been making a voyage of research and discovery. Hundreds of books have been written on the Ark of the Covenant and the Garden of Eden, the Holy Grail and the Dead Sea Scrolls. All of them confuse fact with speculation. There are said to be sacred bloodlines from the union of Jesus Christ with Mary Magdalene and their children. There are, perhaps, cosmic patterns linking temples and churches and megaliths and peaks in the Near East and the South of France. A claim has been staked for the finding of the Ark of the Covenant in Ethiopia. The Grail has been sighted serially across the Levant and Europe and even in North America. The Dead Sea Scrolls and Essene mysteries deriving from earth-mother worship in Egypt have spawned claims that these reached the Knights Templars in Jerusalem and Europe and Scotland. The lost city of Atlantis has been located in Peru and off Land's End. How will this ever end?

I hope in this book. I am a trained historian. I deal in probability, backed by fact, rather than speculation. I intend to demonstrate how the ancient Gnostic heresy of the personal vision of God came with the Knights Templars and the Cathars and the medieval Grail romances into the early Masonic movements, which now have tens of millions of followers. The secret lies in the Kirkwall Scroll in Orkney, where the answer would be revealed. At last, the mysteries of the Ark and the Garden of Eden and the Grail were to be explained by this vast Scroll, hanging as Christ once did, but now in a Masonic Lodge on an island in the North Atlantic ocean.

Roots are rarely important to youth, and middle age tends to be preoccupied with present families. Old aunts or cousins delving into genealogies seem little better than cranks. Only when your children begin to look like their predecessors do you begin to wonder about the distant links of your ancestry. Edmund Burke called it the great chain of the living and the dead. Although I had a recognition at Muirfield golf course near Edinburgh in Scotland when I was twenty years old, I had done nothing to pursue the history of my family. At that age, I knew no better or worse.

National Service in the Coldstream Guards, so far as I was concerned,

1

consisted in doing public duty in a red tunic and a bearskin hat – guarding Buckingham Palace and St James's Palace and the Bank of England, and their contents. War was not a part of it. The army had it on file that I was a golfer, or tried to be. Accordingly, I was asked to be the fifth and last member of the regimental team in the Army Championships at Muirfield. When I arrived in the club house, the rest of the team, a major-general, a colonel and two majors, hooted at me, a poor ensign. Over the chimneypiece of the main room hung a portrait of William St Clair of Roslin. Although he wore knee breeches, a red coat and a black hat and carried a wooden baffy, his face was the spitting image of my own, long and hangdog, the four lines of melancholy splitting both of our faces from nose to lower cheek, from mouth to chin.

Later I would find out about him, the last of seven centuries of male St Clairs, who had ruled at Roslin Castle, but now had only daughters to marry off. A member of the Royal Company of Archers, the royal bodyguard for Scotland as I was in England, he was a founder of Muirfield in the late eighteenth century, and also admired by Sir Walter Scott, who wrote of him:

> The last Roslin was a man considerably above six feet, with dark grey locks, a form upright, but gracefully so, thin-flanked and broad-shouldered, built, it would seem, for the business of war or chase, a noble eye of chastened pride and undoubted authority, and features handsome and striking in their general effect, though somewhat harsh and exaggerated when considered in detail. His complexion was dark and grizzled, and as we schoolboys, who crowded to see him perform feats of strength and skill in the old Scottish games of Golf and Archery, used to think and say amongst ourselves, the whole figure resembled the famous founder of the Douglas race . . . In all the manly sports which require strength and dexterity, Roslin was unrivalled; but his particular delight was in Archery.

The similarity with my ancestor had slipped my mind, when I went out on the tee in the morning. I performed in the Army Scratch Competition in the early hundreds. The officers in my team were in despair. Yet in the matchplay, erratic Andrew Sinclair struck two rounds in the low seventies. For the first time since they had marched south to restore Charles the Second to the throne, the Coldstream Guards had won a coup or a cup in the north. The major-general in charge summoned me to a drink that night, knowing that I was leaving shortly for Cambridge and another career. Would I stay on for a third year and the next army tournament with promotion and pay? I admitted I was a reluctant soldier and said that I had never pulled a trigger once in the last eighteen months: I had been guarding Her Majesty and fooling around with debutantes in the Season. The major-general looked at me with twinkling contempt, and said, 'Whoever joined the army to fight?'

I felt small, very small. Of course, the Coldstream Guards were the bravest of the brave as well as serving as the royal guardians, as the St Clairs had long done in Scotland. Yet I did not accept the offer and went on to be a historian at Cambridge and Harvard, and the other admirable institutions of learning which taught me to analyse past facts and put the chosen ones in a credible order. No paragraph without proof; no speculation without confirmation. I did not know in those early days that I was being prepared for a quest into my own roots as well as into the Grail and the Garden of Eden. In a strange way, the personal may inspire the inspirational, the particular may push towards the general. If I did not join the army to fight, I have pursued this cause to the finish.

I

A Templar Stone

Seem'd all on fire that chapel proud,
Where Roslin's chiefs uncoffin'd lie.
Each Baron, for a sable shroud,
Sheathed in his iron panoply.

Sir Walter Scott,
The Lay of the Last Minstrel

WE HAD LEASED the redstone Rosslyn Castle for two weeks, a crusader stronghold built to protect Edinburgh from the enemies of Scotland. Its modern spelling had superseded Roslin, just as St Clair had become Sinclair. Roslin had meant Rosy Stream, perhaps a reference to the Blood of Christ, while St Clair in Latin had been Sancto Claro or Holy Light. Yet before going to Rosslyn Chapel on the hill above the moat, I had noticed in the drawing-room of the restored part of the castle a white engrailed cross on the stucco ceiling, the emblem of the medieval St Clair barons, and a huge white scroll, gathered on a wooden wheel. Once unrolled, it was seen to be covered with the signatures of all the Lodges of Scotland to their Masonic Grand Master, an Earl of Rosslyn in the Victorian age. These appeared strange testimonies to an unknown heritage. The castle windows looked down past flying ravens to the green glen of the Esk, flowing to the Firth of Forth and the North Sea.

Then I visited the fifteenth-century Rosslyn Chapel and I asked the sympathetic and knowledgeable curator Judith Fisken about possible connections with the Templars, the Knights of the Temple of Solomon. She seemed reluctant to say much; Rosslyn Chapel was a part of the Church of Scotland, the Templars had been condemned as Catholic heretics and their Grand Master had been burned at the stake. Although there were two branches of the Order of the Temple of Solomon in existence in Scotland, Freemasons had always held an ambiguous position within the Christian Church. I was shown, however, a mounted knight with a lance carved on a boss by a chapel window: behind him, an angel bearing a cross. Later I was brought to a carved Templar Seal of two hands opening a curtain to reveal the device of the Lamb of God with the Cross, and also of Pegasus, the winged horse of the Greek

5

gods and a Templar symbol. I also saw a carving of a group carrying the 'Mandylion' of Christ's head on a banner, thought to be taken from the Veil of St Veronica or the folded Holy Shroud of Turin.

On this first visit, I was merely shown marks scratched on the wall-stones by the masons who had built the chapel in the fifteenth century. The eight-pointed crosses were said to be crosses of rededication. Legend had it that an apprentice had built an ornate pillar in the chapel while the master mason was absent on a pilgrimage in Rome. He, enraged on his return at the excellence of his pupil's work, killed the youth with a blow to the head. Abandoned in a dark corner I also found an obscure oblong slab, small enough to be the tombstone of a dwarf. Crouching down in the gloom, I could just make out the design of a sword carved upon it, also some octagonal tracery at its head like the outline of a rose window.

A month later, a rubbing was made of the stone by an expert, using flower and vegetable dyes – petunias and marigolds from Rosslyn churchyard, also woad and red cabbage, rhubarb and beeswax. The stone revealed clues to some mysteries, but suggested many more. The small tombstone was the first to be recently discovered with the Grail carved upon its length. Inside the communion cup was an eight-pointed cipher of the Templars in the shape of an 'engrailed' octagon with a rose at its centre – a reference to the Holy Light within Christ's blood. The cup bore the name of the dead man, carved in Lombard lettering Willhm De Sinncler. The base of the Grail or chalice formed the pattern of the steps to the Temple of Solomon.

Moreover, the corrupted spelling of the name of the man who had been buried under the stone was included within the bottom of the Grail. The last two letters of his name, E R, had been turned up at a right angle in the set-square of the Templars and the Master Masons. E R usually signified in the Middle Ages Et Reliquiae, Latin for And His Remains or Relics. The battle sword that ran down the other side of the stem of the cup had a hilt that curved down at either end, characteristic of knights' swords in the first part of the fourteenth century, when Lombard lettering was inscribed on tombstones. While the communion cup of the Grail signified the grave of a Scottish Master of the Temple, the stone seemed to date from a time after the Templars had been dissolved and their leaders had been tortured and burned alive in France.

The knights and masons of the period were mostly illiterate, and names were rarely spelt consistently in the Middle Ages. The tombstone was certainly that of a William de St Clair of Rosslyn. It had been removed from the original Collegiate Church of St Matthew, which is situated in the graveyard below the present chapel – only two of its buttresses survive. Although the name of William was common in the St Clair family at the time, the dating of the sword hilt and the lettering pointed to one particular Sir William de St Clair, who fought with Robert the Bruce at Bannockburn and died in 1330, while taking Bruce's heart in a silver casket to be buried at Jerusalem. Surrounded by the Moorish cavalry in Spain, he and Sir James Douglas and two other Scottish knights had flung the casket into the enemy ranks, and had charged the whole Muslim army and been slaughtered. Their courage had so earned the respect of their foes that the Heart of Bruce and the relics of the four knights were returned to the sole Scottish survivor, Sir William Keith, who took them back to their native land. The Heart of Bruce was buried at Melrose Abbey and the heart of Douglas at his family chapel, while the bones of William de St Clair were apparently buried at Rosslyn. The remains of the Templars were often interred in the position of the skull over crossed leg-bones, an important symbol in their ritual and later Masonic ceremonies. If William de St Clair, as a Master of the Temple, were buried in this fashion, the small size of his tombstone was explained.

Visiting the Douglas chapel later, I found the embalmed heart of Sir James Douglas still on show beneath the floor in a casket of silver and lead, set beside the gigantic effigy of the heroic knight, who seemed even taller than my ancestor described by Scott, the William St Clair of Roslin, archer and golfer. Opposite lay the stone figures of his great-grandson, the fourth Earl of Douglas, the husband of Beatrice St Clair, who became the mother of four more Scottish earls. A broken Templar gravestone in the chapel proved the Douglas connection with that Military Order as well as with the St Clair family, both strong supporters of Robert the Bruce. I also found drawings of buried tombstones at the chapel and cemetery of Old Pentland near to Roslin and endowed by Sir William de St Clair. These showed foliated Templar crosses incised within circles, stems leading down to the steps of the Temple of Solomon or to an upturned chalice base, swords on both, but a measuring rod on the left of one stone. The connections between the Templars and the St Clairs were beginning to be revealed in geography and carvings.

Exploring Rosslyn Chapel further, I found it a medieval stone herbal, bursting with carved vegetables and leaves and fruits. At the east end, steps led down to a crypt, probably the site of the earlier eleventh century chapel and castle. On the walls were scratched architectural designs to aid the masons who had built this extraordinary holy place. One of these designs demonstrated how the cross-section of the building conformed to the sacred geometry of the encircled octagon and crossed triangles, which were used by the Templars in the construction of their churches and castles.

The present chapel had been built by the third St Clair Earl of Orkney. He had brought craftsmen from all over Europe to construct his building to the glory of God. His personal crusade, he had made it a work unique in its symbolism and profusion of styles. Nordic and Celtic influences as well as Templar and Masonic iconography decorated this one wing of an intended cruciform church that was never completed. The famous Apprentice Pillar within the chapel was as pagan and Gnostic as it was Christian. At its base, eight octagonal serpents with their tails in their mouths surrounded an apparent stone tree-trunk, which supported the roof. This was clearly Yggdrasil, the tree of Norse myth that held up the heavens from the earth, which itself was kept together by a serpent or dragon twining its body nine times round the circumference of the world. The mysterious chapel also referred to the Tree of Life as well as to the Tree of the Knowledge of Good and Evil in the Garden of Eden, for the serpent with its tail in its mouth was not only Lucifer, but also part of the secret wisdom of the Cathars and the Templars. The Apprentice Pillar derived from Nordic myth in spite of the four strands of stone that twined as ivy about it, probably a posy to the Four Gospels.

A similar accretion of Christianity overlaid the carvings in the rest of the chapel. The representation of a man with a wound in his forehead was associated with the legendary apprentice who had carved the pillar and was killed by his master mason. In fact, he appeared to represent Hiram, the biblical builder of the Temple of Solomon. The legend of the murdered apprentice seemed only a Christian cover story for an apocryphal saint and martyr, who had inspired the Military Order of the Temple of Solomon and all Masonry with its symbols of the sword and the trowel, the compasses and the maul. There were also twenty small Temples of Solomon carved about the walls, as well as a poem by Sir Walter Scott about twenty St Clair knights held to be buried in the hidden vaults, who burned at Pentecost with sacred fire.

To see Rosslyn Chapel was to see Christ on the Cross overlaid on pagan beliefs. There were dozens of carvings of the wild face of the Green Man with serpents and stems of green leaves erupting from his mouth. For that was the wonder of this curious chapel. On every pillar, from each architrave and boss, the plants of the earth multiplied and replenished the innumerable carvings. I might have been watching the Third Day of Creation in stone, the day before the God of Genesis made man in His own image. Each one of these lush and distinctive fruits and herbs and leaves had its symbolic meaning in medieval herbal and arcane lore. Nobody had begun to unravel all the designs. They merely proved that the architect and designer of Rosslyn Chapel, William St Clair, was privy to the Gnostic and cabbalistic knowledge of the Templars and the alchemists and their believers.

I was stimulated in this quest by the remarkable Niven Sinclair, a distant cousin from Caithness and a man of decisive action and belief. He was obsessed with the Templar connection with the St Clair family, in particular with Henry St Clair, the first Earl of Orkney as well as Rosslyn, said to be an early colonist of North America. Commissioned to do a film with a book on the subject, I committed myself to proofs of that connection. I looked for more evidence carved in stone near Roslin, with the aid of the erudite Templar archivist in Scotland, Robert Brydon. At Currie, south-west of Edinburgh on the Water of Leith on a bridle-path from Roslin over the Pentland Hills, the Templars had built an industrial base, using river-power to grind flour and crush iron and silver ore from their Hilderston quarry near Linlithgow. In fragments outside the Georgian church there lay broken carved stones, recently unearthed and set as a border to the path. Two of them were Grail and Templar stones, the chalice ending in the steps of the Temple of Solomon. One of them had a strange and beautiful cup, containing two circles with an opening between them, as if Christ's blood were pouring down into the hollow stem of the Grail. On one side, a dirk was incised, on the other a knight's sword with rounded pommel and square hilt. The other chalice enclosed five circles within a star, the symbol of the Virgin Mary: only one sword was carved on the stone with a triangular pommel and down-curving hilt. Two other broken tombstones showed the Templar octagonal cross within a disc-head, while one was incised with a mallet and a compass on either side of the stem of the Grail cup.

Within the church was another Templar knightly tomb engraved with sword and cross, but on either side of the church door, two primitive burial stones had been set, probably of lay brothers or squires attached to the Military Order at Currie. Both showed rough Templar octagonal crosses within jag-toothed circular heads, and both had hilts protruding from a stem that carried down the stone to an oblong base scratched with lines. They bore a pair of scissors or shears to the left, while one had a dirk with a double hilt to the right. The tools suggested work at woollen or building trades, although the dagger showed a military role as well.

I also discovered a church at Corstorphine near Edinburgh, with Templar and St Clair tombs and a hidden Grail. Sir Adam Forrester

9

had founded the chapel fifty years before the new chapel at Rosslyn, and had married Jean, the daughter of Henry St Clair, the first Earl of Orkney. Forrester still lay beside his wife on a tomb in the chapel, she in a long dress with stone pleats, her Bible clasped in her hands. Below her was carved the St Clair coat of arms of ship and Engrailed Cross, matched by the Forrester arms of three bugles. On the opposite wall of the church was set a huge Templar stone with a cross fleury inside a circle and a stem leading down to the steps of Calvary and the Temple of Solomon: a crusader sword was etched by its side. By the priest's door another memorial stone was inscribed to a medieval chaplain named Robert Heriot. Its only ornament was a chalice or Grail, which looked like two triangles set on end with the world as a ball dropping within. On the first floor of the church in the old tower, a fireplace was set on high to lead travellers by night to safety across the marshes.

My quest for Templar stones continued across the Firth of Forth in Fife. At Westkirk near the ruins of the Cistercian abbey of Culross, a cemetery and a roofless chapel lay among pastures and wheatfields. Masonic gravestones of the eighteenth century filled the graveyard as at Currie and Corstorphine with their symbols of the skull and cross-bones and the hourglass of time as well as the tools of the trade – plumb and hammer, maul and set-square. At Westkirk, shipwrights were also buried, so that the stones showed sailing vessels and carpenters' planes as well as hammers. Their ancestry was proved in a remarkable way. Three Templar tombstones had been used as lintels for the doorways of the ruined chapel. And beside the swords and the stems of flowering crosses leading down to the steps of the Temple of Solomon were carved a hammer-axe and a set-square above a measuring-rod. In four churchyards near the Firth of Forth, Templar tombstones, sometimes showing building tools, were to be found near the grave slabs of the later Masons of Scotland, often with the same mechanical shapes carved on the stone.

At the old Cistercian abbey of Culross nearby, the octagonal rib vaulting of the chapter house was in the style of Templar architecture. The white monks were heavily engaged in the wool and salt trade for Baltic timber. The merchant's house of Sir George Bruce at Culross Harbour was called 'The Palace': on its inner wall was the insignia of the Guild of Hammermen and Shipwrights, which met in a panelled room where there was a painting of the Temple and the Judgement of Solomon. As at Westkirk, there appeared to be a direct link between the Military Order of the Temple of Solomon and the beliefs of the later Masons and Lodges of Scotland. Again in the Magdalene Chapel in Cowgate in Edinburgh, there were stained-glass windows of the fifteenth century depicting Hammermen with their emblems and the Temple of Solomon. In paint as well as in glass and stone, the link between the Templars and the Masons began to be proven.

I discovered another Grail and Templar stone in the Commendator's House of Melrose Abbey. The dark crimson ruins of this Cistercian institution, the first of that Order in Scotland, was founded seven years after Hugues de Payens had come to the country in 1129 to initiate the Templar centre at Balantrodoch. Melrose had been built on the southernmost tip of a swathe of land stretching up to Edinburgh that included another major Cistercian foundation near Dalkeith at New-battle and the St Clair lands in the Pentland Hills. Even smaller than the Rosslyn Chapel Grail stone, the Melrose one bore a different design. Inside the cup of the chalice was a small eight-pointed cross fleury within a large eight-pointed foliated cross. An elongated dirk pointed down beside the stem of the cup to the base, again depicted as the steps of Calvary and of the Temple of Solomon. The name of the dead knight was lost and not engraved on the stone.

Nearby were other fragments from Templar graves, floral crosses contained within a circle or a disc-head, and a boss of the five-petalled rose and the symbol of the Virgin Mary. Another boss was carved with clam-shells, the emblem of the pilgrimage route to Compostela in Spain, which had been guarded by the Military Order of the Knights Templars. A diagram showed the octagonal roof arches of the original central vaulting of the abbey, signifying the Trinity and its offshoots. This was reminiscent of the Templar practice of 'working the octagon' to reveal the secret of its ritual and its architecture. A lead badge belonging to a monk from the abbey was in the form of a rebus, a play on the word melrose, showing a mason's mallet or *mel*, which contained a *rose*. A mason with his mallet was also carved on the exterior walls of the chapel.

The connection between the Templars and the Cistercians as the architects of their age was further emphasized in the abbey, where the master of the works in the mid-fifteenth century, John Morow, had left his mark on the lintel of the doorway to the wheel-stair – a shield charged with two mason's crossed compasses and a fleur-de-lys. This device was surrounded by an inscription: SA YE CVMPAS GAYS EVYN ABOVTE S VA TROVTH AND LAVTE SALL DO BVT DIVTE BE HALDE TO YE HENDE Q° IOHNE MORVO. (As the compass goes evenly about, so truth and loyalty shall do without doubt. Look to the end quoth John Morow.) Morow also left another inscription, declaring that he was in charge of the mason's work in six major Scottish ecclesiastical buildings, and he prayed to God And Mari Bathe & Swete Sanct: Iohne

11

To Kepe This Haly Kyrk Fra Skathe. Mary and St John were also venerated by the Military Orders as the protectors of holy places from harm. The exuberance of some of the carvings on the ruined chapel at Melrose, poppies and roses and a Moor's head along with devil's masks and Green Men, also suggested the influence of Morow on his contemporary Sir William St Clair, who built Rosslyn Chapel with its profusion of stone ornaments.

The *Chronicle of Melrose*, the principal monastic record of medieval Scotland, ran for a hundred years between the late twelfth and late thirteenth centuries. Its most interesting entry dealt with the disinterment of its second abbot Waltheof, to whose relics was ascribed the power of working miracles. When his lead coffin was opened, his body was discovered to be uncorrupted, probably because it had been embalmed. More proofs of this technique were buried in the abbey, and recently verified by exhumation. On a low wall by the ruins, a plaque read: An Embalmed Heart Within A Leaden Casket, Supposed By Many To Be The Heart Of King Robert Bruce, Is Interred Nearby. This was the Heart of Bruce, which the William de St Clair beneath the Grail tombstone in Rosslyn Chapel was carrying to Jerusalem when he died in Andalusia, charging ahead of Sir James Douglas and other Scottish knights into the heart of the massed Moors. He was showing that berserker streak in the Norse and Norman St Clairs which made them rush to an almost certain death. The Templars had that recklessness in battle which often resulted from a willingness to surrender the life of the flesh in support of a just cause.

In the three centuries between the reigns of the Scottish King William the Lion and James the Second, the St Clairs signed fifteen charters and grants of land concerning Melrose Abbey. Sancto Claros in Latin, their names were also spelt DE S, DE SCO, DE SCO CLER, DE SCO CLARO and SANTCLER. One was a Viscount of Edinburgh, one a Bishop of Glasgow, and one a Rector and two Archdeacons of Melrose Abbey at the time of their kinsman St Waltheof in the twelfth century. The documents usually asked God to bless 'the Virgin Mary of Melrose and the monks there'. Henry, the father of the William de St Clair of the Grail tombstone, had also helped to win the Battle of Bannockburn with his brother, the fighting Bishop of Dunkeld, and he signed three charters at Melrose for Robert the Bruce as well as the Scottish Declaration of Independence at Arbroath. The last charter signed by the family before the abbey was finally destroyed at the Reformation bore the name of the William St Clair who was the builder of Rosslyn Chapel. The *Munimenta de Melros* were proof of the close connection between the Kings of Scotland, the St Clairs from Roslin, the Knights Templars and the Cistercian monks. The monastic Order in its white habits and the Military Order in its white cloaks and red crosses were founded in the same age and sponsored by the same saint, Bernard of Clairvaux. Both were architects and builders. In their example and ritual, the ancient crafts and guilds of Scotland might well have had their roots.

To find the roots of the family genes and the reason for a hereditary and gloomy look that seemed to bear the impress of the medieval knight in *The Seventh Seal*, I went to the origin of the name St Clair on the borders of Normandy. I had discovered that we were an Orkney breed from the Norwegian Møre line, who controlled some of coastal Norway, the Orcadian Isles and Caithness in Scotland. The founder of its power was Earl Rognvald, celebrated in saga and folk memory. While one of his sons, Torf Einar, took over the Orcadian Isles and became the father of the formidable Thorfinn the First, another of Rognvald's sons – Rolf the Ganger or Rollo to the French – was outlawed by the King of Norway and took a marauding expedition down the North Sea to conquer most of Brittany and Normandy. On the Epte river, he concluded the Treaty of St Clair in 911 with King Charles the Simple, whose daughter he married after he was converted to Christianity. He refused to be a vassal and to kiss the King's foot. 'Not so, by God,' said this Viking seaman, who performed the act of homage by raising the royal foot to his rude mouth and toppling the seated King.

The saint who had given his name to St Clair-sur-Epte was a Scotsman called Guillermus or William, a favourite Christian name of the later Lords of Rosslyn. He lived at the beginning of the seventh century in a cell near a well, the waters of which were held to cure eye diseases. Healing wells were always associated with St Clair; there would be one dedicated to St Catherine near Roslin. Guillermus was executed for refusing the advances of the local Salome. The well still exists by the river Epte, surveyed by the statue of St Clair holding his severed head in the palms of his hands. His cult became widespread in Normandy, perhaps because the treaty ceding the land to the Vikings had been signed in his native town, and also because he resembled the beheaded St John the Baptist, revered by the Military Orders for his sacrifice. Across the Epte, the Møre cousins, who were left to guard the borders against a French attack from Paris, took the name of St Clair and built a castle with a round keep. Its ruins still dominate the lush cornfields that roll down to the little river that runs into the Seine.

Another two legendary saints of Normandy and Brittany were also called St Clair. The first was held to have been the founder of the Holy See of Nantes in the first century. He was said to have been converted

13

by Drennalus, the disciple of Joseph of Arimathea who had brought the Holy Grail to Glastonbury Abbey in the West Country of England. And indeed, the ragged cross of the arms of the Bishops of Glastonbury would become the St Clair family emblem, although in its quarterings, sailing ships would be substituted for its two cruets or Grails catching the blood and sweat of Jesus Christ. A holy healing well at St Cleer in Cornwall, which existed until the Victorian age, also attested to his journey and his powers. Another St Clair associated with the founding of the See of Nantes was dated to the third century, sent by the Pope to convert northern France with the nail used to pierce the right hand of St Peter at the time of his crucifixion. As with the blind St Longinus, who recovered his vision at the foot of the Cross, this St Clair was invoked for the restoration of eyesight. Until the French Revolution, his skull was venerated in a silver reliquary, an example of the head worship of the Knights Templars and the time.

Without divine sanction, Rollo made himself the first Duke of Normandy. By his second wife, Poppa, he had a son, William Longsword, the second Duke, who extended Norman control as far as the Channel Isles. He granted further lands to his St Clair cousins and hunting reserves near Cerisy. The Bruce family, which had also accompanied Rollo from the Orcadian Isles, was given grants in the Contentin. These two Norman neighbours were to play an important role in later Scottish history. William Longsword's son Richard, the third Duke of Normandy, had a son Mauger, who became the Count of Corbeil. His eldest son Richard became the fourth Duke and had another son called Mauger, the first to take the title of the Count de St Clair. After serving as the Archbishop of Rouen, he was given the jurisdiction of the town of Saint-Lô and the land to the north between the rivers Vire and Elle. He built a castle and a church in his domain, giving his foundations the name of St Clair and himself the title. The castle was to be destroyed in the Hundred Years' War, the church to be rebuilt in the nineteenth century, while the river Elle disappeared in cattle ponds.

Walderne was the second son of the first Count de St Clair. With his two brothers, Hamon and Hubert, he opposed the rise of the bastard William to the dukedom of Normandy after the death of his father, Robert the Devil. Hamon and Walderne were killed at the Battle of Val-es-Dunes, which gave a victory to the future William the Conqueror. Walderne was reputed to have married Helena, a daughter of the Fifth Duke of Normandy, and thus to have been a cousin of the Conqueror. Certainly, the surviving brother Hubert de St Clair was received back into favour and joined other nephews and cousins in the expedition to conquer England. Nine knights bearing the name of

St Clair fought at the Battle of Hastings; one of them was recorded by Wace in his *Roman de Rou* as having charged with three other knights 'a body of the Angles who had fallen back on a rising ground, and overthrew many'. They were richly rewarded by the Conqueror and became some of his instruments in the rule of England.

Before the conquest, the Normans had many contacts with the ancient Saxon and Cerdic royal house of Wessex and England. A Cerdic King Ine had founded the monastery at Glastonbury, later associated with the legend of King Arthur and the Knights of the Grail – the cup holding the Blood of Christ which Joseph of Arimathea was supposed to have carried there. The last of the Cerdic kings, Edward the Confessor, had a Norman mother and ran a court permeated with Norman influence. Indeed, Walderne's youngest son, William de St Clair, was attached as a youth to the English household of Margaret, the granddaughter of Edmund Ironside, who was buried in Glastonbury. During her exile to Hungary after the Battle of Hastings, he would serve as her cupbearer and travel with her in her later marriage to the King of Scotland.

These first discoveries about the Templars and my Viking and Norman roots at Roslin were only signs by the wayside. I saw through a glass darkly; the more I knew, the less I perceived. How did the Templars become the Knights of the Grail as carved on the Rosslyn tombstone? How did they reach Scotland after their trials and excommunication? What were the mysterious principles of sacred architecture and the symbols which lay behind the overwrought St Clair chapel? Some evidence had begun to emerge on my journeys to Lothian and Fife and northern France. Yet now I had to pursue the quest to sacred places in Italy and southern France, in Israel and Jordan. Books, in particular, had to be my foundation. Without research, you may not understand what you see. As yet, I knew little about Gnosticism, the great heresy, and what the Templars had to do with it.

2

The Hidden Inspiration

Do not think that the resurrection is an illusion. It is no illusion, but it is truth. It is more suitable to say, then, that the world is an illusion.

From *The Epistle to Rheginos*,
a Coptic-Gnostic text from Nag Hammadi

GNOSTICISM IS A SERIES of secret beliefs. Wherever there has been orthodoxy, the holders of these hidden mysteries have been declared to be heretics. They share a common faith, that the Adept may make a direct approach to the Wisdom of God. He or She need not reach grace and understanding through a priest or a church. By leading an exemplary existence in a present world of evil, the perfected few will be received into an eternal life on another sacred plane. Official worship is at the best a delusion, at the worst, the work of Satan. For only the Gnostics perceive the true ways to heaven.

The word 'Gnostic' comes from the Greek *Gnosis*, meaning higher knowledge. As the original four Gospels were written in that language, the term was applied to the many thinkers who examined the teachings of Christ and His disciples in the centuries of Roman persecution before Constantine founded an imperial Christian Church in the second Rome of Byzantium with bishops to impose their interpretation of the scriptures on the faithful. From the fourth century to the present day, in convocations and congresses and curias, in anathemas and inquisitions and curses, the Greek and the Roman orthodox faiths have insisted on sorting the good texts from the bad, the sheep from the goats of inspired writing. The Bible is the sifted gravel on the prescribed track to God. Gnosticism is the condemned delta of the eastern tributaries flowing from the infinite essence of the divine.

A city on one of the mouths of the sacred river Nile, indeed, was the source of Gnosticism. Alexandria was the confluence of Egyptian mythology and the apocalyptic fervour of Jewish sects, of the cosmic struggle between God and the Devil of Zoroaster as well as the spiritual searches of Plato and his followers, of Near Eastern astrology and alchemy intermingled with Hellenistic geometry and mathematics. These ancient speculations and traditions infused the ongoing inquiry into the meaning of the life and death and words of Jesus. The past bubbled inside this seething vat of Christian commentary in a fervid mixture of the old and new.

From Egypt and Greece the original alchemists and astrologers, who until the Renaissance were to serve as the scientists of Europe, merged Thoth and his ibis head with the winged Mercury, and called them one Hermes Trismegistus, the inscriber of divine truths on emerald tablets. The goddess Isis, the wife of Osiris, was also remembered as the carrier of arcane knowledge from nature and the realm of the dead; also Ishtar from Mesopotamia, the sister and lover of the shepherd Tammuz: then Astarte, the bride of Baal, and Cybele, the Earth Mother of Asia Minor. All of these feminine principles of life would be recreated by the Gnostic prophets as Sophia and as Mary Magdalene, the new Eve who had listened to the wisdom of the Serpent, another cult from the Nile. The endless struggle described by Zoroaster between the ruler of light and the prince of darkness depicted the earth as the arena of devils in battle against a host of angels. These were strong streams in Gnostic thought.

Further currents reached Alexandria from the cults of Mithras and Orpheus and the Eleusinian mysteries. They involved a sacrificial resurrection through rising towards energy and fire. Another source was the prehistoric Samothracian rites of the Tau Cross in the shape of a Greek T, promising a rebirth as a trinity in one being. The Platonic vision of the cave, which perceived human existence as the mere shadow of the spiritual flame, was joined by the radical and otherworldly asceticism of the Essenes, now believed, following the discovery of the Dead Sea Scrolls, to have influenced Jesus himself. These elements were parts of the heady brew of the early Christian mystics and prophets in their attempt to approach religious verity.

Prominent in the second century was a visionary teacher Valentinus, who made a reputation for himself first in Alexandria, then later in Rome. He preached a spiritual illumination, said to derive from the secret lessons of Christ and St Paul, revealed in apocryphal texts known as the Gospels of Thomas, Philip and Mary Magdalene, and in the *Dialogue of the Saviour* and the *Testimony of Truth*. Extracts from these writings, translated from Greek into Coptic, were discovered at Nag Hammadi in Upper Egypt at the end of the Second World War, two years before the Dead Sea Scrolls and the Essene fragments came to light. These Coptic texts contained many of the later heresies of Christianity, stating that the Virgin Birth and the Resurrection of the Body were only symbols, that the Serpent was wise in Eden in giving the apple of knowledge to Adam and Eve in spite of the jealousy of

God, and that Jesus loved Mary Magdalene more than all the disciples, kissing her often on the lips. In *Thunder, Perfect Mind*, she became the Sophia, the feminine principle of divine knowledge, the first and the last, honoured and scorned, a holy prostitute, wife and virgin and barren with many sons.

The surviving pages of another Gnostic text, *The Epistle to Rheginos*, began by stating that there were some who wanted to learn much, but they were occupied with questions which had no answers. They had not stood within the Word or Logos of Truth. They sought their own solution, which could only come through Jesus Christ, who had denied death, which was the law of humankind. "Those who are living shall die. How do they live in an illusion? The rich have become poor and the kings have been overthrown, everything has to change. The cosmos is an illusion." All was a process, the transformation of things into newness. The Truth was Jesus and the Word and the passage of the spirit to eternal life.

The unknown authors of these early works chose insight rather than the sermons of early Christian bishops to interpret the Gospels and reach revelation. On this count they were denounced in the late second century by Irenaeus, Bishop of Lyons, for 'inventing something new every day'. His chief target was Justin Martyr, who had been a Stoic and a Platonist before becoming a Christian philosopher. Justin praised the heresies of Simon Magus, while treating Christ as the Logos or Word, Who mediated between the sinful earth and the light of heaven. Simon Magus, indeed, had claimed that Genesis and Exodus mystically represented the womb of Paradise and the placenta of Eden. The passage of the Red Sea was that of all living things in blood from the feminine divinity. These inspirations were called Gnosis, which now came to mean a personal vision, a direct and individual perception of truth. The first appearance of Jesus to Mary Magdalene after his Crucifixion in the garden was interpreted in her apocryphal Gospel as no actual event or even a spiritual flash: she saw Him in her mind. This vision she reported to His disciples. They could now see the risen Christ as she had; any believer could see Him. When questioned by the disciple Peter, Mary denied that she lied, and Levi defended the truth of her vision, saying, "If the Saviour made her worthy, who are you to reject her?"

Of course, the direct approach to Christian revelation put in doubt all religious authority. Why listen to a bishop if an inner voice told you what Christ wanted you to do? Already in St Mark's Gospel, it was stated that Jesus had given the disciples the secret of the kingdom of God, while He spoke to the rest of the world in parables. While Saints

Peter and Paul professed to pass on these secrets to the churches later established in Rome and Byzantium, the Gnostic Gospels claimed that the living Jesus could at any time reveal His hidden mysteries to a woman who was not a disciple, to a Mary Magdalene or to any of her successors through her immediate experience. He would show Himself to the person who was fit to see and hear the divine message.

For the Gnostics, there were two distinct worlds, split by a war zone and a veil between heaven and earth. On the shining and dividing screen were the pictures of things, created by the Logos or Word and interpreted by Christ. Flaming walls separated wisdom from matter with angels as messengers across the horizon between sky and sea and land. For many Arab and medieval Christian geographers and astronomers, the preferred shape of the world and the planetary system was the ancient Tau Cross with the top of the T marking the boundary between the profane and the sacred, between the temporal and the eternal. The Tau had also been the last letter of the Hebrew alphabet, and so signified the end of this plane of existence. In his celebrated world map of the thirteenth century, William of Tripoli would follow the works of the Arab geographer al-Qabasi in treating the upper stroke of the Tau as an equator, below which lay Africa and Europe, while above was the Holy Land and the fabled Eastern areas ranked under the arch of heaven towards Paradise, which was set within the rising sun.

The Tau Cross became the symbol of the first Military Order, for its patron saint Anthony had been crucified upon it. Left a large estate by his rich Christian parents in Egypt in the third century, Anthony gave away his inheritance to the poor and took to the life of a desert hermit. Tormented by sexual fantasies and the loss of secular power, he offered a spiritual example to the rich. Privation was his direct path to divine knowledge. He exercised his soul and mortified his body as a solitary in order to fire an inner light and revelation. He was the icon in the Near East for feudal barons who took up the Cross, swearing to renounce the flesh and the Devil and all his works.

The Florentine and Venetian Order of Altopascio was founded in 1056 before the First Crusade and took the Tau Cross as its insignia. The Order had one foundation in Scotland at Leith beside a monastery dedicated to St Anthony. These Scottish knights also built a chapel on Arthur's Seat by Edinburgh, where their seal with the Tau Cross and the figure of the Egyptian hermit is still preserved in the Advocates Library. The holy relics of the ascetic had allegedly been discovered during the reign of the Emperor Justinian and carried to the Church of John the Baptist in Alexandria, from where they were removed in

1070 to Vienne by Joscelin of Poitiers, another case of eastern mysticism reaching western chivalry before the Christian attempt to regain Palestine from Islam.

For the Normans who were descended from the Vikings, another cosmic tradition complemented the Tau Cross. This was the myth of the sacred tree Yggdrasil, which held up the Nordic heaven from its hell, with Middle Earth dividing the gods from the demons and kept within its circle by a wise serpent girdling the circumference and eating its own tail. Dragons and snakes were frequently incised above the cross of the sword hilt and emblazoned on shields as in the Viking and Norman St Clair family crypt and chapel at Roslin. Carved as late as the fifteenth century, the cosmic and spiral Apprentice Pillar was given a knot of serpents coiling about its base.

Moreover, the fear and veneration of the snake had been insinuated into the most ancient illuminations. In the Egyptian myth of the creation of the world, the serpent Âapep was the ruler of the underworld, pitted in eternal struggle with the sungod Rê and trying to swallow the divine river Nile until it ran dry. Among Mesopotamian peoples, the writhing Illouyanka was in conflict with the tempest god, while in Semitic legends, the divine ruler Baal was eaten by the devil python Mot, which was forced to disgorge him before he could be assembled to reign again. The wily serpent in the Garden of Eden had also condemned humanity to sin in the Jewish and Christian faiths, while Aaron's rod and Jehovah's fiery serpent given to Moses attested to the persistent power of the satanic snake in early beliefs. These wise serpents, often with wings and crowns, would become key symbols in medieval alchemy; in the *Practica Musice* of 1496 by Gafori, a cosmic snake would even link the seven planets to the four elements of Earth, Air, Fire and Water, bringing the music of the spheres to Apollo and all living things, as the python or Pythia had brought prophecy and the Muses to the interpreters of the oracle at Delphi.

Without appreciating its significance at the time in the pattern of my quest, I discovered that the crest worn in tournaments in the fourteenth century by another crusading Henry St Clair, the first Earl of Orkney, was the head of a great serpent or dragon with a crown round its neck to hide the join to the peak of the helmet. Its shape was that of the monstrous heads which had topped the curved prows of the longships of the Vikings, when they had crossed the seas to set up the Norman empire in Britain, France and the Mediterranean, and to spearhead the conquest of Jerusalem. On his shield, as the *Amorial de Gelre* of Flanders showed, Earl Henry also bore the Engrailed Cross with its ragged edges. The heraldic devices which he chose, with their allusion to the myths of the Great Worms, bore evidence of his Nordic inheritance, as well as of the Gnostic faith in a wise serpent – beliefs also designated by his grandson for the base of the Apprentice Pillar in Rosslyn Chapel.

Curiously, I then discovered that the crusading father of the Venetian Procurator Carlo Zeno, who had saved embattled Venice from the Genoan fleet and encountered Earl Henry in Denmark before sending his brothers to aid him in a proposed Northern Commonwealth, was called Pietro Zeno 'the Dragon' for his courage in conflict. He had carried that emblem on his shield when serving as Captain-General of the Christian Confederation against the Turks in the Levantine wars.

Behind the logistics of the military assault on the little-known Near East, a strange cosmogony and geography had inspired the crusaders. For they believed that Jerusalem was a heavenly city as well as an earthly one, and that they might achieve the light of paradise by battling the dark forces of Islam below. They did not reckon that many of their doctrines derived from the enemy places and peoples encountered in this holy war in the East. And certainly they could not foresee that they would turn their weapons on themselves, to exorcize in blood and fire the condemned heresies that were to spread back through Bulgaria and the Balkans past the Alps to Provence, where the Cathars or Perfect Ones would become the Adepts of the West.

THE EARLY CRUSADES

The First Crusade, which ended in the creation of the Kingdom of Jerusalem, had been preceded by many others in Spain and Norman Italy. The Popes had used the Normans to make war on their enemies, particularly the German emperors. When an anti-pope was installed in Rome, Pope Gregory VII had called on the Norman freebooter and lord of southern Italy, Robert Guiscard, to leave off his attack on Byzantium or Constantinople and return to restore him to power in the Eternal City. The Normans treated Rome as brutally as had the Huns, pillaging and burning and even selling many of its citizens into Muslim slavery. Yet their forcible reinstatement of Gregory as pope excused the crime. The rape of the most sacred Christian city after Jerusalem was justified by the motive for the deed.

The death of Pope Gregory in 1085 opened the way to the First Crusade against Jerusalem. The new pope, Urban II, had met the most charismatic preacher of the time, Peter the Hermit, at Bari on his return from a pilgrimage to Palestine. Peter had been a French monk from Amiens and was said to look like his donkey; but his sermons and his visions were compelling. He swore to Pope Urban that he would 'rouse the martial nations of Europe' in the holy cause of aiding Constantinople against the Turks and retaking the Christian shrines of the Holy City from Islam. The Pope held a council at Piacenza in 1095, where the Byzantine emperor Alexius Comnenus sent envoys to plead for help. He followed it with a second synod at Clermont in south-central France, where his chances of attracting the support of the Frankish warlords would be greater, and where the masses inspired by Peter the Hermit and his fellow preachers might congregate to hear the call.

Behind the call for a crusade lay millennial yearnings. The Byzantine Church of the Holy Sepulchre in Jerusalem had been destroyed by the Fatimid ruler al-Hakim, who saw himself as the Mahdi, an avenging archangel for Islam, the counterforce to the warrior saints James and Michael. Seen as the Anti-Christ by the Catholic Church, he personified the spirit of Evil that now, a thousand years after the eschatological visions of Saint John the Divine on Patmos in the Book of Revelation, was to be confounded in the final struggle with the Good, which had been foreseen by the Persian sage Zoroaster and later by the Manicheans. The seizure of the Holy City would be the prelude to this final battle against Satan and lead to the sovereignty of God.

An aristocrat from the court of Champagne as well as a Cluniac monk, the Pope Urban believed in sacred wars fought for the faith by his old countrymen. His proclamation of a divine mission to aid the rich Byzantines and seize back Jerusalem was pitched to the ears of his audience. The Eastern adventure combined strategy and hope of salvation, greed and penitence, risk and absolution. Urban invoked the words of Jesus from the text of St Matthew: "And every one that hath forsaken houses, or brethren, or sisters, or father, or mother, or wife, or children, or lands, for my name's sake, shall receive a hundredfold, and shall inherit everlasting life." This verse, used habitually for the induction of monks, was now used to recruit soldiers who were expected to behave as monks with swords, believing that the hundredfold they would receive could be measured in rewards on earth.

When the Pope's address was finished, the crowd shouted, *"Deus hoc vult!"* (God wills this!) This shout of approval was for the expansion of Europe in the name of a religion that united it in spite of its schisms, a search for the mystical city where the founder of the Faith had died and risen to heaven. Jerusalem was the focus of creed and of spiritual quest; it was set in the words of the prophet Ezekiel 'in the midst of the nations and countries that are around her'. The Holy City was the magnet, too, for the scattered tribes of Israel and Christian pilgrims. As Isaiah had declared of Jerusalem, "The mountain of the Lord's house shall be established in the top of the mountains, and shall be exalted above the hills; and all nations shall flow unto it." When the words of the Bible were a matter of literal belief, the call for a crusade to Jerusalem was an exhortation as well as a battle cry. This was the opportunity to forsake a brutish life in medieval Europe for the place where God came down to his Chosen People on earth, where the Second Coming might be provoked after the reign of the infidel Anti-Christ, where the Saviour and the prophets of the Holy Book were buried, and where the gates of the heavenly city and Paradise awaited their opening.

After his rousing sermon, Urban went on a recruiting mission in Provence and on to Poitiers and the Loire and Tours before crossing the Alps to return to the Papal See. The first magnate to join, Count Raymond of Toulouse, wanted to lead the holy venture. He enrolled knights mainly from the South of France, although northern barons were also induced to take the Cross. William the First of England had flown a papal banner in his Norman 'crusade' in 1066 for the conquest of his new kingdom. He used this occasion to send to the Near East the two leading rivals to his authority, Robert, the Duke of Normandy, and the Anglo-Saxon heir and pretender, Edgar Atheling, who had spent many years as a refugee in Hungary and had accompanied his sister Margaret to Scotland for her marriage to King Malcolm Canmore. A devout Catholic, she had brought with her a piece of the True Cross or Holy Rood, which was placed in a chapel of that name in Edinburgh. Its guardian was her Norman cupbearer, William de St Clair, now known as 'the Seemly' because of his demeanour and appearance – "well proportioned in all his members, of middle stature, fair of face, yellow hair'd."

King William of England did not relish the Atheling claimants to his crown over the Scots border, and he persuaded Edgar to leave for Apulia in Italy with two hundred knights. At the approach of the First Crusade, Edgar recruited further support from his and his sister's vassals in Scotland, particularly in Lothian near the court in Edinburgh. One of these was Robert, the son of Godwin, a cousin of the King Harold killed at the Battle of Hastings. Another was the son of the royal cupbearer by the daughter of the first Earl of March. Henry de St Clair had been granted lands on the Pentland Hills south of Edinburgh to defend Holyrood and the royal treasures from English attack: one of these would kill his father, who died in a berserker charge on enemy raiders. These Scottish crusaders joined Edgar Atheling in Italy, while four professional armies marched overland past the Balkans to Constantinople and on through Asia Minor to besiege Antioch. These expeditions were led by Raymond of Toulouse and Godfrey de Bouillon,

23

Duke of Lower Lorraine, and his brother Baldwin, and the two Roberts, the Duke of Normandy and the Count of Flanders. Edgar Atheling and his northern knights, however, sailed to Constantinople to pick up supplies for the crusading forces at the walls of Antioch, before sailing on to the strategic port of Lattakieh, which they seized and handed over to Robert of Normandy to keep in trust for the Byzantine emperor.

After the fall of Antioch in 1097 and the mysterious discovery of the Holy Lance, which had pierced the side of Christ and cured the blindness of the Roman centurion Longinus, now revered as a soldier saint by the crusaders, the combined Christian forces proceeded through Syria on the improbable conquest of Jerusalem. They were only preserved on their journey to the outskirts of the Holy City by the bickering and quarrels between the local Muslim enemies. When Jerusalem fell to their hymns and siege-towers, and to the sound of the trumpets which had caused in the Bible the walls of Jericho to come tumbling down, there was a terrible slaughter. One Arab contemporary wrote that the population of the Holy City was put to the sword, and the Franks spent a week massacring Muslims, mostly in the al-Aqsa mosque where they had fled for sanctuary. According to another Arab commentator, "The Jews had gathered in their synagogue and the Franks burned them alive. They also destroyed the monuments of the saints and the tomb of Abraham, may peace be upon him!" The invaders expelled the oriental Christian priests, Greeks, Copts and Syrians alike, from the Church of the Holy Sepulchre, torturing some of them to make them reveal where they had hidden the True Cross.

The earthly Jerusalem was cleansed by the crusaders in an orgy of violence. They also sacked the mosque of Umar, built to commemorate the second successor of the Prophet Muhammad. Ironically, Umar had saved the Church of the Holy Sepulchre when he had entered Jerusalem. As he was escorted by the Greek Patriarch round the Christian holy places in the city, the time for Muslim prayer arrived when he was present in the Church of the Holy Sepulchre. Although the Patriarch agreed to his praying there, Umar realized that if he worshipped within the church his followers would make it into a mosque. So he knelt and prayed outside, and a mosque in his name was built on that spot. This mosque was now destroyed by the crusaders, who were still far from learning that accommodation with other religions which their civilized Arab enemies were to teach them.

Of the leading Christian Military Orders founded in the Near East – the Knights of the St John or the Hospitallers, the Knights of the Temple of Solomon or Templars, and the Teutonic Knights – the Templars would become the stuff of medieval Grail romances and

Wagnerian operas as well as the historical protectors of pilgrims to the holy places. Their role was to defend the faith and to live the life of armed monks in the manner of the ascetic religious warriors of their Muslim enemy, the Sufis and the Isma'ili sects. At the Muslim Dome of the Rock in Jerusalem in 1118, the nine original founders of the Templars, led by Hugues de Payens of Champagne, took their sacred oath to serve as protectors of the pilgrims to the Christian holy places. They transformed the al-Aqsa mosque into their headquarters and built a chapel there modelled on the Church of the Holy Sepulchre which, lying below their citadel, was guarded by the Knights Hospitaller of St John, the defenders of the site of the tomb of Christ.

Through Count Hugues of Champagne, Hugues de Payens had been to Byzantium in 1104 and had encountered the Gnostic Order of the Brothers of the East, founded by the diplomat Michael Psellos, with its grades of Grand Master and Adepts and Disciples. The successor of Psellos, indeed, took the name of the divine priest-king Melchizedek, and from him Payens learned of their practices. Of the nine knights who formed the first members of the Order of the Temple of Solomon, three were connected with the court of Champagne – Hugues de Payens, Geoffroy de Saint-Omer and André de Montbard, uncle of St Bernard of Clairvaux, who would promote the Order to its rapid ascendancy. Both the third and the fifth Grand Masters of the Order, Everard de Barres and André de Montbard, would give up their leadership to return to Clairvaux as monks. Of the other six founding knights, Payen de Montdidier and Achambaud de St-Amand were connected to the court of Flanders, while Geoffroy Bisol, Gondemare, Rosal and Godefroy appear to have been wandering poor knights who found themselves in the right place, while Baldwin the First was crowned as King of Jerusalem.

The legend that these nine protectors of pilgrims did little for nine years led to later beliefs that they had spent their time excavating holy treasures such as the Ark of the Covenant. But had their good service not been proven, neither the Kings nor the Patriarchs of Jerusalem would have ensured their rapid rise and recognition in western Europe in 1129 at the Council of Troyes, where St Bernard was their advocate. Also important in their early success was Fulk of Anjou, who succeeded Baldwin the Second as the King of Jerusalem, and played a decisive role in the election of the second Templar Grand Master, Robert of Burgundy and Anjou. By means of the papal bull, *Omne datum optimum*, the Military Order became independent of local control and answerable to the Pope alone. Priests could even be received into the Order on probation and dismissed after a year if they refused to sanctify Templar practices. The knights became a state within the state, the Grand Master a king among kings.

St Bernard of Clairvaux had been a neighbour of Hugues de Payens and was the promoter of the fledgling Military Order as the lance and armour of his Cistercian white monks. He had much to do with writing the official Rule of both Orders, although the Templar battle-cry came from the prologue of the Benedictine Rule used by St Bernard in his treatise *De Laude*: "Not for us, Lord, not for us, but to Your name may glory be given." The most able political priest of his age, St Bernard oversaw the rapid expansion of the Templars and the Cistercians, siting military commanderies and monasteries often side by side. Both the saint and the Templar Grand Master went on recruiting tours to bolster their alliance. The *Anglo-Saxon Chronicle* described the success of Hugues de Payens in 1128 in Britain:

> In this year Hugues of the Knights Templars came to the king (Henry the First) in Normandy from Jerusalem; and the king received him with great ceremony, and sent him thereafter into England, where he was welcomed by all good men. He was given treasure by all, and in Scotland too; and by him much wealth, entirely in gold and silver, was sent to Jerusalem. He called for people to go out to Jerusalem. As a result more people went, either with him or after him, than ever before since the First Crusade, which was in the days of Pope Urban.

King David the First of Scotland gave Hugues de Payens the land for the Scottish headquarters of the Military Order. There was no coincidence in the site. Balantrodach, now called Temple, was only six miles away from Roslin Castle, where the St Clairs protected Edinburgh from English attack from the south. Married into the St Clair family before he took his vows of chastity, Hugues de Payens made Balantrodach one of the first of the six hundred properties which the Templars would acquire in Scotland. On his return from the First Crusade, Henry de St Clair and his son Henry by the drowned Rosabelle, daughter of the Earl of Stratherne, had become the defenders of the southern marches and commanders for David the First, who began the building of Holyrood Abbey and House around the chapel, which held the precious relic of the True Cross brought from Hungary. The St Clair family at Roslin would continue to serve as guardians of the sacred treasures and as canons at the neighbouring abbeys of the white monks at Newbattle and Melrose; they also held religious posts at Selkirk and Kelso, Dunkeld and St Andrews, Dornoch and Dunfermline. The Templars maintained their ascendancy over the Scots crown. According to Ailred of Rievaulx, King David "committed himself to the counsel of religious men of all kinds, and surrounding himself with very fine brothers of the illustrious knighthood of the Temple of Jerusalem, he made them guardians of his morals day and night." By the thirteenth century, indeed, a Templar was always the almoner of the royal household.

Most important for the Order, St Bernard secured from Rome recognition of the Templars as defenders of the Temple Mount and all Christian pilgrims. "These warriors are gentler than lambs and fiercer than lions," Bernard wrote of them, "wedding the mildness of the monk with the valour of the knight so that it is difficult to know what to call them: men who adorn the Temple of Solomon with shields instead of crowns of gold . . . They come and go at a sign from their commander; they wear the clothes which he gives them, seeking neither garments nor other food. They are wary of all excess in food or clothing, desiring only what is needful. They live all together, without women or children . . ."

In Jerusalem, the Templars put their chargers into the ancient caves below the Temple Mount, known as the Stables of Solomon. The neighbouring octagonal Dome of the Rock was believed by pilgrims to be the original Temple of Solomon and was shown on the seal of the Grand Master of the Military Order. The knights would absorb a great deal of contemporary Arab philosophy and science, as well as building techniques which derived from classical Greek thought. Having many masons in their Order, they used biblical descriptions of the Temple and building tools in the symbolism of their designs and their ceremonies. Influenced by Neoplatonism, as many Masons after them, they believed in One God, the Architect of the World, in Whom the members of all religions, Christian and Muslim and Jew, might believe. This was central to their creed and led to later charges of heresy. The Templars would also become the conduit from the Near East of hermetic and cabbalistic knowledge, conveying this to the original Scottish Masons and so eventually to all Freemasons.

Also influential in Templar beliefs was the secret knowledge, the Gnosis, of early Christian and oriental mysticism. Central to its sacred geometry was the octagon contained within the circle. The Dome of the Rock was built by Islamic architects as eight equal walls holding up a golden dome, with at its centre a holy stone. During the ninety years of the Christian Kingdom of Jerusalem the building was guarded by the Templars and its shape influenced all their architecture. Octagonal chapels are found in many Templar commanderies, particularly at their base in Portugal, Tomar, while the eight-sided design was favoured

27

for the chapter houses of many medieval Gothic cathedrals in Britain and France. The mysteries of Templar building design were preserved through the *compagnonnages*, the early masonic guilds which constructed the holy places of the Middle Ages.

The Templars were not only the bankers of the Kingdom of Jerusalem during its century of survival, but also its diplomats within the Muslim world. Only when unschooled Grand Masters preferred confrontation did the kingdom fall. One story told by the emir Usamah Ibn Munqidh, a diplomat and writer from Damascus, showed how far the Templars had learned tolerance from their Muslim neighbours. When he visited Jerusalem, he wished to pray at the al-Aqsa mosque, which was now converted into a Christian church. The Templars placed a small chapel beside it at his disposal. When the emir began his prayers, a knight, newly come from Europe, turned him forcibly toward the east, saying, "We pray that way." The Templars took the newcomer away, but when the emir resumed praying towards Mecca, the knight repeated his outrage. This time he was ejected by the Templars, who apologized to the emir with the words, "He is a foreigner. He has just arrived from Europe and has never seen anyone pray without turning to face east." The emir ceased from his prayers, but forgave his Templar friends. Among the crusaders, he explained, "We find some people who have come to settle among us and who have cultivated the society of the Muslims. They are far superior to those who have joined them more recently in the territories they now occupy."

Although dependent on new recruits and the income from their commanderies in Europe, the Templars were a permanent standing army in the Holy Land, a few hundred knights holding the Holy City and a broken necklace of castles across Palestine. Their existence depended on playing off one Arab ruler or warlord against another. Any combination of the Muslim states against them would have spelt their end. They were particularly influenced by the rival Muslim warrior Shi'ite and Isma'ili sect of the Assassins, who held castles and lands in the mountains near the Caspian Sea and in Syria, and were supporters of the Fatimid caliphs of Egypt. The founder and first Grand Master of the Assassins, Hassan Ibn al-Sabbah, was a poet and a scientist and the forerunner of modern terrorism. He indoctrinated fanatical young men to murder his enemies, usually at the cost of their own lives. From these suicide squads derived the word *fedayeen*, still used of Palestinian guerrillas. The Assassins found the Templars to be willing allies in overthrowing the Sunni rulers of Syria and other Arab states, as well as susceptible converts to some of the secret practices of their organization.

The Isma'ili sect held that Muslim law and scriptures contained an inner meaning that was known only to the imams. They taught that there were seven prophets: Adam, Noah, Abraham, Moses, Jesus, Muhammad and the imam Isma'il. In the order of creation, the prophets stood at the level of Universal Reason, second only to God. Last in the sevenfold chain of creation stood man. Though God Himself was unknowable, a man could work through these grades as far as Universal Reason, and a new aspect of the teaching would be revealed to him at each level. Because such views were heretical, every Isma'ili initiate was required to conceal his beliefs in accordance with the Shia demand of secrecy and to conform, outwardly, to the state religion. Central to Isma'ili writings was the quest of an obsessed wanderer like Perceval in search of the Grail. The initiate sought truth through trial and suffering until he was at last accepted into the faith by an imam, who revealed to him the true meaning of Muslim law and scriptures.

Such a quest was described by Hassan Ibn al-Sabbah. In his memoirs, he told of how he pursued spiritual power by means of political power and transformed the role of the Isma'ili believer by turning him into an assassin. At the same time, Hassan modified the grades of initiation. The only descriptions of these mysteries were written by later European scholars, who saw the Isma'ili hierarchy itself as mere brainwashing. According to their accounts, the teaching given at each level negated everything that had been taught before. The innermost secret of the Assassins was that Heaven and Hell were the same, all actions were indifferent, and there was no good or evil except the virtue of obeying the imam.

Little is known of the Assassins' secrets, because their books of doctrine and ritual were burned when the Mongols in 1256 sacked their library at Alamut among the Persian peaks. Hassan emphasized the Shia doctrine of obedience and made changes in the Isma'ili hierarchy. Persian tradition had it that below Hassan, the chief *da'i* or Grand Master, came the senior *da'is*, the ordinary *da'is*, the *rafiqs* or companions, the *lasiqs* or laymen, and the *fidais* (devotees) who committed the murders. The division of the Templars under their Grand Master into grand priors, priors, knights, esquires and lay brothers was closely to follow this hierarchy.

In his asceticism and singleness of purpose, Hassan was an ideal revolutionary leader and conspirator. He is said to have remained continuously within his home in his fortress for more than thirty years, going out only twice and appearing twice more on his roof. His invisibility increased his power. From his seclusion he strengthened the defences of Alamut, purged the ranks of his followers, putting to death two of his own sons, and continued with his strategy of seizing hill positions as centres of local subversion. He elevated his authority to tyranny over life and soul. The will of the so-called Old Man of the Mountains was the unspoken will of his Shi'ite caliph, and thus the will of God. By winning over garrisons and assassinating local governors, he occupied strongpoints and terrorized the Sunnis – Persian and Turk alike. The conspiracy of the determined few, as usual, met little resistance from the fearful many. On the model of Muhammad himself, who had fled to Medina to rally support and reconquer Mecca and all Arabia, Hassan hoped to take over the caliphate of Baghdad.

By the authority of his rank and by the use of drugs, Hassan trained *fidais* in such blind obedience that, like the Japanese suicide pilots of the Second World War, they welcomed death during an attempt at assassination. They preferred the dagger as a weapon, and the court or the mosque as a place of execution. They scorned the use of poison and backstairs intrigue, for their code was that of soldiers rather than of harem murderers. Legend tells of one *fidai*'s mother who rejoiced when she heard that her son had died in an attempt on a ruler's life, then put on mourning when he returned alive. Similar legends grew up around other loyal *fidais* who stabbed themselves or dashed out their brains on the rocks below the battlements to prove their obedience to the Old Man's command.

The founder of the Templars, Hugues de Payens, knew of the Assassins when he formed his organization. The Christian and Muslim Military Orders were aware of each other in Syria before 1128, when the Templar Rule was written. Even the colours worn by the knights, red crosses on a white ground, were the same as those of the Assassin *rafiqs*, who wore red caps and belts and white tunics. Some claimed that the Templars adopted the Assassin 'hues of innocence and blood, and of pure devotion and murder' only because the rival Knights Hospitaller wore black. However that might be, the function of the Templars was virtually the same as that of the Assassins – to serve as an independent power on the side of their religious faith.

When the Assassins murdered the Count of Tripoli, the Templars forced the Syrian branch to pay them a yearly tribute. And when the Shi'ite caliphate of the Fatimids finally fell in Egypt, the Assassins in Syria were in such despair that they offered to convert to Christianity. The Templars, however, were reluctant to lose their income and they had the Assassin envoys killed as they returned from their interview with the King of Jerusalem – an action which spelt the end of co-operation between the two warrior Orders of Christianity and Islam. Equally rash decisions by the Templar Grand Master in 1187 would put an end to the Kingdom of Jerusalem itself.

Three years before that disaster, the Andalusian traveller Ibn Jubayr had noted the understanding and respect that Christian and Muslims had for each other's rights and commerce in Palestine. This, however, was doomed; with increasing raids by the Franks on the Red Sea trade routes and the pilgrim caravans to Mecca, the great Kurdish general Saladin succeeded in uniting the divided Muslim states in a *jihad* or holy war against the infidels. He sent a reconnaissance force of seven thousand cavalry under safe conduct, but these were attacked by the Templar and Hospitaller knights, who were decimated. The survivors berated the King of Jerusalem for dealing with the Muslims, as they had done themselves for so long. They persuaded him to march out and fight Saladin's united army.

At the Horns of Hittin in Northern Palestine, the Christian army was trapped without water and cut to pieces. For once, Saladin abandoned his usual policy of mercy to punish infidel perfidy. All prisoners from the Military Orders of knights were beheaded by their Muslim equivalents, the Sufis. Yet in contrast to the Christians' massacre of the citizens of Jerusalem during the First Crusade, Saladin spared the sacred place. The leader of the resistance, Balian of Ibelin, threatened to destroy the Holy City, including the Dome of the Rock, unless the defenders were ransomed, and Saladin accepted the terms. He even put guards in the Christian places of worship and refused to raze the Church of the Holy Sepulchre in retaliation for the brutality of the Christians when they had taken Jerusalem. Its walls freshly sprinkled with rosewater, the al-Aqsa mosque became an Islamic shrine again.

The fall of Jerusalem put an end to the proper purpose of the Templar Order, founded to provide guardians for the Temple of Solomon and protection for pilgrims to the Christian holy places, now in Muslim hands. Although they were to survive for another one hundred and twenty years as a Military Order, the Templars would have to find a new role. They fell back to the sea and built fortresses there, preparing for a new assault on Jerusalem. Only the Third Crusade with King Richard the First of England would come near to achieving this second objective; but Saladin would prove a match for the Lionheart himself. More and more, the Templars would become merchants and bankers and administrators of their estates.

Their fate was foreshadowed by another crusade, now directed by Christian against Christian in France. The victims, the *cathari* or pure ones, were condemned as heretics, as the Templars were to be in their turn. Since their foundation by Hugues de Payens, the Templars had been closely connected with the court of Champagne and Provence and the local Langue d'Oc, while writers of the medieval romances were

31

identifying them with the Knights of the Grail. The cultural patrons of the South of France, the richest and most civilized in Europe in the twelfth century, supported the crusades and sometimes died while serving upon them. Yet the Kings of France coveted the independent principalities of the south, and the Popes distrusted the increasing power of the Cathar priests, the *perfecti*, who wanted to reform the faith by instituting the direct approach of the Chosen to the grace of God.

Both the Cathars and the Templars were influenced by Manichean, Sufi and Islamic doctrines as well as by early Christianity and the Cabbala from the previous millennium. They believed the flesh was corrupt and life was an ascension to the spirit rather like the quest for the Grail. Lucifer or the devil had brought about the creation of man. Plato was right in the *Gorgias* when he quoted Euripides, "Who knows if life be death, and if death be life?" The Grail king in the German *Diû Krône* spoke true: "We only seem to be alive, in reality we are dead." Through the mystical feast known as the *manisola* and the chaste kiss of reception into the faith called the *consolamentum*, the *perfecti* took their initiates into the path of the spirit. This religion was certainly more pure and personal than Catholicism at the time, for an individual was made responsible for his or her own soul by the pursuit of an ascetic way of life. Cathar influences are evident in the romances about the quest for the Grail and in the early crusading desire to capture the Holy City of Jerusalem. The tragedy was that the Albigensian Crusade against the South of France was diverted to the ground which had inspired previous crusades to the East.

Catharism was covertly opposed to the feudal system as well as to the Church of Rome. According to the most radical of its thinkers, Peire Cardenal, even the crusades were a way for the clergy to exploit the knights. "In truth, the priests throw them right into a massacre. After giving them bread and cheese, they send them into the fray, where they are pierced with barbs." The southern barons however, did not see the libertarian Cathar message of a direct approach to God as a threat to their own authority, only as a menace to the Papal See. Had not the first troubadour, William the Ninth of Aquitaine, been excommunicated many times for his repeated attacks on ecclesiastical privilege? In Provence, indeed, the rulers saw the Cathars as almost a national church, not as an attack on their legitimacy.

For the Cathars, as for the knights of Grail romances, Pentecost was the most important religious festival. Then the *perfecti* were touched by the fire of the Holy Spirit, as the Apostles had been. Baptism by water at the font was insignificant. By their purity of life on earth, and their repudiation of the powers of evil, they might achieve the gift of tongues and the passage of the soul to heaven above. That was their heresy – the denial of all bishops and kings as intercessors on the journey to salvation.

The lands and cities of the Langue d'Oc were to be as thoroughly ravaged by poor and unemployed mercenary knights as the Holy Land had been before them. Predictably, the last castle of the Cathars to hold out at Montségur was held to be the Grail Castle, where spiritual food and life were available to the *perfecti*. A chalice used at the *manisola* was meant to have been smuggled out of Montségur before its fall and to be buried still – another real Grail – in the caves beneath the fortress. Although some of the Templars joined in the Albigensian Crusade, most of the Cathar knights who escaped the slaughter were received into the Military Order of the Temple of Solomon, which was itself permeated with oriental influences. These mysteries would become the basis of the charges levelled against the Order by later French magistrates and papal inquisitors, who had doomed the Cathars and would destroy the Templars for their wealth and their pride and their heresy, if those were the names for them.

3

The Eastern Mysteries

*And the Lord said unto Moses, Make thee a fiery serpent, and
set it upon a pole: and it shall come to pass, that if a serpent had
bitten any man, when he beheld the serpent of brass, he lived.*

From *The Book of Numbers*

A T THE TRIALS of the Templars, they would be accused of abomin-
able practices no more real than the Gnostic belief in a Satanic
world, which was the shade of the divine Light above. Many of
the mystic beliefs of the Grand Masters of the Military Orders would
be transmuted to the ultimate and thirty-third Masonic degree of the
Royal Arch. Elements from the Torah and the Old Testament, from
the Ark of the Covenant and Hiram's building of the Temple, from fire
worship and serpent veneration and a sexless Garden of Eden, from
the divine Sophia and the evil Jehovah, would join with the inspirations
of the three Johns – the Baptist, the Evangelist and the Divine – as
well as Jesus Christ, to create an arcane knowledge, based on the personal quest for a Grail, the illumination of God. This bubbling vein
would burst out in the incessant rebellions against the orthodox
churches by sects such as the Gnostics and the Cathars, the Sufis and
the Templars, eventually leading to the Protestant eruption against the
Church of Rome.

For the Jews and the Christians, the first mystery was the interpretation of Genesis. How was the world created? What was the relationship
of human beings with God? And of man with woman, and both with
nature? The myth of Eden derived from ancient traditions, and the
commentaries upon them were multitudinous. One of the paradoxes
most sympathetic to the Gnostics, the Military Orders and the Cathars,
and even to the Roman Catholic Church, was the sexlessness of Adam
and Eve in their state of innocence. *Elohim*, the spirit of God in the
Old Testament, was androgynous, both male and female. Plato in his
Symposium spoke of original beings of a combined sex, while Genesis
itself had Eve created from Adam's rib. According to the apocryphal
Gospel of Philip, Adam was immortal until Eve was separated from
him. And in the New Testament, the promise in Galatians was that
there was neither male nor female, 'for ye are all one in Christ Jesus.'

Belief in a hermaphroditic Adam-and-Eve in the original paradise would be discovered at the head of the only major Templar Scroll still to survive.

The interpreters of the Garden of Eden always drew the line between eternal God and temporal Creation. Even those who proposed a total union with the divine stressed the imperfection of matter. Yet in most Gnostic texts, Adam represented the soul and Eve the spirit of intelligence; their marriage united these two genders. In the text called *Reality of the Rulers*, the intelligent Eve was in the Serpent which gave the apple to Adam. In the *Testimony of Truth*, the Serpent was wiser than any of the animals in Eden, but was cursed wrongly by Jehovah. The enlightened snake did not poison Adam and Eve. He was unjustly condemned to crawl on his belly in the dusk and arraigned himself against humanity and God in the shape of Satan, the fallen archangel.

For the Gnostics and many other thinkers and poets even to the time of William Blake, the Jehovah of Genesis was a wrathful and a vengeful God. He burned cities with fire and ordered the Israelites to exterminate rival tribes. When his chosen people, led by their high priest Aaron, worshipped the Golden Calf, Jehovah commanded Moses on his descent from Mount Sinai to order the slaughter of three thousand male idolaters by the untainted sons of Levi. "Thus saith the Lord God of Israel, Put every man his sword by his side, and go in and out from gate to gate throughout the camp, and slay every man his brother, and every man his companion, and every man his neighbour." This incentive to sacred slaughter proved a splendid absolution to the Military Orders in their holy wars against Islam. Jehovah was distinguished from God the Father or the Creative Force. Indeed, in the *Apocryphon of John*, Jehovah was given the attributes of Zeus and the pagan gods, who might appear in the shape of bulls or asses, lions or eagles as well as serpents. Essentially, Jehovah was on the side of Satan and the seven deadly sins, which ruled over the material world with the seven planets. In the words of the *Poimandres*, human beings lived in a "darkness downwards, coiled like a snake, moist and confused, uttering an inexpressibly melancholy sound, and giving off smoke as from a fire."

According to the Talmud, Jehovah made a number of worlds which he obliterated, before settling for the present unsatisfactory one. As the modern Rumanian philosopher Cioran has commented, the Creation was the first act of sabotage, since it destroyed all alternative versions. The wrath of Jehovah against living things was attributable to his knowledge of their imperfections. Yet he was responsible for putting the apple into Eden and allowing the Serpent to enter the Garden and offer the fruit to Eve from the Tree of the Knowledge of Good and Evil.

If that were so, the Serpent was wise and virtuous. In many Gnostic formulas, Lucifer as the fallen angel was the reverse side of God, while Satan was the elder brother of Jesus, and the Serpent was the sign of the Saviour. The Gnostic Cainites revered the snake on the tree and the figure of Cain, who offered God first fruits and not his brother Abel's bloody sacrifices. The Ophites, who used asps and vipers at their ceremonies to consecrate the holy bread, showed a Satanic dragon enwrapping the seven circles of the earth. As declared the *Pistis Sophia*, the Greek for Faith and Wisdom: 'the outer darkness is a huge dragon whose tail is in its mouth', an image also adopted by the alchemists of the Middle Ages. And the Naasenes believed that Christ was both a reincarnation of the Serpent from Eden and of Aaron's rod. For had not that supernatural wand been converted by the Lord into a serpent in front of the Pharaoh and the magicians of Egypt? "For they cast down every man his rod, and they became serpents: but Aaron's rod swallowed up their rods." For the Gnostics, this verse of Exodus was a parable symbolizing that their wisdom had swallowed up all previous eastern mysteries, while Aaron's rod then turned the great serpent of the Nile into blood.

Further use of such imagery was seen in the mysterious episode of the fiery serpent of God, when the Israelites questioned the divine wisdom of their desert travail towards the Promised Land. As the Book of Numbers declared:

> And the people spake against God, and against Moses, Wherefore have ye brought us up out of Egypt, to die in the wilderness? for there is no bread, neither is there any water; and our soul loatheth this light bread.
> And the Lord sent fiery serpents among the people, and they bit the people; and much people of Israel died.
> Therefore the people came to Moses, and said, We have sinned, for we have spoken against the Lord, and against thee; pray unto the Lord, that he take away the serpents from us. And Moses prayed for the people.
> And the Lord said unto Moses, Make thee a fiery serpent, and set it upon a pole: and it shall come to pass, that every one that is bitten, when he looketh upon it, shall live.
> And Moses made a serpent of brass, and put it upon a pole: and it came to pass, that if a serpent had bitten any man, when he beheld the serpent of brass, he lived.

In this biblical myth, the serpent was both the vengeance and the messenger of God. The recognition of this role was the antidote, as the venom of a snake still cures the strike of its fangs. To this day, in the Ancient Rite of the present Knights Templars of Scotland, the serpent entwined round the Tau Cross or pole is a symbol of veneration and belief in the power of the holy writ and will.

Among the Military Orders, belief in the divine feminine intelligence also appealed to their cult of chastity and the pursuit of truth. In Gnostic texts such as the *Pistis Sophia*, she was an angel of inquiry who sought the ultimate knowledge of God and so fell into chaos and the world of matter. She was also judged for trying to produce children without a male ethereal partner. Now condemned to the vileness of the earth, she was associated with the fate of Jerusalem, and in the *Second Treatise of the Great Seth*, she was called a whore, the keeper of profane knowledge. In this incarnation, she became another Mary Magdalene, the sinner brought to redemption by the love of Jesus. Both of these feminine principles were called the Bride of Christ, symbolically and literally. Yet Sophia was, like Eve, equated with the Holy Spirit, the bringer of supreme understanding to humanity, while Mary Magdalene was said in the *Dialogue of the Saviour* to speak 'as a woman who knew the All'. In the *Gospel of Nicodemus*, she became the carrier of the Grail, while she served as the witness of Christ, in the *Great Questions of Mary*, when He had intercourse with a woman produced from His side.

Such self-contained sexuality in the Gnostic mysteries was sublimated by the knights of the Military Orders in their cult of the Virgin Mary, who was impregnated by the divine essence to produce Christ. A man had nothing to do with the birth of the Son of God. The cult of Mary also included the veneration of her attributes, particularly the Ark of the Covenant carried on its poles as may be seen in her window at Reims Cathedral. For she, Sophia, was the life-giving spirit of intelligence. The human mind came from her womb. The monkish brotherhood of the Hospitallers, the Templars and the Teutonic Knights took comfort in the concept of procreation without intercourse, although the Templars at their trials would be accused of imitating the Cathars in their initiation ceremonies with the kiss on the mouth and other parts of the body as a rite of birth, not of passage. Both heresies were also accused along with the Brethren of the Free Spirit or Perfectionists of practising open love of all kinds in naked rituals, although these accusations were not proven. The Templar symbol of two men riding on one horse referred to the duty of a knight to look after his poor brother, not to sodomy or too intense a fraternity. At a higher level, the two riders represented the flesh and the spirit, and, as shown in Perceval's vision in the Grail manuscript at Le Mans, the twin nature of Christ as crowned God and human Word, rising from the birthplace of the holy vessel.* That Templar symbol would soon be replaced by a winged horse or Pegasus, representing spiritual illumination.

The dualism of Gnostic thought supposed the world made by Jehovah and Satan to be dark and evil, set against the light and heaven with Jesus as the messenger. This was the ideology of the Military Orders in their struggle with the devil of Islam, a struggle in which death would mean a translation to paradise. In the more esoteric level of understanding of the Grand Masters, such as those who exchanged knowledge with the Assassins, even Judas became a saint. The name *Iscariot* derived from the Greek word for assassin and denoted also the carved dagger worn by the extreme Jewish sect of the Zealots, who believed that the coming of the Messiah could only occur by force and self-sacrifice. This belief was shared by the members of the Military Orders, who believed that Christ had ordained them to their sanguinary role. Had He not in St John's Gospel ordered Judas to betray him, "That thou doest, do quickly?"

As the Knights Templars grew in wealth and power, their questioning of orthodox faith became more elaborate and they began to take issue with the conventions of society and the pretensions of the Papacy. They became less the warriors of the Holy See and of the Cistercian Order than the avenging angels of a sinful world, whose Grand Masters spoke directly to the All as Mary Magdalene had in her time. Their leaders looked for their intelligence directly to divine inspiration. When at their trials, the Templars would be accused of worshipping Baphomet in the shape of a cat or a devil, they were only guilty of receiving Islamic wisdom in the mythical shape of the wise Serpent.

The knights of the Temple of Solomon would be particularly feared for their long tenancy of the site of the Temple. Had they discovered their arcane knowledge there? Had they discovered the sacred wealth of King David and even the Ark of the Covenant? Although the Old Testament never declared what was the divine intelligence contained within the Holy of Holies, its treasures and those of the Temple were described, while its very construction and nature were the ordinance of the Almighty, as written in Exodus:

> And they shall make an ark of shittim wood: two cubits and a half shall be the length thereof, and a cubit and a half the breadth thereof, and a cubit and a half the height thereof.
> And thou shalt overlay it with pure gold; within and without shalt thou overlay it, and shalt make upon it a crown of gold round about.

* See Illustrations.

38

And thou shalt cast four rings of gold for it, and put them in the four
corners thereof; and two rings shall be in the one side of it, and two
rings in the other side of it.

And thou shalt make staves of shittim wood, and overlay them with gold.

And thou shalt put the staves into the rings by the sides of the ark, that
the ark may be borne with them.

The staves shall be in the rings of the ark; they shall not be taken from it.

And thou shalt put into the ark the testimony which I shall give thee.

The tabernacle erected round the Ark and later the Temple of Solomon was a treasurehouse of precious metals and stones, some of which
the Templars were meant to have excavated as the capital for their
banking wealth. Architecturally, they may have translated to some of
their chapels the two pillars, Jachin and Boaz, which held up the
Temple, but they rejected its shape as a cube – adopted at the Ka'aba
at Mecca – in favour of the sacred octagon crowned by a dome. This
was the design of the Islamic Dome of the Rock, thought by Christian
pilgrims to be Solomon's holy place, even though it was celebrated in
Islam as the place from which Muhammad was held to have stepped
into the seventh heaven.

In fact, the Templars seem to have acquired a foundation for their
riches, when they lost their headquarters in Jerusalem. In 1185, the
Patriarch Heraclius of the Church of the Holy Sepulchre had travelled
to London to consecrate the Temple in that city. Two years later, when
Islam conquered the Holy City of Israel, Heraclius was allowed by
Saladin to depart with all his sacred treasures, many adorned with gold
and jewels, for the Templar castle at Acre which served as the strong-
room of the Levantine bank of the Order. Also gathered there were
the spoils of Constantinople, when it was seized by the warlords of the
Fourth Crusade. The Holy Shroud and the Holy Veil of Veronica were
meant to have passed into Templar possession along with their golden
vessels which contained the cloths of the Passion, and so were given
the name of Grails. For they held the body and blood of Christ. After
the fall of Acre and the flight of the Templars from Palestine, these
precious objects were carried overseas. In 1306, one year before the
condemnation of the Military Order, the Templar treasury was moved
from Cyprus by sea to Marseilles, and then on to the Temple in Paris.
The Holy Shroud would surface in France, the Holy Veil in Rome,
after the annihilation of the Templars for heresy.

Further favourite symbols and saints of the Gnostics were also held
dear by the Military Orders. God called to Moses in fire out of a
Burning Bush, which was not consumed, as it was set alight by an

angel. St John the Baptist was martyred and his head put on a platter, a sign of the Grail in one medieval romance. His example and the symbol of the martyred Lamb of God holding up the cross on a banner were important, particularly to the Templars. The opening of the St John's Gospel was so imbued with Gnostic belief that John's adoption by the Hospitallers as well as the Templars was clear evidence of their sympathy with the eastern mysticism that he and the Baptist conveyed:

> In the beginning was the Word, and the Word was with God, and the Word was God.
> The same was in the beginning with God.
> All things were made by him; and without him was not any thing made that was made.
> In him was life; and the life was the light of men.
> And the light shineth in darkness; and the darkness comprehended it not.
> There was a man sent from God, whose name was John.
> The same came for a witness, to bear witness of the Light, that all men through him might believe.
> He was not that Light, but was sent to bear witness of that Light.
> That was the true Light, which lighteth every man that cometh into the world.

Such paradigms of Light and Darkness, with the Word or Logos of God sent through His witness to an ignorant earth long before authority was assumed by Rome, appeared clear in their meaning, as did other statements in the Gospel which drew parallels between the wisdom of Moses and the resurrection of Jesus:

> And as Moses lifted up the serpent in the wilderness, even so must the Son of Man be lifted up:
> That whosoever believeth may in Him have eternal life.
> For God so loved the world, that He gave his only begotten Son . . .

Only in St John's Gospel too, was the story told of Christ's appearance after his death to Mary Magdalene in the garden, from which she bore the news of her visitation to the unbelieving disciples. Indeed, so numerous were the Gnostic references in that Gospel that its inclusion in the Bible was surprising. The same held true of the Book of Revelation of St John the Divine, with its millennial visions of the Alpha and Omega, the beginning and the ending, which is, and which was, and which is to come, the Almighty. The saint was, as he wrote, 'in the Spirit of the Lord's day', when he saw and heard the glory of God telling him, "Worthy is the Lamb that was slain to receive power, and

riches, and wisdom, and strength and honour, and glory, and blessing."
No wonder that John the Divine's promises to those who sacrificed
themselves for Christ were so attractive to the crusading knights. His
later visions of Michael and the angels at war in heaven with a seven-
headed red dragon were also coloured by Gnostic beliefs. "And the
great dragon was cast out, that old serpent, called the Devil, and Satan,
which deceiveth the whole world: he was cast into the earth, and his
angels were cast out with him." The same serpent even tried to destroy
the winged mother of the divine man child, who was to rule all nations
with a rod of iron. He first nourished her in the wilderness from his
face, then spat out a flood to drown her, but "the earth helped the
woman, and the earth opened her mouth, and swallowed up the flood."

With ancient beliefs in the earth mother combined with Gnostic
sayings all finding a place within the Bible before they were condemned
as heresies, no wonder that the Grand Masters of the Military Orders
felt free to select the saints and texts necessary to justify their position
in this world and the next. The most important of these holy figures
for Christian knights and for those civil powers who sought to confront
the authority of the Church of Rome, was Melchizedek, priest and king
of ancient Israel.

The Gnostic sect of the Sethians had believed that the 'secrets of
Adam' were passed through Seth, the third son of the first father by
Eve, on to Illuminati, who came upon the evil earth to enlighten humanity. The chief of these were Melchizedek, priest-king of Salem at the
time of Abraham, then Zoroaster, then Jesus Christ. Elements of this
cult influenced the early Byzantine emperors, who wanted to assert
their dominance not only over their own imperial Greek church, but
over the See of Rome. Their buildings and images at Ravenna would
influence Charlemagne and later German rulers as well as the French
kings in their assertion of divine right against the Papacy. There, beside
the sea at Sant' Apollinare-in-Classe in Italy, two key mosaics of the
royal and holy Melchizedek are to be found. In the first a gold chalice
is set before the Old Testament ruler on a table altar or Ark covered
by a white cloth; Abel offers to his sacred majesty and to Almighty
God a sacrificial white lamb. On the altar are a pair of round loaves in
the shape of sun discs and a pattern, two misaligned squares making
up an octagon within a circle – the sacred building shape of the Baptisteries at Ravenna, both of which have exquisite and naturalistic mosaics
of Jesus being baptized in Jordan with the Holy Spirit as a dove
descending on Him.* Opposite the mosaic stands the bearded Byzantine

* See Illustrations.

emperor Constantine the Fourth granting privileges while holding a bowl. The first imperial Constantine had turned Byzantium to Christ: he and his heirs were the rulers of state and church: that was the message of the Melchizedek mosaics. Their significance was repeated in the statues of the biblical priest and sovereign made for the benefit of the Merovingian and early Capetian kings of France, and placed by them in the cathedrals of Reims and Chartres.* Like the Byzantine emperors, they needed to show that their succession was blessed by God. To be of the blood royal was to rule by divine right, whatever the Church had to say on the matter.

This was no message for the later Popes of Rome, who not only opposed the Greek rite and eventually sent out their crusaders to take Constantinople, but also found themselves in frequent conflict with the German Holy Roman Emperors, contesting their claim to be supreme in religion as well as politics. In Byzantine Ravenna, no potentate went on his knees to Canossa to seek papal forgiveness. The churches were intended to celebrate the glory of the imperial family. The second mosaic of Melchizedek is in San Vitale, a huge octagonal church consecrated in 547 by the great Archbishop Maximian along with Sant' Apollinare-in-Classe. At the head of her court the Empress Theodora, dripping with pearls, is shown as a priestess holding a golden chalice studded with gems: on her robe are embroidered the three Magi, who appear time and again in mosaic and marble, pressing their generosity on Christ, as the Byzantines did. Theodora faces her husband, the emperor Justinian, who holds a large gold paten – the monarch here usurping the role of Archbishop Maximian, whose last resting place this is. The building remains an encyclopedia of early signs of the Holy Vessel. On the archbishop's sarcophagus are two doves drinking from a flowing Grail; on his ivory throne is carved the feast at Cana and the miracle of the loaves and fishes, while the four Evangelists surround the Virgin Mary, two of them bearing a dish, one with little loaves and one with the Lamb.

The link from Melchizedek at Ravenna is forged at Notre-Dame in Reims. There, in the most sacred royal cathedral in France, is a highly significant representation of the early ruler of Israel, presenting a wafer of bread and a cup of wine to the Patriarch Abraham as he returns from victory over the enemies of the King of Sodom. As Genesis tells the story:

---

* See Illustrations.

And Melchizedek king of Salem brought forth bread and wine and he was
priest of God Most High.

And he blessed him, and said, Blessed be Abraham of God Most High,
possessor of heaven and earth:

And blessed be God Most High, which hath delivered thine enemies into
thy hand.

In the carvings, the bearded Melchizedek in his long robes offers a
wafer with his right hand, holding a large chalice in his left. Behind
him, a cloth covers a table altar. Standing before him is Abraham in
medieval chain-mail armour and helmet, with surcoat, swordbelt and
spear, and his hands joined in prayer. Another knight faces us, holding
up his right arm, broken off at the wrist, perhaps representing the King
of Sodom. His armour consists of dragon-like scales, his round ridged
shield resembles the sun, its rays spiking from the boss.* This ensemble
is remarkable for the thirteenth century in its portrayal of the knight
receiving communion directly from the priest-king without the benefit
of the Church, which did not yet exist. Such an ancient assertion by
the Kings of France of a primordial divine sanction was transposed to
the age of chivalry and crusade and expanding royal power. The gravest
accusation against the Templars at their trials would be that, like Melchizedek, their leaders gave communion to their knights after battle.
Indeed, Melchizedek had been praised in a Psalm of David for his
prowess in holy war:

The Lord hath sworn, and will not repent. Thou art a priest for ever, after
the order of Melchizedek.

The Lord at thy right hand shall strike through kings in the day of His
wrath.

He shall judge among the nations. He shall fill the places with dead bodies;
He shall strike through the head in many countries.

Nearby in the small rose window of the litanies of the Virgin Mary,
the Ark of the Covenant is displayed as one of her attributes. Shown
as a brown pouch with a red diamond in its middle, it hangs from two
carrying poles. On its golden top sit two brown and yellow birds – owls,
phoenixes or eagles – representing wisdom. A blue sun encompasses it,
the light of heaven.

At the rival cathedral of Chartres, there is another carving of Melchizedek, holding a chalice with a stone inside its rim. Also to be found
there are two reliefs of the Ark of the Covenant, this time carried on

* See Illustrations.

43

spoked wheels and not on the prescribed staves. A mysterious Latin inscription, *Archa cederis*, may be translated, 'You are to work through the Ark'. The Templar architects of Reims and Chartres and the *compagnonnages* they directed appear to have taken this ancient wisdom to heart, for both French cathedrals have been constructed on many of the principles of the lost art of sacred geometry.

The importance of Melchizedek was also recognized in the New Testament. As King of Salem (an early name of Jerusalem), and thus the heir of Aaron, who first wore the sacred breastplate of the High Priest studded with twelve gems, on which were inscribed the names of the Twelve Tribes of Israel, he was declared to be a divine source, "having neither beginning of days nor end of life; but made like unto the Son of God." Paul himself wrote of Christ that He was "called of God, an high priest after the order of Melchizedek." According to the early Jewish historian Josephus, Melchizedek built the first Temple and served there as a priest. One of the Dead Sea Scrolls extolled Melchizedek as a heavenly figure at the right hand of the Almighty, who judged the guilty and the innocent like another archangel Michael. Through Jewish interpretation, Melchizedek thus became for the Templars a forerunner of Christ: the bread and wine given to Abraham was an early Eucharist without a church. In the Epistle to the Hebrews, he was described as "without father, without mother, without descent, having neither beginning of days, nor end of life; but made like unto the Son of God; abideth a priest continually." This biblical emphasis on his importance would enhance his significance to those who opposed the later Christian orthodox establishment, unable to condemn the example of Melchizedek because of his holy provenance.

In these forms and by these means the Knights Templars passed their secret knowledge to the West. They influenced not only iconography but also the medieval romances of the Round Table, in which connections between the chivalry of King Arthur or the court of Charlemagne and the Templars proliferated. There was a cult of the skull.

4

Idol or Skull

God be in my head
And in my understanding.

Old English Prayer

A STRANGE ELEMENT in many medieval romances connected with the Grail was the severed head; it might speak and be made of metal as with the Celtic god Bran, or set on a gory platter like the head of John the Baptist – sometimes held to be another embodiment of the Grail. At their trials the Knights Templars also confessed to the adoration of a magic head, known as Baphomet, whose name perhaps combined that of the pagan god Baal and the Prophet Mahomet in its old spelling

When interrogated in 1307, the Templar Hugues de Payraud declared that he had felt and kissed and worshipped a head at Montpellier, and that it had two feet in front of the neck and two behind. For Pierre d'Arbley, the head was silver with a silver beard; for Hugues de Bure, it was gold or silver or copper with a narrow cord about the neck, such as was later given to a brother to admit him to the Military Order. Some Templars asserted under torture that the idol looked like the devil, and that the initiates cried out, 'Yah Allah', when they kissed it, the words suggesting a belief in Yahweh or Jehovah and Islam. For Raoul de Gizy, this was the image of a demon, while Guillaume d'Herblay swore that the object had two golden faces like a mask of the Roman messenger god Janus, with one face bearded and another with smooth cheeks, denoting the apparent dualism of the Templar doctrine. All witnesses confessed to honouring the head as the Saviour with the generative power of making the trees green and the plants grow.

I had become familiar with some of these beliefs when I bought a ruined farmhouse and barn in Normandy near the village of Mantilly. Built from stones said to have been plundered during the French Revolution from the abbey of Savigny, it lay at the heart of the country of Lancelot of the Lake. That Arthurian knight was held to be an evocation of the popular local saint, Fraimbault, whose cult was as widespread as that of St Clair, commemorated in twelve different places all the way to Senlis on the Oise, the first capital of the Capetian kings of France.

There all the relics of the sixth-century Norman saint had been buried except for the crown of his head, which was kept as a venerated relic in an old church near his home town at Lassay.

The correspondences between Lancelot and Fraimbault were well documented. Both of their names signified the lance of the lake. Both were sons of kings or chiefs who lived at the time of King Arthur. Both were carried away to live by water in the Pays d'Erne in Normandy. Both had adventures in carts and ended as hermits. And both sought the Grail or Holy Light, the name carried by their neighbours the St Clairs, who seemed to associate themselves more with Perceval than the erring Lancelot. Indeed, the silver reliquary containing the skull of an original St Clair had been venerated at Nantes until it too was destroyed by the French Revolution.

Visiting St Fraimbault-de-Lassay, on two weathered tombstones built into the north-east outer wall, I discovered two more Templar grailstones. Just visible was a mallet chiselled above a chalice, then another chalice with a cross above it in the shape of a four-pointed clover leaf. Within the church was a statue of St Fraimbault holding a spade like Christ the Gardener and a book of the Word of God. Yet more remarkable was the bust containing the crown of his skull, locked away in the church sanctuary. On the Monday of Pentecost, it used to be paraded by the villagers through various parishes, carried on a litter on poles as the Ark of the Covenant had once been. And what was this reliquary but the shining metal head and shoulders of a bearded man, enclosing the relic of the local saint. Indeed, along with St Clair, decapitated for resisting the advances of a temptress, the severed head seemed a Norman as well as a Templar cult.

At the nearest large centre to Mantilly, the Angevin fortress of Domfront, there was another eleventh-century church in the shape of a cross on the river Orne. By the water, masonic gravestones lay incised with skulls and the usual craft symbols. Yet exceptionally, placed at the foot of an ancient stone Tau Cross as high as a small tree with the bearded head of Christ at the join, a tombstone as small as the Templar one at Rosslyn Chapel bore the incised chalice or Grail. Its size made it likely that only skull and crossbones were buried beneath.

Yet at the nearest town to Mantilly, Passais-la-Conception, the enduring proof of the Grail myths was still evident at Pentecost. The whole farming neighbourhood packed into the church of Notre-Dame as the Grail knights had around the table at Camelot, to receive the gift of the Holy Spirit and eat curious generative pastries called *cônets* and *trous*. What had Sir Thomas Malory written about the divine fire and the gift of tongues?

In the midst of this blast a sunbeam entered clearer by seven times more than ever they saw day, and they were all enlightened of the grace of the Holy Ghost. Then every knight began to behold each other apparently fairer than they ever saw before. There was no knight who might speak one word for a great while, so they looked every man on the other as if they had been dumb. Then covered with white samite, the Holy Grail entered into the hall, but there was no one who might see it, nor who bore it. And good odours fulfilled all the hall, and every knight had such meat and drink as he best loved in this world.

There was even a Grail tour in the area, taking in a dolmen called the Devil's Table at Passais, the Tomb of Baudemagu, Arthur's Seat and the lake where Excalibur was found. More credible was an illuminated *History of the Holy Grail* or *Joseph of Arimathea* at Le Mans, probably written by Walter Map, the chaplain of King Henry the Second of England. This contained a remarkable illumination of Perceval seeing two Christs in the holy vessel, displaying Templar dualism as well as Jesus as both Logos and divine ruler. Other illuminations showed the knights of Camelot as Templar crusaders, bearing the red cross on the white shield, one of them with the image also of the crucified Saviour.* I seemed to be in the middle of the ancient legend.

Further afield, I visited the port of Fécamp, the first capital of Normandy and a centre of pilgrimage. There, the scabs scraped off the body of Jesus by the knives of Nicodemus, as reported in the Gnostic Gospels, were meant to have been washed up, concealed in two lead caskets within the trunk of a fig tree, which took root at Fécamp without disclosing its secret in the manner of the flowering thorn at Glastonbury, said to have been planted by Joseph of Arimathea. These had been the subjects of two of the Grail romances by Robert de Boron and Walter Map, telling of how the Holy Blood reached Sarras in the South of France and Logres in the West of England, which became the Waste Land.

When the first Duke of Normandy, Rollo, began the construction of the huge abbey church at Fécamp in the tenth century on the site of a nunnery sacked by the Vikings, a miracle was necessary to bless the place. An old man appeared in a vision and left one of the knives of Nicodemus on the altar, incised in Latin with the inscription, 'in the name of the Holy and Indivisible Trinity'. Later, at a mass in a nearby village church at Saint-Maclou-la-Brière, the wine in the chalice was turned into blood, signifying the presence of Christ. When the abbey of the Holy Trinity was rebuilt in the twelfth century, the knife

* See Illustrations.

of Nicodemus and the two lead cylinders of the Holy Blood were found in a hollow pillar eighteen years before the discovery of the tomb of King Arthur at Glastonbury. The lead tubes are still housed in a tabernacle behind the high altar, on which three angels are carved holding vessels to catch the sacred fluid from His wounds. Below are testimonies to miraculous cures: MARIE PROTEGEZ NOUS. HOMMAGE AU PRECIEUX SANG.

While I was there, in the Chapel of the Virgin opposite the shrine, an aged priest was raising a silver-gilt communion cup and celebrating mass. Over the entrance to the Chapel was a remarkable marble relief of St John the Baptist. His severed head was carried on a platter by two angels. Fécamp is rich in venerable images associated with the cult of the Grail, although the bone of St Mary Magdalene which was claimed to be there in the Middle Ages has since disappeared. The abbey church contains a Chapel dedicated to the Magdalene, while in the modern village church at Saint-Maclou where the wine turned to blood a thousand years before, windows show a Grail arriving from the sea at Marseilles, confirming the French link between south and north in the cult of the Holy Blood.

At the great royal cathedral of Saint-Denis outside Paris, which I visited later, I found another statue of a venerated saint, walking with his head in his hands. A decapitated saint was also meant to have arrived by sea at a greater medieval shrine, Santiago de Compostela in northern Spain. Like St John the Baptist, the warrior and martyr St James had been adored by the Knights Templars, who had guarded pilgrims on the sacred routes from France across the Pyrenees to Compostela as well as in the Holy Land.

Further links between the Templars and the cult of the skull were evident in the two Celtic stories, Peredur and the *Perlesvaus*, said to have been written by Joseph of Arimathea himself at the dictation of an angel. In the latter romance King Arthur is cured from his sloth by the blood from the severed head of a Black Knight, brought to his court by the sister of Perceval, who is followed by a bald maiden with a cart containing the heads of 150 knights sealed in caskets of gold, silver and lead. This horror sends Gawain off on his adventures towards the Grail Castle, where he is refused entrance until he returns with a sacred Templar relic, the sword which beheaded St John the Baptist. "If you bring that sword," a priest tells Gawain, "you may freely come into the castle, and everywhere in the realm of the Fisher King, you will be made most welcome."

Gawain wins the relic from the cannibal Gurguran, ruler of Scotland who is now converted to Christianity – a memory of the first Irish missions to the pagan Picts. Conducted by angels the knight rides over the perilous bridges into the Grail Castle, where he hands over the biblical sword to the maimed Fisher King, whom he finds there reclining on an ivory bed before a cross of gold in which is embedded a piece of the True Cross. There Gawain meets a group of initiates, each with a red cross on his breast. After a feast with twelve of the knights, however, Gawain repeats Perceval's mistake in failing to ask the right question of the diseased Fisher King. He is struck dumb by the sight of the Grail and the three drops of blood falling from the Holy Lance, held in the hands of two maidens. He is not the perfect knight. He cannot heal the king's wounds.

Lancelot now takes up the Quest. The brutality of the period again intrudes on the story. Martyrdom is presented to Lancelot in the guise of mutilation. He sits with the lady of a castle:

> The first course was brought in by knights in chains who had their noses cut off. The second by knights in chains who had their eyes put out, so that squires led them. The third course was brought in by knights with one hand and chained. After that, other knights with one foot brought in the fourth course. And with the fifth course came tall and fair knights, each with a naked sword used to cut off their heads, now given to the lady.

Perceval resumes the Quest for the Grail, carrying the azure and silver shield with the red cross of Joseph of Arimathea. Meeting his sister, he learns of the death of the Fisher King and the disappearance of the Grail. The Lord of the Moors has taken Camelot from his mother. In delivering that castle from Islam, Perceval shows himself more pagan Celtic knight than crusader. His killing of the Muslim chief and his warriors is a scene of ritual slaughter, worse even than that inflicted on the Templars by Saladin after his victory at the Horns of Hittin.

> "Our Lord God commanded in both the Old Law and the New," Perceval said, "that justice should be done to mass-killers and traitors, and justice will be done upon you so that His Law is not transgressed." He had a great vat made ready in the middle of the court, and ordered the eleven Moorish captive knights to be brought out. He had their heads severed into the vat with all the blood drained from their bodies, then he had the flesh taken out so there was only the blood in the vat. After that, he disarmed the Lord of the Moors and took him before the vessel filled with blood. Perceval had the Lord's hands and feet bound fast, and after that he said: 'You were never satisfied with the blood of the knights of my lady mother, now I will satisfy you with the blood of your own knights.' So he had the Lord of the

49

Moors hanged by the feet in the vat with his head in the blood as far as his shoulders, until he was drowned and quenched. After that, Perceval had all the twelve bodies and heads dumped in an ancient burial pit beside an old chapel in the forest, while the vat of blood was cast into the river, so that the waters were all red.

King Arthur's son has been killed by treachery, but again the head is returned to the father in a casket, smelling of sweet spices. He now sees the Grail 'in five different forms that none ought to tell,' before civil war breaks out in his kingdom. Perceval is carried over the sea to the Castle of the Four Horns, where he finds a company of white monks with a red cross on their breasts – an allusion both to the Cistercians and the Templars. They lead him to a glass casket entombing an armed knight. Perceval is given a white shield and directed to a Plenteous Island where he redeems the knights' heads sealed in their gold, silver and lead caskets in the cart of the maiden, as well as the head of its king and queen. He takes back all the severed remains and is given a golden cup of healing for his chivalry and pains. Eventually he takes the Grail and the body of Joseph of Arimathea to another world on a Ship of Solomon with the Templar markings of red crosses on white sails.

Such an association by the author of the *Perlesvaus* of the cult of the severed head with the Cistercians and the Templars was enhanced by the dedication of the work to its patron, Jean de Nesle, who had served on the Fourth Crusade, which took Constantinople rather than Jerusalem. This crusade had brought the two sacred heads – on the Veil of St Veronica and on the Holy Shroud – into the possession of the Templars. The cult was even more sanguinary in the other Welsh romance of *Peredur*, the name of the hero. Witnessing a horrific Grail procession, he sees two youths carrying 'a spear of huge size, and three streams of blood running along it from the socket to the floor'. All present cry out in grief. And then 'two maidens came in holding a great platter between them, with a man's head on the platter bathed in blood'.

This version of the Grail procession was a Celtic blood ritual, commemorating the sacred head of Bran, as well as alluding to the gory death of St John the Baptist. Later in the story, Peredur hears the truth about the spear and the platter. The head is that of Peredur's cousin, who has been killed by the Caerloyw Witches, and whose death Peredur must now avenge. At the same time, this being a Grail romance, the spear symbolizes the Holy Lance of Longinus and the platter represents the Holy Vessel of the Last Supper and the Crucifixion. This startling confusion between pagan and Christian was paralleled in the *Perlesvaus*, where the maiden had brought the hero his cousin's remains in an ivory vessel with the caskets containing the remains of all the other knights. Eventually becoming the ruler of the Grail castle, Peredur, with the help of King Arthur, kills off in a last act of vengeance the Witches who had maimed the previous Fisher King. He also cuts off the head of his cousin – the trophy on the bloody platter of the Grail.

These old romances, along with the reliquary of St Fraimbault or Lancelot of the Lake, suggest that the Templar heresy of the adoration of the bearded head of Baphomet might be an inquisitorial twisting of the medieval Christian worship of images of Christ and relics of the skulls of saints. Two renowned examples of the head and face of the bearded Jesus, after all, had fallen into Templar hands after the Fourth Crusade of 1204, when the Military Order had joined the Frankish invaders in seizing Constantinople. Under attack from the crusaders, the keeper of the Pharos Chapel, Nicolas Mesarites, had warned the enemies of the Byzantine emperor not to attack the place. "In this chapel," Mesarites wrote, "Christ rises again, and the Shroud with the burial linens is the clear proof . . . They still smell of myrrh and are indestructible since they once enshrouded the dead body, anointed and naked, of the Almighty after his Passion." A crusader, Robert de Clari, saw another Holy Shroud or Veil in the Church of St Mary Blachernae. Here "was kept the Shroud in which Our Lord had been wrapped, which stood up straight every Good Friday, so that the features of Our Lord could be plainly seen there."

Following the fall of Jerusalem to Islam, Constantinople had become the greatest repository of holy relics in Christendom. Along with the golden *capsula* containing the veil of St Veronica and the jewelled receptacle of the Holy Shroud, there were a host of other sacred objects. Nicholas Mesarites stopped a mob seeking the blessed relics by telling them of three other instruments of the Passion which he held in the Pharos. The first was "the holy Crown of Thorns, which remained intact because it took on incorruptibility from touching the sacred head of Jesus." The second was the last "Holy Nail preserved just as it was when it penetrated the most holy and merciful Flesh." The third was the *flagellum*, the whip with the thongs that still bore the blood of Christ. These five remains of the Passion were among the blessed treasures of Constantinople, which remained for the looting.

There were many other objects of veneration, as well. As early as the fourth century, the bodies of the saints Andrew, Luke and Timothy had been disinterred for reburial in the Santa Sophia. Most of these relics were now plundered by the Venetians and the crusaders. By a long and elaborate process of international bribes, King Louis the Ninth of France arranged for the Byzantine Crown of Thorns to be redeemed from Venice and to be enshrined in Paris in the miraculous building of the Sainte-Chapelle. And an engraving of the other treasures in that most sacred place – all dispersed at the French Revolution – shows a reliquary containing Moses' rod of the fiery serpent and another gold and bearded bust, claimed to contain the crown of St John the Baptist's skull.*

The two Byzantine images of the Holy Shroud and the Veil of St Veronica came into the possession of the Templars with the sack of Constantinople. How the Veil reached Rome is unknown, but the Shroud or its copy emerged after the burning for heresy in 1314 of the Templar Grand Master, Jacques de Molay. Royal permission and authentication was given to a favourite supporter, Geoffroy de Charny, to exhibit what is now called the Shroud of Turin at a collegiate church, constructed for its exposure, at Lirey near Troyes in Champagne. Although the Knights Templars had been outlawed, de Charny tried to found another religious and Military Order of the Star, which developed into the Order of Notre-Dame of the Noble House. Nearly all its members, however, were cut down at the Battle of Poitiers in 1356, following de Charny with the sacred oriflamme in a charge to the death, and leaving the Holy Shroud to pass into the possession of the House of Savoy.

The mania for parading and viewing evidence of the Crucifixion and the bones of the saints was part of a faith which believed in the resurrection of the body. More than a pagan cult of the dead hero, orthodox Christianity continued to venerate the flesh as the home of the Holy Spirit. St Augustine himself had complained of travelling salesmen dressed as monks, who sold pieces of martyrs; but he had praised the carrying of the remains of St Stephen to Tbilisi, where they continued to work miracles. Although this traffic was condemned by Rome, ambitious abbots and bishops went on buying sacred bits and pieces and housing them in precious boxes to attract contributions from their congregations. Pope Gregory the Great had refused to donate the head of St Paul to the Byzantine Empress Constantina, yet his condemnation of cutting up the bodies of the martyrs and distributing them for profit was ineffective. Another attested head of St John the Baptist turned up in its jewelled case in San Marco in Venice, while three skulls of St Mary Magdalene were on view – one still remains in the crypt of Vézelay. The skull of St Andrew is said to be held in a hollow pillar of St Peter's in Rome; another skull is in Scotland. Yet perhaps of all the venerated

* See Illustrations.

heads, the prize was kept at the Dom of Cologne, the embroidered skulls of the three Magi, who had brought their bountiful caskets of riches, frankincense and myrrh to the cradle of the infant Christ at Bethlehem. The Empress Helena had found these relics in the Holy Land, and they had been transported by way of Constantinople and Milan to their final resting-place: the donor and thief of the skulls was said to be the alchemist Albertus Magnus, rumoured himself to possess a talking head in the manner of the Celtic god Bran, which acted as an oracle.

Indeed, part of the condemnation of the Templars for their purported worship of a saintly skull within a reliquary of precious metal was the widespread belief in magic. The talking head was a stock-in-trade of the alchemists, whose mixture of astrology and hermetic knowledge passed as the science of the Middle Ages. Not until he wrote that superb mockery of chivalry, *Don Quixote*, did Cervantes expose the bronze and speaking head on its jasper table, said to be cast by the enchanter Escotillo. When the deluded knight had asked the oracle whether he had truly seen a Grail procession in the Cave of Montesinos, the brazen mouth replied, "There is much to be said on both sides." The metal bust was then revealed to be mechanical and was broken up by the command of the Inquisition, 'the sentinels of our faith'. They, too, had broken up the heads of the Cathars and the Templars for their spoken heresies.

Later, at an old commandery in the English village of Templecombe, I was to see the bearded face which the Templars had truly worshipped. Painted on a plaque was a copy of the Mandylion, the head of Christ as depicted on the Holy Veil and other Byzantine paintings. Only discovered in 1951 with the collapse of a ceiling in a storm, the image of Baphomet was at last shown as the image of Christ. In all their searches of the Temple in Paris and of other commanderies, the Inquisitors of 1307 had only found a single skull wrapped in a red cloth and labelled *Caput L V III m*, either a holy relic or the remains of a Grand Master. The monstrous idol of Baphomet seemed the product of a nightmare under torture. Still later, at the village of Anzeghem near Courtrai in Flanders, there was discovered in the ancient Templar church dedicated to St John the Baptist, a bearded wooden head, a reliquary said to contain the skull of John the Baptist similar to that shown in the engraving of the treasures of the Sainte-Chapelle.

More evidence appeared on one of my many visits to Rosslyn Chapel. The Templar archivist Robert Brydon showed me an old polished wood skull, still used in the ceremonies of the Ancient Scottish Rite of that Order – an object reminiscent of the terrifying bearded head on a pole said to have been brandished by Henry of Silesia as he led the Teutonic and Templar knights into battle against the Mongols. The chapel was festooned with dozens of heads, chiefly of the elemental Green Men with all nature sprouting from their distorted visages, but also of Hiram the Masonic martyr with a gash in his forehead, and on the starry ceiling, the bearded Christ with raised right hand. Behind the altar was a smooth-faced portrait, said to be the death mask of Robert the Bruce. He had become undisputed King of Scotland with Templar assistance at the Battle of Bannockburn, and had appointed, as I now learned from Brydon, the St Clairs to represent him as the hereditary Grand Masters of all the crafts and guilds of Scotland, more proof of how the Templars would pass their ceremonies on to the early Masons in the north. The new national symbol, indeed, of the St Andrew's Cross was based on the Templar burial pattern of the skull and crossbones.

Most intriguing were three carvings around the top capitals of three of the pillars of Rosslyn Chapel. One showed St Veronica holding up the Mandylion or Head of Christ on her stone veil, as He carried the cross through the crowd. Another showed Him being taken down from a Tau Cross by Joseph of Arimathea and Nicodemus with the warrior saint and centurion Longinus standing by and holding the Holy Lance, with Mary Magdalene at His feet beside three other holy women. The third carving depicted a bearded angel or Baphomet with a curved sword and Templar cross on his shield delivering Christ from the Tomb guarded by four sleeping soldiers in armour, one with a battle-axe. These were the very symbols of Gnosticism and the Grail.

An eroded carving on the outer wall of Rosslyn Chapel was later recognized by two Freemason writers as a Knight Templar initiating a kneeling and blindfold novice into the Order by placing a noose round his neck. This was given as a proof in stone of the existence of a Templar rite at Rosslyn as late as the fifteenth century, using the symbol of the death to come which has passed into modern Masonic ceremonies. What the two Freemasons did not know was that some of the Templars at their trials in France had confessed to a similar act, when they put cords of white thread round the head of Baphomet as a baptism into wisdom. Once the relic of the head had received these cords, they were placed by the Templars round their belts or bodies as talismans, not as reminders of mortality. Another recent claim by Keith Laidler that the Head of Christ Himself was buried within the Apprentice Pillar at Rosslyn owed more to hope than fact. The Templars worshipped the head of St John the Baptist, not of Christ, and if some of their archives and relics reached the St Clair chapel vaults in Midlothian, this Baphomet would be a reliquary of the Baptist, as in the Sainte-Chapelle in Paris.

A further problem for the Templars was their admission at their trials that the head they venerated was called Baphomet. The simplest explanation of the name – as a devilish amalgam of Baal and Mahomet, led to a possible variant – that of John the Baptist and Mahomet, alluding to the Templars' veneration of the Christian saint and their collusion with Islam. Such an explanation of BAP-HOMET was plausible, and accounted for the supposed cry of the initiates, 'Yah Allah'. The first learned commentators on the Order in Napoleonic times, Nicolas de Bonneville and Joseph von Hammer-Purgstall, looked to the possible Greek origins of the word, the Gospels having been written in that script. For them the term derived from *Baphe*, or Baptism, and *Meteos*, an Institution into Wisdom. Other suggested deviations from Greek split the word into three, signifying *Bios* or Life, *Phos* or Light, and *Metis* or Prudence. Such hypotheses gave a Gnostic content to mere idolatry.

The reasoning made sense. This was the Order of the Temple of Solomon. The knights venerated St John the Evangelist as well as the Baptist. His Gospel stressed that in the beginning was the Word, and the Word was God. In Gnostic philosophy, Jesus had always been the Logos or Word, the interpreter between the divine above and the flesh below. Solomon himself was renowned for his wisdom and had built the first Temple at Jerusalem. This was the head of the faith, the fountain of all knowledge. The very word, temple, was applied to the part of the skull containing the brain. That portion of John the Baptist's remains formed the holy of holies in known reliquaries representing bearded men in the Sainte-Chapelle and at Anzeghem, as well as in the metallic bust containing the crown of St Fraimbault at Lassay. The Knights Templars did not worship the image of Baphomet, but the initiation into wisdom through the head.

The supreme sin of the Gnostics, and their successors the Cathars and the Templars, was to preach the approach to God through personal inspiration and action outside the rules of the orthodox churches. This was true also of such Islamic philosophers as Averroës, who believed that a particle of the Divine Mind lay in each person's head. By reason as well as faith, we might partake in the ultimate wisdom. Whatever that wisdom might be, and however infinite and mysterious the ways of reaching it, all seekers shared a belief in a single creative Intelligence, the fount of knowledge, the architect of the universe, and all that therein was and is and will be. This was the hidden message of the Brahmins and the Magi, the Adepts and the Perfecti and the Grand Masters of the Temple. They did not worship a skull, but the divine light within the bone. As a baby learns a step or two before it may walk, so the initiate could only kiss an image or a bust before he came to understand more. That was the significance of the worship of the head.

My Grail trails now led me towards another mystery from the Near East. The worship of Mary Magdalene had been the supreme female cult in the Christian west of Europe in the Middle Ages. The Gnostic Gospels and the Grail romances had her bringing the holy vessel with Joseph of Arimathea to Sarras and the South of France. At the crossroads of the pilgrimage ways in central France at Vézelay, where St Bernard of Clairvaux had preached the Second Crusade after creating the power of the Cistercian monks and the Knights Templars, the skull and bones of the Magdalene are still kept in the crypt of the abbey church. What had this saint and sinner to do with the Divine Mind?

5

The Magdalene

In honour of Our Lady our Order was founded and in
Her honour it will come to its end whenever it pleases God.

The Templar Rule

ALTHOUGH IN ST JOHN'S GOSPEL the risen Christ is shown
appearing to Mary Magdalene alone in the garden, she was often
portrayed at the foot of the Cross or carrying a gold pot of
myrrh to the Tomb with two or three other women, including the
Virgin. In the early third century, Bishop Hippolytus of Rome, com-
menting on the Canticle of Canticles, held that the Bride was not the
Shulamite, but Mary Magdalene, seeking the Bridegroom, who was not
Solomon, but Jesus Christ, so that she might anoint His wounds in the
garden and at the Tomb. With her sister Martha, she asked the watch-
men, now angels at the empty Tomb, "Saw ye Him whom my soul
loveth?". They answered, "Whom do you seek? Jesus of Nazareth? See
He has risen." To St Augustine, Mary Magdalene saw with her own
eyes the resurrection She was the vital witness of the risen God.

She was also the saved Eve. She found in the garden Jesus as the Tree
of Life, turning away from the Tree of the Knowledge of Good and Evil.
Her early identification as the Bride of Christ and as the new Eve was
emphasized in the Gnostic gospels, where she was often confused with
the repentant sinner or prostitute in St Luke's Gospel and with Mary of
Bethany, who wiped the costly ointment off the feet of Jesus with her long
red hair. In the early Syriac Church, the Magdalene was even merged
with the Virgin Mary as the mother of the Church and of Jesus:

> He drew Mary Magdalene
> To come and see His resurrection.
> Why was it first to a woman
> He showed Himself risen, not to men?
> Here He showed us a mystery
> Concerning His Church and His mother.

So the Magdalene took on the identities and attributes, not only of
Eve, but also of the three Marys of the Gospels and the penitent sinner

in the house of the Pharisee. How many Marys were at the Tomb, the Christian Father Ambrose asked in the fourth century, before going on to stress the role of the Magdalene, telling believers to hold on to Christ, the Tree of Life, as she did, even though He told her not to touch Him. Gregory the Great finally settled the issue in 591 in a sermon in Rome, declaring of the passage in Luke:

> She whom Luke calls the sinful woman, whom John calls Mary, we believe to be the Mary from whom seven devils were ejected according to Mark. And what did these seven devils signify, if not all the vices? . . . She displayed her hair to set off her face, but now her hair dried her tears. She had spoken proud things with her mouth, but in kissing the Lord's feet, she now planted her mouth on the Redeemer's feet. For every delight, therefore, she once had in herself, she now immolated herself. She turned the mass of her crimes to virtues, in order to serve God entirely in penance, for as much as she had wrongly held God in contempt.

Gregory had sent apostles to England to convert the pagan south of the island, not yet touched by Irish and Scottish missionary saints. His version of the Magdalene as the sinner absolved by her adoration of Jesus made her into the most popular and useful female saint of the Middle Ages. Still the new Eve and the Bride of Christ, she was also the sinner forgiven by the love of God, the model for the Church's divine power of absolution. Like Gomer, the unfaithful wife of the prophet Hosea, she also represented the Chosen People, who were unfaithful to God in the flesh. Another medieval confusion of her name with the desert hermit, Mary of Egypt, led to the two women being painted naked and clothed only with their long hair, unique among the female saints, as Eve was originally in the Garden of Eden. At the first resting-place of her supposed bones at the basilica of Saint-Maximin-la-Sainte-Baume, there is a fresco of her nude, carried by angels from her alpine cave to her sepulchre there before most of her remains were removed to Vézelay.* Prints by Dürer and the Altarpiece of the Apocalypse from the Magdalene cloister in Hamburg also show her bare with long tresses, rather too voluptuous for an ascetic.

Her voyage to Marseilles was a golden thread in the legends of the Grail. Two early lives of the woman saint, written in the ninth century by Saxer and Rabanus Maurus, the Bishop of Mayence, moved her cult overland to the Atlantic from the Mediterranean, where she was meant to have landed with the Grail and many pilgrims. The myth spread north through Bruges and Vézelay, Semur-en-Auxois and

* See Illustrations.

The Grand Master of the Knights Hospitallers of St John prays to St John the Baptist, holding the Paschal Lamb with banner on a green Grail platter.

From the Burdett Psalter, c. 1285.

On Matthew Paris's strip map of the Near East, we see crusading and Templar ships sailing into the Holy Land, then probing at fortified Jerusalem, and even seeking to take Cairo in Egypt.

Priest and King Melchizedek at the altar of sacrifice with an ancient Grail and two loaves as sun-discs. He is attended by Abel and Abraham.

From the sixth-century mosaic at Sant' Appollinare in Classe, Ravenna.

The Holy Spirit with the divine sun-disc comes down at Pentecost to St Mary Magdalene and the twelve Apostles, St Peter with the key, another with a crusading sword.

From the Burdett Psalter.

Sir Bors, Perceval and Galahad at Sarras in search of the Grail.

From *The Quest of the Holy Grail*, the *Le Mans MS*.

King Arthur bids farewell to his knights as they leave on the Quest of the Grail.

From a thirteenth-century French illustration.

King Arthur, the overlord of thirty kingdoms, many of them legendary.

Charlemagne on horseback.

From a fourteenth-century French illustration.

The naked St Mary Magdalene with the Grail.

From a fresco in her basilica at Maximin la Sainte Baume.

St Mary Magdalene bears the Grail while the Christ child plays cat's cradle with the rosary.

From a medieval Flemish painting.

St Mary Magdalene carries the Grail with the cosmos falling into the cup towards the Christ child above the Cross.

From a medieval painting in Nuremburg.

A ritual sacrifice beneath the Crucifixion, with St Longinus and the Holy Lance, also the sponge on the reed being offered to Christ.

From the Floreffe Bible, c. 1170.

Two Magi present jewelled chalices to the Infant Christ.

From *The Adoration of the Magi, Tapestry, Brussels*, c. 1480. The Treasury of the Cathedral of Sens.

The crucified Christ on the Templar Cross on the shield of the blood of Joseph of Arimathea.

From *The Quest of the Holy Grail*, the *Le Mans MS*.

Sir Perceval perceives the dual nature of Christ, divine king and human, contained in the Grail.

The perfect octagonal arched round tower at Charroux, built in the twelfth century.

The crusaders besiege Damietta on the Nile.

From the Templar Map on the Kirkwall Scroll.

St Veronica holds the head of Christ on her veil.

From the painting by the Master of St Veronica, c. 1420.

The octagonal Chapelle Saint Clair below the Chapelle Saint-Michel on its lava pinnacle at le Puy-en-Velay

The Garden of Paradise with the hermaphrodite Adam/Eve under the sun and moon and stars and over a medieval Royal Arch to heaven above the Cross on the steps and many other Templar and Masonic symbols.

From the Kirkwall Scroll.

The Serpent on the Tau Cross and the crusading Paschal Lamb with banner and the Royal Arch above the Ark of the Covenant.

The Ulster Boyne Society wallchart, dating from the 1690s.

The Ancient Ark Mariners Degree.
    a. The Royal Arches
    b. The Templar Lamb and Flag
    c. The two Cherubim above the Ark
    d. The Serpent on the Cross
    e. The Ten Commandments
    f. The Triple Tau Cross
    g. The Tabernacle or Holy of Holies
    h. King and Priest Melchizedek
    i. The St Clair and Mariners ship seal
    j. Two sea dragons worshipping the Serpent on the Cross in the disc of the sun
    k. The Ark of Noah and Moses

From the Kirkwall Scroll.

The two Cherubim guard the Ark of the Covenant between the two pillars of the Temple, Jachin and Boaz, under the Royal Arch beside the breastplate of the High Priest, showing the twelve Tribes of Israel and the sacred serpent.

Two priests carry the Ark on its poles by the Tomb of Sarah, while below, two other priests worship the Golden Calf, set on an inverted Tau Cross.

From the Kirkwall Scroll.

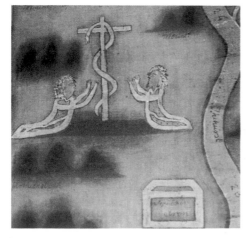

The prophets worship the serpent on the Tau Cross above the Tomb of Aaron.

Troyes, Châteaudun and Chartres and Verneuil-sur-Avre, Bayeux and Bellevault, Besançon and Le Mans, Châlons-sur-Marne and Reims to Fécamp in Normandy on the Channel, the first stronghold and port of the invading Vikings under Rollo, and then across the sea to Glastonbury and Cambridge, where a college was founded in her name. William of Waynflete, the founder of Magdalen College at Oxford where five statues of her can still be seen, read the Maurus manuscript and revered the saint as much for her knowledge as her repentance. She had been regarded in the Gnostic Gospel of Philip as 'the symbol of divine wisdom', while Maurus stressed that her jar of ointment symbolized the secrets of the heart as the sanctuary of faith and charity, the very container of spiritual life.

Odo of Cluny connected the ancient myth of the Grail, as the womb and sin of Eve, with Christ first appearing to the Magdalene after the Crucifixion in His healing garden as the Doctor of her soul. His hymn for his fellow monks celebrated her story:

> After the scandal of her frail flesh,
> From a cauldron she made a cup afresh.
> Into a vase of glory, she altered
> The vessel whose worth she had bartered.

> To her Doctor she ran, spent and sick,
> Bearing her vase so aromatic.
> All the illnesses she had endured
> By the word of the Doctor so were cured.

In the South of France, legend had it that Mary Magdalene had landed at Les-Saintes-Maries-de-la-Mer near Marseilles, the Sarras of Arthurian myth where Joseph of Arimathea also brought the Grail on his way to Britain. The cult of the Magdalene was so widespread that the number of her shrines or churches increased in the five centuries after the eighth from thirty to one hundred and fifty; they were often associated with the veneration of the Black Virgin. In Germany in the first eighty years of the thirteenth century, thirty-two shrines were founded in her name alone. The Gnostics adored the Magdalene as the favourite disciple of Jesus. Her history was told in *The Golden Legend*, the most popular medieval version of the Lives of the Saints. She was identified with Mary of Bethany and was said to own castles and lands near and in Jerusalem with her brother Lazarus and her sister Martha. One home of hers was a tower at Magdala on the Sea of Galilee, another at her home town. She was engaged to John, the other beloved disciple; but when Jesus changed the water into wine at Cana, John left with

Him, and Mary became promiscuous before being redeemed by Jesus, who also brought back her brother Lazarus from the dead.

Her role at the Crucifixion identified her as the Grail-bearer. The Gospels made her out to be the leader of the three women who came with spices to anoint the body of Christ in His Tomb, only to find it gone. The Magdalene was also with another Mary, the mother of James, at the Crucifixion, 'beholding from afar', although not with the Virgin Mary. She would have seen Joseph of Arimathea catching the Holy Blood in a vessel from the Cross, although she did not herself prepare Christ for burial, as the Tomb was empty when she arrived there. Other legends had her accompany Joseph to Sarras with his Grail containing the Holy Blood and her own.

Many medieval windows and tapestries depicted the Magdalene and Mary, the mother of James, holding golden vessels rather like the three Magi; these held the spices for His Body, and they gave out one of the properties of the Grail, the sweetness of delectable aromas. This jar of ointment was also the one which the Magdalene used to collect the body fluids of Christ on the Cross and at His Deposition, although some claimed that she was given the Grail by Christ Himself in the garden. On the sea voyage to France, the Magdalene, like her companion Joseph, was frequently shown carrying a cup or precious vessel. Although the Grail princess with the chalice in the processions at the Castle of the Fisher King was not identified as the Magdalene, her legend was surely in the imagination of the romancers.

With the Magdalene came many early Christians including her brother Lazarus, said to be the first bishop of Marseilles, and her sister Martha, who quelled the dragon of the Rhône at Tarascon, and the first Bishop of Aix, St Maximin. She retired to a cave on a cliff at Sainte-Baume, the name of the holy balsam for the Body of Christ. There she meditated and fasted for thirty years, fed only by manna from heaven as if from a Grail. According to Saxer, she was naked and penitent, only clad in her long red hair. On the point of death, angels carried her to the hermitage of Maximin. He had her body embalmed and put in a mausoleum. It was later transferred to a sarcophagus in the church that bore his name, where the incorruptible flesh gave off sweetness and her cheek was still rosy where Jesus had touched it at the time of his Resurrection. The flask of the Holy Blood which the Magdalene had brought with her was seen to liquefy on every Good Friday. One arm was given to the fortified church of Les Saintes-Maries, where it was put in a precious reliquary and is still said to perform miracles of healing, also blessing the waters of the Mediterranean that brought her safe to Provence.

The crossroads of the pilgrim trails of France was at Vézelay. The shrine in the crypt of the cathedral church is said to hold the skull and bones of Mary Magdalene. According to local historians, the relics were removed by the 'holy theft' of the monk Badilon from her hermit cave at Sainte-Baume near Marseilles, although the clerics of the nearby basilica of Saint-Maximin also claimed the sacred remains of the beloved companion of Jesus, some of which are still kept in a Gallo-Roman sarcophagus that serves as an altar. In Marseilles itself, the church of Saint-Victor used to flaunt its possession of the spiced jar of unguent, with which the Magdalene anointed the feet and the wounds of Christ. Both churches denied the claims of the abbey of St Stephen at Halberstadt and of St John Lateran at Rome to be the final resting-place of the saint. According to the rival story, Mary Magdalene had died as a penitent in the Cave of the Seven Sleepers outside Ephesos, and was taken to Byzantium to be buried beside her brother Lazarus in a monastery on the Bosphoros, only to be spirited away by Conrad, the Bishop of Halberstadt, after the sack of the imperial city during the Fourth Crusade.

Vézelay was in no way the first church dedicated to Mary Magdalene. Nearby at Auxerre, indeed, the feast day of Martha and Mary was introduced as early as the sixth century, while King Athelstan four centuries later gave a finger of the saint to Exeter cathedral. In the eleventh century, shrines to the saint were erected at Bayeux in Normandy, at Bellevault and Besançon, Le Mans and Verdun and Reims, where her great statue stands above the entrance beside the Virgin Mary, received into heaven with the black ball of the world at her feet. In England, her first sanctuaries were in the West Country, at Barnstaple in Devon and Beckery near Glastonbury, where Magdalen Street still fronts the ruins of the abbey, leading to a little church and hospice for poor pilgrims, dedicated to her name.

The origins of Vézelay were laid in a small monastery founded in the ninth century under the patronage of the Virgin Mary. Not until two centuries later did a papal bull from Leo the Ninth make Mary Magdalene the chief patron of the abbey there, while Stephen the Ninth confirmed her as sole patron and authenticated her relics. The growing strength of her cult was shown in this rare case of her displacing the Virgin Mary – a situation that would be reversed in modern times, where most of the Magdalene's churches would be ascribed to the other Mary, the Mother of God. Pilgrims began flocking to Vézelay, expecting miracles; her tomb was soon surrounded by the broken fetters and chains of freed prisoners, who had prayed to her for their release.

In Vézelay, St Bernard had preached the Second Crusade, after founding the Cistercian Order of white monks and promoting the Knights Templars of the octagonal red cross to their power and glory.

Their function was the protection of pilgrims to the holy places, not only to Palestine, but also to Santiago de Compostela in Spain, where many prospective crusaders found themselves fighting the Moors before they managed the voyage on towards Jerusalem. Although the Benedictines from Cluny had already established the Knights of St John as protectors of the sacred way, the Templars were useful allies in the holy war in Spain. The bones of the penitent woman saint brought pilgrims to Vézelay; the arms of the Hospitallers and the Templars accompanied them through the town from the coronation place of the Kings of France at Reims to the cathedral of St James at Compostela. As far as the French border, a way lay through Neuvy-Saint-Sepulchre, Charroux, Civray, Aulnay and Saintes to the pass at Roncevalles, where Roland had died. At each of these places, there remained symbols of the Grail and the Magdalene.

Surviving stained-glass windows in France and Italy still show her as the patron of many trades. Inevitably, following Christ's appearance to her, she was sacred to gardeners. Her vase of unguents brought her the worship of apothecaries and perfumers. Her early life of luxury was celebrated by the drapers of Bologna and the makers of gloves and shoes. The people of Bolzano prayed to her to help their vintages, while the water-sellers of Chartres also sought her benediction. Her healing by Christ, who had also cured her brother, made her an apostle to the sick and to lepers, while her penitence endeared her to prisoners, who dedicated their chains to her at Vézelay. She was the most charismatic woman saint of the Middle Ages.

In the Romanesque churches of France, the weeping Magdalene wiping the feet of Christ with her hair can be seen in many early carvings – on the frieze at Saint-Gilles-en-Gard, and on the capitals at Arles and Autun, where she is sculpted by Ghislebertus as one of the three Marys, going with their spice jars towards the Tomb. Her three attributes are all represented in *The Golden Legend*, first as the bitter sea of sin and repentance, then as the giver of the light of the Spirit and the Ecclesia of the church, and lastly as the enlightened one, the Sophia of Gnostic wisdom. At the castle of Semur-le-Auxois, which Charlemagne himself gave to the monks of St Maurice, the ancient chapel in the basilica of Notre-Dame is dedicated to St Mary Magdalene. Restored along with Notre-Dame de Paris and Carcassonne by the great architect Viollet le Duc in the nineteenth century, the church contains two windows; their seven diamond panels made six centuries previously recount Mary's life and legends. She and her sister Martha can be seen praying with Joseph of Arimathea before a golden Grail placed on a red cushion on an altar; in another scene, she takes a ship to Sarras; in yet another, the saint dies and is entombed in her sarcophagus. On the marble Renaissance altar, Christ is shown after His Resurrection appearing to the Magdalene.

From Semur, past the great Cistercian abbey of Fontenoy, the cult of the Magdalene spread to Troyes, the city of Chrétien, who first gave the Grail its medieval identity by writing the original romance on the subject. The oldest church in the city is dedicated to Mary Magdalene, part of it still dating from the end of the twelfth century, the time of the writing of *Perceval*. My visit there was a revelation. The word *graal* is a Provençal word. Southern troubadours were popular at the court of Champagne. Most likely, they knew of the story of Joseph of Arimathea and the Magdalene from the Mediterranean south at La-Sainte-Baume. The oldest church in Troyes was built to commemorate that legend, and Chrétien would have known why. In a Renaissance extension of the building, the stocking-makers of Troyes presented in 1506 scenes in stained glass from the life of the saint, surmounted by a pair of small windows, showing twin cherubs holding ornate Grails. In one panel, the two blessed Marys bear precious jars of spices for the wounds of Christ. In another, Jesus reappears to Longinus and Joseph, before His apparition to the Magdalene, at whose feet lies a Grail. She and Joseph and her family are then banished from the Holy Land, only to have Christ bless them again as they are converting the King of Sarras at a royal feast. Finally, the saint is laid in her sepulchre, with Bishop Maximin praying for her soul.

Although these windows postdated the writing of *Perceval*, they reflected faithfully the early story of the Magdalene as it was seen in cathedral windows of previous centuries. There is every chance that Chrétien knew of this *Story of the Grail*, the subtitle of his book, because of her church at Troyes. An early stained-glass window in France showing Longinus piercing the side of Christ with the Holy Lance and Joseph of Arimathea catching His Blood in a Grail is in the cathedral of St Peter in Poitiers; it dates from 1165, before the writing of *Perceval*. Other churches and basilicas in Troyes confirm the prevalence of the legends. In the Church of St John, where King Henry the Fifth of England married Catherine of France, there are windows of the Last Supper, of John the Baptist's head on a platter, of the three Magi bearing gifts and of the Circumcision of Jesus, and more rare, of manna falling from heaven, collected in bowls by the believers, the direct gift of the food of life by the Almighty to his Chosen People. This image would occur on the Secret Scroll, which was to end my long quest.

Most strange, however, are the links between Chrétien, the romancer of the Grail, and the Treasury of the cathedral of St Peter and St Paul at Troyes. A reliquary of the Magdalene carried between two angels testifies to the memory of her preserved in the city. But an extraordinary alms purse there connects her Gnostic legend with the pursuit of the divine. On it, two women are shown seated before an altar which bears a naked heart. Above, a flying oblong Ark sends down a fork of lightning or grace. A portrait of St Bernard appears to bless this confusion between human love and divine fire.

Halfway to Reims, to the north at Châlons-sur-Marne, a window celebrates St James wearing a pilgrim's habit as he leads the Spanish crusaders to victory at the Battle of las Navas de Tolosa against the Moors. At another window dedicated to the Compassion of the Virgin Mary, Joseph of Arimathea catches the Holy Blood of the crucified Christ, while a large-scale Mary Magdalene holds a golden chalice as other women receive Him after His deposition. Her story is also repeated – collecting His blood at the foot of the Cross, sailing to Sarras with her sister Martha and Joseph at the prow, their two golden Grails with His Blood blessed by an angel on arrival and used to heal the sick. Most curious is an apparition of Jesus to the Magdalene, in which He plunges the Holy Lance of Longinus into a transparent bucket, as if washing it off.

At Châlons, too, are the double windows of the Brotherhood of the Blessed Sacrament at St Alpin, who saved the city from Attila, King of the Huns. These are rare testaments to the Cathar and Huguenot heresies, which led to the bloody religious wars of France. As in the Grail romances, the crux of the conflict was the granting of grace directly from God. Was the Host a mystery of the Roman Catholic priesthood or were communion and the chalice open to all believers? The Protestants controlled Châlons in the early sixteenth century, when the Brotherhood of the Blessed Sacrament was formed. The windows show manna falling from heaven and the institution of the Last Supper. The Brothers dressed as Apostles take communion directly from the Son of God, as the *perfecti* and the Cathar faithful did at their divine feasts. Christ is shown putting His hand to His mouth, signifying that He is the Word of God speaking individually to each believer through the Bible. And in another Renaissance window, two colourful panels of the miracles of the loaves and the fishes along with the turning of water into wine at Cana emphasize the bounty of God to all who attend His celebrations.

On the way to the Channel lies an early Church of the Magdalene in Verneuil-sur-Avre. It is crowned by an unearthly censer or pepperpot spire, looking like a descending Grail scattering light. The stained-glass windows of the choir show Joseph of Arimathea with the holy vessel blessing St Mary and other pilgrims before their voyage from the Holy Land. An inscription on another window identifies Marseilles as their landing place, with shepherds already kneeling on the rocks in worship and wonder. Although the building, like that at Troyes, dates from the twelfth century, the windows are part of the revival of the cult of the saint inspired by Viollet le Duc, as at Semur and Châteaudun.

There, the abbey church of the Magdalene is stripped as bare as her reputation has been. Yet the exquisite round Romanesque arches set beside those with slight points in the shape of perfect breasts make this white stone edifice the most beautiful of the shrines still left to the saint. There is no altar at Châteaudun, as if religious faith had been removed from the Magdalene. In a battered frieze, her sole statue has had the Holy Vessel broken from her hand. Yet above her gouged head is the scallop shell of the pilgrims on their way to Santiago de Compostela; for her church was traditionally built over a crypt of the fifth century dedicated to St James and hollowed out of the rock. And strangely, on the hexagonal medieval baptismal font, there is a curiously mixed pagan-Christian relief of the back of a naked figure emerging from a cornucopia. Man or woman, this hermaphrodite holds up the lid of plenty. Later, in the Imperial Museum in Vienna, I would see four androgynous statues, said to have been taken from Templar commanderies, and I would learn of the same figures carved on stone coffers, which derived, according to the Chevalier de Blacas, from Templar houses in Burgundy and Tuscany.

Yet the lady venerated by the Templars was meant to be the Virgin Mary, not the ambiguous Magdalene, who represented the repentant sinner as well as the androgynous Gnostic goddess of wisdom. The first and last prayers of the day in the Templar Rule were to the Mother of God. At the initiation ceremony, the novice knight was told, "In honour of Our Lady our Order was founded and in Her honour it will come to its end whenever it pleases God." When the Order did come to an end, the lady they were accused of worshipping and kissing took the form of a hermaphrodite Baphomet, as illustrated by the late classical figures shown in the edition of 1818 of the oriental scholar, Joseph von Hammer-Purgstall, in his book, *The Mystery of Baphomet Revealed*, and in his later work, *The Guilt of the Templars*.

The author worked for the Austrian Chancery, and his object was to discredit Freemasonry, which was then seen as a secret threat to the conservative European monarchies that re-emerged following the defeat of Napoleon. Curiously enough, his research tended to contradict his propaganda. He made plausible connections between Gnostic sects such as the Ophites, Cathars and Templars and the Ismai'ili Assassins and the medieval guilds and the later Freemasons, then he proceeded to vilify all of these confraternities. To him, the Ophites indulged in orgies, denied Jesus, and worshipped the phallus rather than the serpent of wisdom. The Tau Cross, indeed, was another phallic symbol, rather than the shape of the crucifixion of St John and the end letter of the Hebrew alphabet. Inheriting Gnostic beliefs, the Cathars and the Templars were accused not of seeking divine enlightenment, but of free love and sodomy and the worship of androgynous idols such as Baphomet. The Grail was a Gnostic vessel, not a Christian chalice, and as the knights of the Grail, the refugee Templars passed on their subversive knowledge through the Ancient Scottish Masonic rites to contemporary Freemasons. While excoriating the Templars as corrupt devil-worshippers, all Hammer-Purgstall succeeded in showing was that they were an important conduit of Gnostic beliefs through the Middle Ages into later Masonic practices.

For Hammer-Purgstall, 'Our Lady' worshipped by the Templars was the hermaphrodite Achamoth or Sophia who held the Tau, which was the phallus as well as the serpent of wisdom. This was a perversion of the Gnostic beliefs which had such an influence on the Templars. Indeed, they did venerate both the Virgin Mary and the Magdalene because of their sexlessness, their union of the male and female principles in one flesh. This would finally be confirmed to me by the painting at the head of the Secret Scroll. There an androgyne, both Adam and Eve, sat in the paradise, which all the Knights of the Military Order sought to attain, as did the Ismai'ili Assassins, by the sacrifice of their flesh to the divine intelligence – as St John the Baptist and Jesus Himself had done before them.

Almost at the end of my Grail trails, I discovered the ultimate proof that the Templars were the Knights of the Grail. On the route from Toulouse to Compostela, the Templar commandery of Montsaunès was the most important between the Provençal city and the Pyrenees. Founded in 1156, it guarded the pilgrim route to Spain. During the Cathar rebellion, Bernard the Fourth, the Count of Comminges, protected the Templar stronghold from the ravages of Simon de Montfort and his marauding crusaders: the remains of his sarcophagus are still there. The surviving Romanesque chapel confirmed the close connections of the Knights Templars with the early French masons, the *compagnonnage* of Saint-Jacques, the patron saint of Santiago de Compostela. Outside stood a clock tower with five openings, while triple windows enlightened the choir. On the west and south doors, there were triple arcades, sustained by four small columns ending in a sculpture recalling the builders. The rose window chapel was composed of thirteen circles, the twelve apostles and the signs of the zodiac, with Christ the sun at their centre.

On the fresco of the roof of the nave, two plumb-lines beneath a Royal

Arch enclosed a red octagonal Templar cross *pattée*, which supported a chalice bowl, ornamented by the flower with six petals of the *compagnonnage*, and by the entwined worms or serpents of Gnostic wisdom. Arrowheads and stars with the sun and the moon, triangles and pyramids and an encompassing cosmic bowl, argued for greater mysteries within this medieval Military Order. I could perceive Sirius and Sagittarius and the seven disciples of Saint-Jacques, connected to the seven planets and to the biblical Hiram, the builder of the Temple of Solomon. An exact compass was painted on the vault to guide the pilgrims on the right way, while the presbytery once held a Black Virgin representing the Sophia, the Goddess of Wisdom, as well as of Mary, the Mother of God.*

The cult of the Magdalene also spread west along the Mediterranean coast from Saint Maximin-La-Sainte-Baume and Marseilles, where she landed traditionally with the Grail. At Béziers, there is a large church dedicated to her with an octagonal tower constructed by the apse. A Viscount Trescard was murdered in the holy building, and at the massacre of the entire population of the city in 1209 during the Albigensian crusade, the worst slaughter took place in this sanctuary, where the Cathars had fled, seeking a vain mercy. The grim words of Arnald-Almaric, Abbot of Cîteau, inciting the vengeful crusaders against the heretics still resound: "Kill them all: God will look after His own." During the French Revolution, the church was turned into a workshop for the making of bayonets, but now the only sign of war on its outer walls is a crusading knight within a large medallion, while a gigantic scallop shell design reminds the pilgrim today of the holy way to Spain.

In Narbonne, the old Bishop's Palace has a Magdalene tower and chapel, now converted into an archaeological museum. A faded fresco of the Deposition from the Cross has almost expunged the saint, while two clearer cherubim swing their censers on chains above her. At Albi, there are a pair of Magdalenes carrying her vase, almost lost among the exuberant Renaissance portals. But at Carcassonne and Perpignan, there are no traces of her. At the cathedral of Gerona, however, beside the paradise of the cloister with its Tree of Life and fountain of youth, the Treasury contains a brilliant altarpiece of the voyage of the Magdalene to the South of France and of her apotheosis there. Below the region of the Langue d'Oc, the land of the Catalans tended to venerate the Black Virgin, another name for the ancient feminine principle embodied by the Magdalene.

In modern times many signs of the bygone cult of the Magdalene,

---

* See Illustrations.

the St Mary of the Middle Ages with her two hundred and more shrines, have been obliterated. Why should this be? The medieval Church was at its most successful in making Christians feel guilty. Its control of the wilder passions lay in the need for expiation that was mediated by the priest. And much repentance was demanded in that cruel and plundering age. For the warlords and knights, whose violence and greed was the occasion of considerable sins, the Magdalene was their perfect messenger – a stained woman, blessed by Christ Himself. Yet in a later age of materialism and psychiatry, guilt would be at a discount and pardon would become merely the confession from a couch. The Vatican would hold purity to be a better message, particularly for women; transgressions would be expiated by Hail Marys rather than walking with bleeding feet along rocky paths. Jung himself, one of the fathers of analysis, would study alchemy and the Grail, in search of the well-springs of those legends within the human psyche. In the course of this progress, the cult of the Magdalene and the Grail were to be lost or mistaken.

With the waning of the Grail at the end of the Middle Ages, the Magdalene was gradually displaced by the cult of the Virgin Mary or Our Lady, although the Gospels made no mention of her presence at the Tomb or at Christ's first resurrection in the garden. Churches were renamed, the Gospels and the golden legends were forgotten. The Mother of Jesus was shown superseding the Magdalene at the foot of the Cross, washing Christ's wounds there and taking care of His body at the opening of the Tomb. By the nineteenth century, she was dominating the Magdalene at most of the second Mary's sites in France as at Meaux, where the windows of the Lady Chapel even show the Virgin at the feast at Cana and with the disciples at Pentecost. The attraction of the repentant sinner who brought the Grail to Sarras was replaced by the vision of the undefiled Mother of God. The sinful woman, forgiven by Christ, was remade without spot or blemish.

By contrast, the Grand Masters of the Knights Templars had replaced the official veneration of Our Lady recommended to the lower members of the Order with the understanding of the Sophia or the Magdalene as the receiver of the divine wisdom. Only the higher Templar degrees were free to receive this insight, as the modern Freemasons must pass through thirty-three degrees to attain the supreme understanding of the significance of Melchizedek and the Royal Arch and the Temple of Solomon. Even so, I was bound to seek some revelations in the Near East, where the secret knowledge was originally distilled.

6

The Temple

Temple [OE. *templ, tempel,* ad. L. *templum,* reinforced by F. *temple*]
I. 1. An edifice or place regarded primarily as the dwelling place or
'house' of a deity or deities; hence, an edifice devoted to divine
worship. **b.** The sacred edifice at Jerusalem, the 'House of the Lord'
and seat of the Jewish worship of Jehovah OE. **c.** *fig.* 1607. 2. A
building dedicated to public Christian worship; a church; esp. applied
to a large or grand edifice. late ME. 3. Any place regarded as occupied
by the divine presence; the person or body of a Christian (I Cor. iii.
16) OE.
II. The head-quarters of the Knights Templars, on or contiguous to
the site of the temple at Jerusalem; hence, the organization of the
Templars 1656.

Oxford English Dictionary

HE VALUE OF EXPERIENCE is a jigsaw puzzle that may never be
solved in a lifetime. The more we travel and see, the more
pieces are scattered at random on our table of choices. Only
when we find the proper place of each part – perhaps decades later –
does the puzzle fit together. We do not know what we are viewing or
recording, until a particular hindsight or insight serves to fill in the
pattern or reasoning of later understanding. Fortunately, I have long
kept illustrated diaries. I still have one of a trip to the Near East made
some forty years ago, when I could not always discern the significance
of what came my way. Now, looking backwards for the purpose of this
book, I can complete more of the picture. Not all comes back to mind
by chance alone.

I went in winter to Alexandria, the cradle and hotbed of the Gnostic
philosophers. The city on a mouth of the Nile was melancholy and
empty by the sea. Founded by the Greek conqueror who bequeathed
its name, its remains included the sunken Wonder of the World – the
Pharos lighthouse – Roman catacombs, Pompey's pillar, the burned
library of all libraries, Islamic mosques, Ottoman forts and Mameluke
battlements. As I descended to the buried Roman tunnels and chambers
of Kom Al-Shokafa, the easy assimilation of foreign gods by the pagan
invaders and the early Christians became everywhere evident. The
Greek serpent goddess Medusa and Osiris were brought together on a

sandstone carving; indeed, the Roman Serapis had been a combination of the divine bull Apis and Osiris. In front of me was a shield or moon bearing Medusa's severed head surrounded by writhing vipers; below it appeared a rendition of Osiris as a snake with a goat's head, horned and bearded. At that time, I knew vaguely of the serpents of wisdom and the cult of the Nile as a goddess, which I later recorded from tomb inscriptions in the Tombs of the Queens as a winged cobra with two feet and as a sinuous boat, supporting four human figures. Yet such images were still mysteries to me, and the greatest of all arcane libraries had been burned long ago.

At the Temple of Luxor, I saw carved squat pillars supporting stone lintels, which would become the models for the Temple of Solomon. Above the pagan statues and symbols stood the yellow plaster and domes of a mosque: a perfect representation of how the religions of the Near East had built one upon another. Later, in Jordan and Syria, I would find pagan shrines overlaid by Jewish, Christian and Muslim foundations, piled one above the other in the eternal bitter confusion of the religions of the Near East. The lotus pillars of the Ramasseum at Thebes also suggested lost oriental influences, which would result in the decorative palm-trees and pomegranates on the capitals of the Temple of Solomon. In the valley of the Tombs of the Kings, beyond the twin Colossi of Memnon sunk in their paddy-fields, I began to see the motif of the divine snake as beautiful; even a long frieze of beheaded Nubians, their hands tied behind their backs, had a cruel perfection.

Moving to Jordan, I went twice to Aqaba, the second time pursued by an Israeli gunboat while aboard the royal launch on the way to visit the southernmost crusader castle in Sinai. And up at Petra, that wondrous Nabatean city hewn out of pink and blue and coral and purple and yellow sandstone, the pillared porches of the rock temples, the ruined crusader fort, and above all Aaron's Tomb dating from the journey of the Twelve Tribes from Egypt to Canaan, were to have a later and even greater significance for me. Petra was to be named and Aaron's Tomb shown on the Secret Scroll.

The first time I came to Jerusalem on many visits, the old city was occupied by the Jordanians. A medieval tangle within the walls, the narrow winding streets led to steps and under arches. The Christian holy places seemed insignificant; the Via Dolorosa was braying with car horns, the Garden of the Tomb and Golgotha were swallowed up by a bus station, even the Church of the Holy Sepulchre was hugger-mugger with corpulent priests. "The only place to contemplate in town," I wrote then, "is the great Dome of the Rock, which dominates the city. Islam is triumphant in religious awe here." There, the vast octagonal structure built by Byzantine architects for their Islamic masters appeared to displace the Jewish Temple on Mount Moriah; the foundations of Herod's mighty Temple had been reduced to the cyclopean masonry of the Western or Wailing Wall, a continual lamentation for the Holy of Holies, forever lost and gone. "Jerusalem is a Berlin," I wrote, "with the old wall of Suleiman the Magnificent dividing the city, and David's citadel a prohibited Arab military zone, and sudden death standing by the sentry on every wall, and bitterness gagging the voice of the Sunday bells."

In Hebron, again an imposing plain mosque had been built on the great blocks of another temple of King Herod. Over two thousand years, these had housed the remains of Abraham and Isaac, Leah and Rachel. At Palmyra in Syria, from the roof of the great temple of Bel or Baal, I could view the gracious pillars of the capital of Queen Zenobia after her triumph against Rome, while an emir's stronghold dominated the desert valley with its square and abandoned towers. The great chain of Christian and Muslim fortresses stretching from the Red Sea all the way to Anatolia had its culmination in the mighty Krak des Chevaliers, commanding the route from the north into Lebanon. Its size and defensive complexity made it the archetype of crusading fortification. In the exquisite little chapel of the Krak stood the pulpit of a mosque. Islam had again succeeded. Finally, at the Temple of Venus at Baalbek, ancient and pagan could be seen side by side with modern religious relics in the Near East. Once the site of the orgies of Heliopolis and the resting-place of the swallows of Oscar Wilde, the walls of that citadel were still an uneasy divide between the Christian and Islamic sects and warlords, struggling for control of the lost civilization of Phoenicia.

As I have suggested, I did not understand then the value of these experiences. Later, I would write a whole history of Jerusalem, including the making of its three Temples. The biblical accounts of Kings and Chronicles described the building and decoration of the first Temple, but not its precise shape. King David had provided the resources and skilled labour for the sacred place, as he told his son Solomon:

> Now, behold, in my trouble I have prepared for the house of the Lord an hundred thousand talents of gold, and a thousand thousand talents of silver; and of brass and iron without weight; for it is in abundance: timber also and stone have I prepared; and thou mayest add thereto.
> Moreover there are workmen with thee in abundance, hewers and workers of stone and timber, and all manner of cunning men for every manner of work.
> Of the gold, the silver, and the brass, and the iron, there is no number. Arise, therefore, and be doing, and the Lord be with thee.

Arise therefore, and be doing. That was the command in the accounts of the building of the Temple, both to the Jews and later to the Christians and the Masons. These were practical directives for making a home for the Ark of the Covenant and, in the words of the Book of Kings, 'an house for the name of the Lord God of Israel'. Parts of the Old Testament are almost a builder's manual, while the Book of Revelation – the inspiration of St John the Divine on the island of Patmos – is a surveyor's apocalypse and an architect's apotheosis where the Temple is measured with a 'reed like a rod'. The original Temple of Solomon was described as the work of a multitude of hands in the service of a transcendent vision. Labourer, overseer and prophet were one in a sacred purpose. Thumb and brain served together; matter met with mind. That building of Solomon, who was credited with the wisdom as well as the holiness of the oriental priest-king, was a paradigm for those who wished to unify tribes and clans into a people or a society. In that common and divine work was a harmony between rich and poor, high and low.

A specific artist and architect with a Jewish mother and a Phoenician father, Hiram of Tyre, was credited with the decoration of the Temple. He was, according to the Book of Chronicles, "a cunning man, endued with understanding . . . skilful to work in gold, and in silver, in brass, in iron, in stone, and in timber, in purpose, in blue, and in fine linen, and in crimson; also to grave any manner of graving, and to find out every device which shall be put to him." He also was credited with legendary tools that could pierce stone. As the Book of Kings stated, the Temple "was built of stone made ready before it was brought thither; so that there was neither hammer nor axe nor any tool of iron heard in the house, while it was in building." The prohibition of the use of tools within the Temple derived from Exodus, when the Lord had directed Moses to make a stone altar without mechanical means, 'for if thou lift up thy tool upon it, thou hast polluted it'. Rabbinical tradition ascribed the dovetailing of the prefabricated stones and ornaments of the Temple to the Shamir, a giant worm that could cut stones – a tradition not far removed from Celtic and Norse traditions of the dragon's fire which constructed Valhalla and Camelot.

The two pillars of the porch of the Temple called Jachin and Boaz, a feature of every future Masonic Lodge, were probably modelled on the pair of obelisks that fronted many Egyptian temples or the pillar of pure gold and the pillar of emerald that Herodotus saw at Tyre in front of the Temple of Hercules. In the biblical accounts Hiram cast in the plain of Jordan "two pillars of brass of eighteen cubits high apiece . . . And he made chains, as in the oracle, and put them on the heads of the pillars, and made a hundred pomegranates, and put them on the chains . . . And four hundred pomegranates on the two wreaths; two rows of pomegranates on each wreath, to cover the two pommels of the chapiters which were upon the pillars." The altar of the Temple was also made of brass, and the Molten Sea beside it was supported by twelve brazen oxen. As in the treasuries at Mycenae and Etruscan Bronze Age tombs, metal plates were used for decoration far more than carved designs in stone. The whole Temple of Solomon glittered with precious and base metals, as if fired in the forges of heaven.

The square and the cube had been the preferred cosmic shapes used for city planning by the first priest-kings of the Near East, although a small clay tablet from Babylon shows a circle enclosing the regions of the world. The first surviving picture of the Third or Herod's Temple on the coins of the Bar Kochba period around 135 AD depicts a square entrance with four Hellenistic pillars leading to the cube of the Tabernacle enclosing the Ark of the Covenant. This was the shape suggested by the Lord God to Moses in the Bible. The idea of the cosmos as a cube pervaded the thought and planning of ancient India and China and the Near East, which seem to have shared their views on the design of the universe and the mathematical correspondence of its quarters and parts. The oriental traditions of the square and the cube as the basic pattern of creation were bequeathed to the Jews; they in turn passed it on to the Christians, who found in the Old Testament descriptions of the Tabernacle of Moses and the first encampment of the twelve tribes of Israel. These were to be shown in Templo's *Retrato del Tabernaculo de Moseh* of 1654 as a small square surrounded by the twelve larger squares of the tents of the tribes, all contained in one regular field with four equal sides. In mind, if not in fact, the Tabernacle and the Temple were the cubes of symbolic creation.

Not even his kingdom survived the death of Solomon, so wise in his judgement, so pacific in his diplomacy, so voluptuous in his tastes, so prodigal in his works. The northern tribes of Israel revolted, and Jerusalem, capital now only of Judah, found itself unable to attract pilgrims from outside its borders. The priests and the Levites, however, congregated in the religious centre of the faith, and the preaching and the prophecies of Elijah and Isaiah lauded and lamented Jerusalem. Disaster fell on the northern tribes when the kingdom of Israel was conquered in 722 BC by the Assyrians. Ten of the twelve tribes were deported and forced into apostasy and disappeared from history. The remnant joined Josiah, who again unified the Jewish tribes by his insistence on the uniqueness of the Temple, and its sole claim to house the Lord God. Jeremiah foresaw the destruction of Jerusalem and the

Temple, if Judah did not surrender to the rising power of Nebuchadnez-zar, the monarch of Babylon. The survival of the holy places transcended the independence of the Jewish state. But Jeremiah was imprisoned in a cistern, Jerusalem was captured and razed, and the Judean people were taken as hostages and slaves to Babylon to sit by its waters and weep for their burned sanctuary.

Yet the deported were not forced by the Babylonians to assimilate, as they had been in Assyria. They were allowed to form what was the first of the ghettos. In exile by the Euphrates, Ezekiel told the Hebrews that they had lost their sacred house as a divine punishment for their sins. Yet they would return in glory to rebuild the Temple, if they repented. In the meantime, a local house of prayer, the synagogue, square in design, was to be built to guard the faith, as the Tabernacle of Moses had done. Again the people of the tribes of Israel were wandering, the beginning of a cycle of expulsion and return that would mark the eventual Diaspora, or scattering of the Jews over the surface of the globe. As in Babylon, each dispersed community would form a congregation and a synagogue to remember the Temple and to keep the holy law. The rituals and the designs of Jerusalem were carried in words and pictures wherever the Jews were cast abroad by the forces of history.

The destruction of the First Temple had also been foretold in the death of its architect, Hiram of Tyre, the memory of which was preserved in the literature of the Cabbala. As old as the construction of the ziggurats and the pyramids had been the practice of a sacrifice to ensure the stability of a newly founded building. Hebrew tradition identified that sacrificial victim in the human creator of the Temple at Jerusalem. According to rabbinical legend, all the workmen of the Temple were killed so that they should not build another one devoted to idolatry, while Hiram was raised like Enoch to heaven. Later Masonic tradition had it that Hiram was murdered by three fellow master crafts-men, because he would not reveal to them the secrets of how the Temple was made. There are Promethean and Dionysian elements in both the Judaic and the Christian versions of the death of Hiram; yet all saw in the destruction of the Temple the loss of the mysteries of its creator, perhaps in consequence of his own secret knowledge.

When the Persians under Cyrus conquered Babylon fifty years after the destruction of Jerusalem, he permitted the return of those Jewish exiles who wished to rebuild their city. Under Sheshbazzar, the prince of Judah, and his successor, Zerubbabel, first the houses were restored and then the Second Temple, built in the size and shape of Solomon's house of the Lord, but in simple stone and with little decoration. As there were no walls to defend them, each Temple builder – in the words of their later leader Nehemiah – 'with one of his hands wrought in the work, and with the other hand held a weapon'. They set an example for the later Christian knights of the Order of the Temple of Solomon, the Templars; there before them was a concrete example of the making of the house of God as a crusade.

At that period, Jerusalem was still ruinous and scantly populated, until the prophet Ezra led back another group of exiles to rebuild the city wall in its long lozenge about Mount Moriah. The Torah once again became the law of the land, and Persian tolerance allowed the recrudescence of the Jewish faith in a form that was both more pure and subtle. Pilgrims from beyond the borders of Judah began to return for the three sacred annual festivals in Jerusalem, beginning the long quest for the Holy City that was to inform the practice and the thought and even the conflicts of succeeding ages.

When Alexander of Macedon defeated the Persians and conquered the Near East, he did not harm Jerusalem. He usually respected the religions of those lands which he occupied, in order to rule them better. In his history *The Antiquities of the Jews*, the first-century historian Josephus described the Greek king's awe at the priests in their silk robes and the high priest in purple with a plate of gold on his forehead inscribed with the sacred name of God. The grateful Jews assisted their new ruler in founding the city in Egypt which was called Alexandria after him, and there the second largest community of Jews in exile after Babylon would establish itself for the benefit of that great port by the Nile. Yet in their prayers and in their synagogues, those who lived abroad still turned in worship towards Jerusalem although later the philosopher and Christian convert Philo would make the city the crucible of Gnostic beliefs.

After the death of Alexander, the Ptolemaic rulers in Egypt continued to treat their Jewish province with kindness, but when their dynasty was defeated by the Seleucids in Syria, one of them, Antiochus Epiphanes, tried to impose the worship of the Greek gods on Jerusalem, provoking the revolt of those five masters of guerrilla warfare, the Maccabees of the house of Hasmon. They re-established the independence of Judah and Jerusalem, where the Temple was dedicated once more, a celebration that is still commemorated in the Chanuka, or the Festival of Lights. They played the growing power of Rome against the decline of the Seleucids and captured some of the old Philistine ports to gain access to the Mediterranean. The increase in territory of the descendants of the house of Hasmon was dissipated by the quarrels between the reactionary and dogmatic Sadducees, who initially controlled the Temple, and the council of elders called the Sanhedrin, and the Pharisees, who represented a strict but evolutionary Judaism.

These conflicts split the state and allowed for the invasion of the Roman general Pompey, who took Jerusalem and the Temple Mount and made Judah into the Roman province of Judea. Except for an incursion by the Parthians and brief rebellions, the Romans would remain sovereign in the Holy City for four hundred years. They chose as king of their province Herod – perhaps the greatest ruler and builder of Jerusalem after David and Solomon, but with the worst of reputations because he was imposed upon the Jews. An Edomite whose family had once had conversion forced upon them by the conquering Israelites, Herod was a friend of Rome and Hellenism. He set about recapturing Jerusalem with the help of mercenaries and Roman legions. Beheading the last of the house of Hasmon and the whole Sanhedrin in order to establish his authority, he reigned for thirty-three years, dying only shortly after the birth of Jesus Christ.

As a builder, Herod behaved like a pharaoh. The fortresses of Masada overlooking the Dead Sea and Herodium above Bethlehem and the port city of Caesarea were his creations, as well as the magnificent New Jerusalem, which he surrounded with huge walls and watchtowers. He watered his capital with aqueducts and cisterns; he buttressed the Temple Mount and placed above it the citadel Antonia and his own palace by the Jaffa Gate; he rebuilt the remains of the Second Temple of Zerubbabel according to the memory of the original structure, doubling the height of the gold-plated porch in front of the inner cube, and levelling the top of Mount Moriah into a vast, flat rectangle supported by retaining walls.

His wife Mariamne came from the house of Hasmon, and her intrigues to replace him with their children and her relatives led to his vengeance against the plotters. "Better to be Herod's pig," the Roman emperor Octavian remarked, "than his son." Although three sons still survived to inherit his kingdom, their squabbles led to a revolt by Zealots expecting a new Messiah to rescue them from Roman rule. The answer of the new emperor, Tiberius, was to appoint a procurator, Pontius Pilate, to govern his unruly province. A severe and rapacious man, he punished all rebellion and plundered the Temple revenues, but he wisely held aloof from the internecine religious quarrels between the Pharisees and the Sadducees and the Zealots and other messianic sects that kept the city in turmoil with their visions of liberation and apocalypse.

Among those who went from the village of Galilee on an annual pilgrimage to the Temple was the child Jesus. "His parents went to

Jerusalem," as Luke narrated, "every year at the feast of the Passover."
Jesus returned there with his disciples on his last pilgrimage – the
expected Messiah come to the Holy City, according to later Christians
but not the Jews. In the Temple the Bible reported him as driving out
the money changers from the house of the Lord. Condemned as a false
Messiah by the Pharisees and the Sadducees, and feared by Pilate as a
potential leader of another Jewish rebellion, he was crucified to appease
divisions in the Holy City between the Roman garrison and the fierce
rivalry of the Jewish sects. The judicial murder of Christ on Golgotha
was to wreak a terrible vengeance on the sacred places of his travels.
Belief in his sacrifice for the sins of humankind was to change his
pilgrimage into a crusade, his palm branch into a sword.

Twice more, the Zealots among the Jews rebelled against the Romans;
but their second defeat resulted in the laying waste of Jerusalem and
Herod's Temple. Under Roman tax gatherers, thousands of other Jews
were crucified for their resistance, until in 66 AD, the Zealots and the
Sicarii, an extreme group of Pharisees, rose up, crying, "No god but
God, no tax but to the Temple!" The procurator Florus outraged Judea
by looting the Temple and sacking the Upper City of Jerusalem. The
Zealots seized the fortress of Masada and the Lower City, while Florus
fled to Caesarea and massacred the Jews, a crime which was answered
by the destruction of the Roman garrison in the Antonia fortress in
Jerusalem. Faced with the loss of Judea, the emperor Nero sent his
leading general Vespasian with his son Titus to subdue the province
with his legions. On Nero's death, Vespasian became the Roman
emperor and left Titus to retake Jerusalem. After many assaults and a
siege, the troops of Titus burst into the city and washed the walls of
the Temple with Zealot blood and reduced the holy places to rubble.
A final heroic stand by the Sicarii at Masada, which had been built by
Herod as his bastion of last resort, took thirty months of blockade to
reduce its thousand defenders to the necessity of mass suicide. "Let us
go from the world," their leader Eleazer said in the words of Josephus,
"together with our children and our wives, in a state of freedom. This
is what our laws command us to do."

Sixty years later, in 130 AD, the rabbi Akiva inspired the last revolt
which would obliterate Jerusalem. In the Talmud of Babylon, he is said
to have seen with two comrades a jackal run from the fallen stones of
the Tabernacle that once housed the lost Ark of the Covenant. He
smiled when the others wept, for he knew of the prophets who had
foretold the utter destruction of Jerusalem, but also its restoration to
glory. As the first prophecy had happened under Titus, so the second
would be fulfilled.

An even greater destruction would take place after another war of independence. Led by Bar Kochba, who stamped on his coins the façade of a Fourth Temple which he hoped to build again, the Jews resisted the decrees of the Emperor Hadrian that aimed to extirpate all traces of their religion from the Holy City. For three years, this new Maccabee and guerrilla leader defeated the Roman troops and their mercenaries before turning on Jerusalem and destroying the Tenth Legion there. Hadrian himself had to bring out a large army to quell the rebellion, which ended in Bar Kochba and the rabbi Akiva being tortured to death. What was left of the killing streets of Jerusalem was razed to the ground. Only the Western Wall still stood. Upon the broken stones was built a new Roman city named Aelia Capitolina, from which all Jews were barred under penalty of death. Judea was named Palaestina, a name that would replace Israel as the country of the Jews, now in exile or a minority in their homeland with a pitiful Sanhedrin surviving in Galilee. The new Roman city became a side alley in history, while Caesarea dominated the province of Syria Palaestina. The centre of the cosmos founded upon the rock of Mount Moriah appeared to be a speck of sand blown away by the sirocco of time.

Jerusalem was hardly now a place. It was a concept and a faith and a state of mind. Its memory brought sorrow to the Jews. The feast of the Passover was celebrated by laments for the razed Temple, and for the eighteen centuries and more that would pass before an independent Jewish state again possessed the site of ancient Jerusalem, where little was left except a tradition. Yet the destruction of the Holy City coincided with the long decline of pagan Rome along with Judaism, while only the Christian faith rose until it would overwhelm the old empire in its new guise and citadel on the Bosphoros. Barbarian tribes, even fiercer than those of Israel when they had entered Canaan and taken it from its possessors, would pierce the far frontiers and knock at the gates of Rome and supersede the emperors themselves. And in response, a Second Rome would rise to the east in Byzantium, until its power was greater than the might of its mother. The emperor Constantine reunited the eastern and the western parts of the Roman Empire and called for the first ecumenical council of the Christian church at Nicaea, which was near his capital. There Bishop Macarius from the inconsiderable Aelia Capitolina told Helena, the mother of Constantine, that there was no monument to the death of Jesus in the city where he had been put on the cross. A Temple of Jupiter, indeed, now stood where the Temple of Solomon had been. In 326 AD, Helena went on a journey to ancient Israel and selected with Macarius the sites of Christ's birth at Bethlehem and, at Jerusalem, the adjacent places of

His Crucifixion and burial, where she happened to discover three ancient crosses in a cavern, one of which was called the True Cross.

In a grotto at Bethlehem, a Church of the Nativity was built, an octagonal structure adjoining the basilica, supported by rows of columns. In Jerusalem, the tomb of Christ was enclosed in a huge dome modelled on the Pantheon in Rome, while the rock of Calvary was enclosed in a cloistered court that led to a rectangular basilica, or Martyrium, again supported on massive pillars. In terms of sacred architecture, two new geometries reached the Holy Land – the octagon, which was made from two superimposed squares containing a cross and surrounded by a circle, and the dome, which was constructed to top the original cube of the Tabernacle. To the mystical arithmetic of the units of two, eight was added to make up the number twelve, while the sliced dome of the cosmos or God, seen as a perfect sphere by Greek philosophers such as Parmenides, was now overlaid on the concept of a cubical universe.

THE TEMPLE OF THE GRAIL

The Grail romances sought to recreate the Temple of Solomon and its mysteries as a mystic fortress for the medieval knightly imagination. In the early account by Chrétien de Troyes, the ignorant Welsh youth Perceval understands little of the happenings at the castle of the Fisher King. The Grail procession is led by a squire carrying the bleeding Holy Lance, followed by two squires bearing candle-holders, each with ten lights, as in a Byzantine or Jewish ceremony. (These twin lights also represent the golden chandeliers permanently shining above the tomb of the Prophet Muhammad at Medina, which in the *Song of Antioch* and the *Conquest of Jerusalem*, the champion of the First Crusade, Godfrey de Bouillon, swears that he will seize and place in their rightful place by the Tomb of Christ.) Then a maiden appears before Perceval with a jewelled Grail, shining with brilliant light as in the Holy Fire ceremony at Easter in the Church of the Holy Sepulchre. She is followed by another maiden with a silver platter, who passes by the bed of the maimed Fisher King.

This blessed vision of Perceval was nearer to pantheism than to the doctrine of the Roman Catholic Church. Although the bleeding lance was associated with the death of Christ, it also echoed the magic spear of Welsh and Irish literature, which was both lethal and life-giving. It could kill as well as make the desert green. It could destroy all the royal enemies, but also a whole kingdom. Its prick could ravage as well as regenerate.

The harm of its point could only be blunted in a cauldron or bowl of boiling blood and water: the male principle creating birth from the female. Otherwise, its wounds might lay waste to the land of the Fisher King, who was incurably maimed by its thrust between his thighs.

Chrétien de Troyes was not the first to use the word 'Grail'. Meaning a 'dish', the term *graal* had occurred previously in a romance about Alexander the Great, deriving from the Latin *gradalis* or a bowl to serve delicacies. In *Perceval*, the vessel appears to have had a lid, which was removed before its inexhaustible food was served to those present. Platter or closed bowl, it was a giver of plenty, as was the Welsh *dysgl*, one of the legendary Thirteen Treasures of Great Britain. Yet it also contained the host or body of Christ, the sole food of the Fisher King. And it was carried by a young woman.

This was anathema to the Church of Rome. The communion cup could only be borne by a male priest. The Elevation of the Host before the congregation remained a supreme mystery, which could not be unveiled. Yet to Chrétien, all those in search of perfection might be free to see the Grail. In his interpretation the giving by Christ of His Body and Blood was associated with pagan fertility rituals, the chalice representing the goddess's womb. He was also invoking the Gnostic heresies from the Near East that were spreading then across Italy and France. These spoke of a *Sophia*, who embodied divine wisdom. The Grail in her hands was the Word and the Light of God, which blazed like the sun upon the darkness of the earth, where Satan was fighting for mastery of the flesh.

The most significant of biblical texts for the Gnostics and for the Knights Templars came from St John the Evangelist: "God is Light, and in Him is no darkness at all." They saw themselves as successors to John the Baptist of whom St John's Gospel wrote: "He was not that Light, but was sent to bear witness of that Light. That was the true Light, which lighteth every man that cometh into the world." This was the Light that shone from Chrétien's Grail, carried in the female hands of wisdom and rebirth. John's Gospel also contained the stories of Nicodemus and Joseph of Arimathea, so central to the medieval romances of King Arthur and his knights.

The Host within the Grail seen by Perceval was not the communion wafer of Catholic absolution, but rather the blessed bread distributed among all believers at the feasts of the early Christian communities and later the Cathar heretics. This did not so much represent the Body of Christ as the miracle of the loaves and the fishes, where Jesus fed the multitude – the fish was a Greek sign of Christianity, while the Fisher King symbolized the search for salvation within his Castle. In *Perceval*, the maiden carrying the covered bowl of the Grail was followed by another young woman with a silver platter. They were serving not the Eucharist but sacred food to the Knights of the Grail. And Perceval saw no priest, altar or cross inside the castle walls.

Although Chrétien de Troyes was a French-speaking cleric and poet, his influences derived from Britain and Rome, Byzantium and the Jerusalem of the crusades. He might have visited the first two places; he knew of the history and creeds of all four. In the sacred objects of the Grail procession, he combined the Nordic with the Christian and the Cabbala and Islam. As well as the lance with its Celtic and Christian associations and the candelabra with their resonance of ancient Jewish, Byzantine and even Islamic ceremonial, there were further allusions. The golden Grail set with gems was both a Celtic cornucopia and a Christian chalice. The silver platter represented a cauldron of plenty and the dish on which was once set both the head of St John the Baptist and the lamb of the Last Supper. The Grail held many sources and had many shapes. No less was to be expected from a poet who had translated Ovid's *Metamorphoses*.

Chrétien's last romance contributed to the spiritual awakening of Western Christendom at the time. The age was replete with discoveries or rediscoveries in science, mathematics and philosophy; it saw the founding of convents, monasteries and Military Orders, the flowering of chivalry and courtly love, the raising of the great Gothic cathedrals, and the launch of crusades to capture Jerusalem and build there a holy and heavenly city on earth. And that same holy Temple was to be built again and again in the west.

In *The Quest of the Holy Grail*, the Temple appears as the Ship of Solomon as well as the mystic castle. Once on board, Galahad, Perceval and Bors find a bed like that of Ulysses, hewn from a living tree representing the Tree of Life in the Garden of Eden and the True Cross. Its three posts are a natural white, red and emerald green, the colours of alchemy comprehended by Solomon, who was "wise with the knowledge that would be grasped by human understanding; he knew the powers of every precious stone, the virtues of all herbs, and had a more perfect knowledge of the course of the firmament and of the stars than any except for God Himself."

On the bed lies the sword of King David made by Solomon with a stone pommel combining all the colours found on earth, each with its own virtue in magic and science. The sword hilt has two ribs, one made from the salamander or serpent of wisdom, the other from a Euphrates fish, which induces forgetfulness and purpose. Celtic and Gnostic in shape, it resembles the sword of Arthur in the *Dream of Rhonabwy*, with two serpents inscribed upon the sword in gold. When drawn, "two flames of fire burst out of the jaws of the two serpents, and so wonderful was the sword, it was hard for anyone to gaze at it." The Ship of Solomon has been launched by a man descending from heaven, who blessed it with water sprinkled from a silver pail and told its builder that the last knight of his line would lie on the bed and learn of his descent. Galahad takes up the Sword of David and reclines on his forefather's bed.

Later Lancelot replaces Galahad on the Ship of Solomon in search of the Grail Castle across the sea. Finding a fortress guarded by two lions, he comes to a chamber so bright that all the candles on earth seem to be burning there. He observes the Holy Vessel, now covered with red samite on its silver table. Angels swing silver censers or hold candlesticks and crosses. An old man raises the host to a Trinity of three figures. Given one of them in place of the Host, he staggers under the weight of the divine body. As Lancelot goes to his aid, he is struck down. As he recovers in the castle by the sea, the Grail appears at table feeding all with their desires. Although Lancelot may not reach the Holy Vessel, he can benefit from its bounty.

Five years later, Galahad, Perceval and Bors reach the Castle of Corbenic of the maimed Fisher King. There Galahad puts together the two pieces of the broken sword, which had wounded Joseph of Arimathea in the thigh. A heavenly figure in the robes of a bishop carried on a throne by four angels appears as Joseph, the first Christian bishop consecrated by the Lord God in Sarras, the Heavenly City in France, from where the Grail was carried on to Britain. Joseph is set down beside the Holy Vessel on its silver table near the Fisher King. The four angels now bear candles, a cloth of red samite and the bleeding Holy Lance. The candles are placed on the table, the red cloth is laid beside the Grail, while the drops of blood from the raised lance fall into the sacred cup, which is then covered with the cloth. In sight of the knights, Joseph performs the miracle of transubstantiation in which a burning child replaces the Host before disappearing. The bleeding naked Christ then appears from the Holy Vessel and gives the sacrament from it to the kneeling knights; they find the blessed food "so honied and delectable it was as if the essence of all sweetness was housed within their bodies." The vision of Jesus identifies the Grail:

> It is the platter in which Christ partook of the Paschal lamb with His disciples. It is the platter which has shown itself agreeable to those whom I have found my faithful servants, they whose sight has ever stricken the faithless. And because it has shown itself agreeable to all my people, it is called most properly the Holy Grail.

The figure of Christ commands Galahad to remove the sacred dish from the British castle of Corbenic to the heavenly city of Sarras. Yet first, he must heal the wounds of the Fisher King with drops of blood from the Holy Lance. Once the king is healed, the Waste Land turns green, and he enters a monastery of white monks. Here, the Cistercians re-enter the story of the Quest, while the Arthurian knights of the red cross of the Templars are compared by the spirit of Jesus to the apostles: "For as they ate with me at the Last Supper, even so did you eat with me now at the table of the Holy Grail."

Bors, Perceval and Galahad now return to the Ship of Solomon, where they find the Grail resting on its silver table on the bed of the Tree of Life and the Cross. Voyaging home, Galahad carries the great weight of the table into Sarras, where the knights have been imprisoned until his return as king. He orders an ark of gold and precious stones to be made to house the Grail on its silver table and praying before this great reliquary with Bors and Perceval, Galahad sees Joseph of Arimathea, who releases his spirit from his body to be transported to heaven.

> A great marvel followed immediately on Galahad's death. The two remaining companions saw quite plainly a hand come down from heaven, but not the body it belonged to. It proceeded straight to the Holy Vessel and took both it and the lance, and carried them up to heaven, to the end that no man since has ever dared to say he saw the Holy Grail.

More illuminating and specific about the beliefs of the Knights of the Temple of Solomon was Wolfram von Eschenbach in his Grail romance, *Parzival*. He went as far as giving his perfect Christian knight a piebald half-brother Feirefiz born in the Levant. The subtext of the long romance was, indeed, the reconciliation and respect of Christian for Muslim, an intention that underlay also the portrayal of the Grail as a stone fallen from heaven as at Mecca. *Parzival* begins by defining lack of faith as dark and the Christian soul as white, as in a description of Gnostic dualism:

> As one sees the magpie's feathers,
> Which are both black and white,
> Yet one may win no blessing . . .

Wolfram also stresses the hidden significance of his text: "I tell my story like the bowstring and not like the bow. The string is here a figure of speech. Now *you* think the bow is fast, but faster is the arrow sped by the string."

As in the romance of Chrétien de Troyes, Parzival begins his career in chivalry as a fool, a rapist and a robber. So when the Fisher King with his incurable wound, whose 'life was but dying', directs him to the Grail Castle, he is tongue-tied at the wonders he sees. A squire carries the bleeding Holy Lance through the great hall in front of the assembled knights of the Holy Grail, while the Grail Queen bears the Grail stone on a cushion of green silk:

> Root and blossom of Paradise garden,
> That thing that men call 'The Grail',
> The crown of all earthly wishes,
> Fair fullness that never shall fail.

Unknown to Parzival, the Grail Queen is his aunt. She lays the Grail on a pillar of jacinth, and all the knights and maidens in the castle are nourished from its plenty.

Here *Parzival* specifically identifies the Knights of the Grail as *Templeisen*; they wear white surcoats with red crosses as the Templar Knights did. The Templars, of course, had many contacts with their Muslim equivalents, the Sufis, and some of their secret practices derived from oriental mysticism, in particular the belief in selfless obedience and purity. When Parzival finally asks the Fisher King the right question and heals him and becomes the Grail King, Feirefiz is baptized from a ruby font standing on a round pillar of jasper, which has been filled with holy water from the Grail. Feirefiz now marries the princess of the castle, who gives birth to the Christian African emperor Prester John, whose role is to appear with his armies to save Jerusalem for the true faith.

Wolfram promotes the semi-divine rule of nations by a company of mysterious monastic Knights Templars hailing from a sacred castle. The Knights of the Grail are the heirs of classical and oriental, Celtic and Christian tradition. Most significantly, Wolfram writes:

> By a stone they live,
> And that stone is both pure and precious.
> Its name you have never heard? . . .
> But young you will live for ever –
> And this stone all men call the Grail.

This stone had been brought down from heaven by angels, who then returned on high because of the sins of mankind. On Good Friday, a Dove flew down with the white Host to lay on the stone – the Body and Blood of Christ, sent to nourish all.

The Templars were believed to be the guardians both of the Grail and of the Temple of Solomon. The Temple of the King of Israel stood upon a rock at the centre of the world, and it contained the Ark of the Covenant, the fount of the Christian faith. As Raphael Patai writes in his considerable work, *Man and Temple*, Solomon's original building, now the great domed mosque on Mount Moriah, was celebrated in Jewish legend as an *Omphalos*, a navel of the earth:

> This rock, called in Hebrew *Ebhen Shetiyyah*, the Stone of Foundation, was the first solid thing created, and was placed by God amidst the as yet boundless fluid of the primeval waters. Legend has it that just as the body of an embryo is built up in its mother's womb from its navel, so God built up the earth concentrically around this stone, the Navel of the Earth. And just as the body of the embryo receives its nourishment from the navel, so the whole earth too receives the waters that nourish it from this Navel.

The cornerstone 'which the builders refused' in the Psalms was another symbol of Christ as was also the rock upon which St Peter founded the Christian Church. In the Book of Revelation the Holy Spirit is also represented as a stone or a green gem, or as fire and crystal. As St John the Divine wrote in his vision, "Straightaway I was in the Spirit: and, behold, there was a throne set in heaven, and one sitting upon the throne. And he that sat was to look upon like a jasper stone and a sardius; and there was a rainbow round about the throne, like an emerald to look upon . . . There were seven lamps of fire burning before the throne, which are the seven Spirits of God. And before the throne there was a sea of glass like unto crystal . . ." These visions were also shared by the legendary Knights of the Grail in *Parzival*, who saw the Holy Vessel as a sacred stone. Such imagery later helped me to understand the stone roof of Rosslyn Chapel, which culminates in the Dove bearing the Host down to the Grail, a crescent cup overflowing with divine grace.

The sacred stone as the source of heavenly light was also embedded in Islamic practice. For thirteen hundred years, pilgrims on the *hajji* to Mecca have been directed to enter the Ka'aba and kiss the black meteorite set in the wall. Associated in religious tradition with Adam and Abraham as well as with Allah, the sacred stone is said to have been brought to earth by an angel to record the deeds of the faithful, to be examined hereafter on the Day of Judgement. Worn smooth by tens of millions of lips, the stone was the sole object from the pagan temple which the Prophet Muhammad kept when he converted the idolatrous shrine at Mecca into an Islamic temple. Apparently, a flash

85

of lightning persuaded the Prophet to retain this Muslim Grail. As the poet Ikbal Ali Shah wrote, the Ka'aba was the heart of the body of the world:

> And the stone that you call the Black Stone was itself a ball of dazzling light. In ages past, the Prophet said, it shone like the crescent moon, until at last the shadows, falling from the sinful hearts of those who gazed on it, turned its surface black. And since this amber gem, that came to earth from Paradise with the Holy Ghost, has received such impressions upon itself, what should be the impressions which our hearts receive? Indeed, whoever shall touch it, being pure of conscience, is like him who has shaken hands with God.

Wolfram von Eschenbach, himself a German knight, died before completing *Titurel*, another Grail romance. This tale was elaborately finished as the *Jüngerer Titurel* by the poet Albrecht. Titurel had given the crown of the Grail Castle to his last surviving son, Frimutel, who was soon to die. His abdication was mourned by the Templars, "whom he had often saved from many a difficult situation when he was defending the Grail with his own hand and with their aid." The castle was presented as a version of the Temple in the Heavenly Jerusalem. On the top of its columns flew angels. Its altars were of sapphire beneath velvet canopies. The doves which brought the Host of the Grail in *Parzival* were sculptures. God was the source of all the architecture. The dome of the castle was the cosmos and set towards the east. An astronomical clock charted the movements of the heavens. In the small temple in the centre, there was an organ with singing birds, a sculpture of the Last Judgement, and bells and gargoyles and all the embellishment of Gothic cathedrals.

The Grail of Albrecht enhanced that of Wolfram. In his temple within the jewelled Grail Castle, a floating stone was the centre of the world. It represented the Stone of Destiny of the Celts, the meteorite in the Ka'aba at Mecca, and the step into heaven of the Prophet under the Dome of the Rock in Jerusalem. Yet Albrecht also took his version of the Grail into alchemy. For him the Grail was also a crystal, a compound of fire and water. These two of the four humours of medieval chemistry, other than earth and air, were capable of birth and resurrection. In that stone was the secret of life.

7

The Shape of the Temple

But he that is highest of all dwelleth not in temples made with hands.

From *Acts* in the Tyndale Bible

THE GRAIL ROMANCES had identified the Knights Templars not only as the knights of the Grail and the guardians of its esoteric mysteries, but also as the architects of new Temples of Solomon, which were usually sited within a castle or on a ship serving as an ark. Gothic architecture was much influenced by Templar ideas distilled from the Near East, particularly by their use of the octagon, which was an early Christian holy and cosmic shape. At Hierapolis in ancient Phrygia, now in southern Turkey – a city mentioned by St Paul and a centre of pilgrimage from the fifth century – are rock carvings showing two interlaced squares containing the cross and within a circle. Remarkably, this symbol was the architectural plan for the neighbouring shrine of the apostle and martyr St Philip, itself built as twin octagons enclosing one another inside a square border of porticos. This pattern would be repeated both at the first Church of the Holy Sepulchre at Jerusalem and at the Dome of the Rock, built after 687 AD for the Caliph Abd al-Malik by Byzantine architects.

Only on my final visit to Jerusalem to see the remarkable tombstone of the Templars, excavated from their castle at Athlit and displaying the same masonic marks as in their burial ground at Westkirk in Fife, did the significance of the octagon strike me relating to medieval architecture. Crowning the Holy City on the Temple Mount, the eight sides of the great mosque supporting the golden dome sheltered the rock, sacred to Jew and Greek and Roman Christian for its connection with Abraham, and doubly holy to Islam as the place of the Prophet Muhammad's journey to the seventh heaven. Since the three Temples of Solomon, Zerubbabel and Herod had been destroyed, the first nine Templar knights in their occupation of Jerusalem seemed to have chosen its shape to fuse the main faiths of the Near East into a common belief in One God. They took the octagon within the circle to enclose their black or red crosses with their eight points, also to uphold the roofs of their chapels. For this was the cosmic design. In geometric symbolism, the number 8 signified 'The Resurrection and the Life', and so became the shape of early baptisteries, while 888 denoted Jesus. The eight-pointed badge worn by the Knights Templars and the pilgrims to Compostela was known as the Hermetic or Solomon's Star, and was even confused with the alchemical Philosopher's Stone, capable of translating brass into gold, or matter into spirit.

Architecture rather than alchemy preserved the Templars' reverence for the octagon. They inherited the building practice not only from the Byzantine architects of the holy places in Jerusalem, but also from Charlemagne's translation of the eight-sided baptisteries at Ravenna to his capital at Aachen. There the octagonal marble chapel in the Dom predicted in mosaics and marble patterns the Gnostic symbolism of the Knights Templars of the Grail. Over the entrance is a mosaic displaying the Heavenly Jerusalem, surrounded within its circular walls by four men in white robes pouring from Greek jars the four sacred rivers of Eden. The Temple of Solomon with its two pillars and quartet of arches appears classical, but is surmounted by a cross, while below are curtains concealing the Ark and above them a hanging lamp. Beside the windows are chalice patterns made of coloured marble; over a door is an eight-pointed cross with a round stone or cosmos dropping from it. Yet most prophetic of all is the mosaic over the golden altar, which shows the Holy Spirit as a dove descending with rays of fire, some in the shape of the Cross, while holding in its beak the Word of God to lay on the empty throne of Charlemagne. This allegory of the divine emperor bringing revelation to his people as King David did to Israel is confirmed by a Latin inscription declaring that God has given Charlemagne the right to build his Temple because he ruled so well.

The ultimate Templar cosmic symbol, the circle containing the octagon, was not to be found in Aachen, however, but at the wonderful abbey of Charroux in the south-west of France, a major resting-place for pilgrims on the way to Compostela. Its supreme circular surviving tower on its soaring octagonal series of arches derived from Charlemagne's chapel at his capital. In the museum within the abbey ruins are also three jewelled reliquaries, one of which housed the Saint Vertu, presented to the abbey by the Holy Roman Emperor himself. The name of this last relic of the body of Christ was in fact a euphemism, for it was meant to be the foreskin of Christ taken from Him at His circumcision. As the original benefactor of the abbey, Charlemagne might well have wished to own part of the virility of God as a symbol of his own sacred power and virtue, and as sire of a race of sanctified rulers in the manner of King David of Israel.

Before Charlemagne took the little piece of sacred skin from the

Church of St Mary in Aachen to present it to Charroux, it had a strange provenance. The emperor was said to have been handed it by an angelic youth in a vision during the saying of mass in the Church of the Holy Sepulchre in Jerusalem. In this vision the emperor saw the right Hand of God descend and place a small thing on the communion chalice – the Saint Vertu, capable of curing and restoring to life. In point of fact, Charlemagne had never visited the Holy City; he learned of the architecture of the octagon in Byzantine Ravenna.

Even more moving than the round octagon of the Templar chapel at Laon and at Segovia is the delicate Santa Maria de Eunate on the pilgrim road to Compostela in northern Spain near Puente la Reina, where a perfect pediment bridge still takes voyagers across the river. Close to a Templar commandery, the little church was built in the sacred shape of the Military Order; the eight sides of the cloister arches enclose the eight walls of the church with its tiny curved apse. Standing isolated, yet surrounded by sheep grazing on brown grass, this holy place is the most contemplative on the blessed road.

The essential octagonal presbytery of all, surpassing even the one within the Templar headquarters in Portugal at Tomar, was built at Ely in the Fens near Cambridge. Its architect was prior of the cathedral, Alan de Walsingham, who took his name from the most famous shrine to Our Lady in England. The Templars' influence on Prior Alan is unknown, but may well have reached him through the medieval masonic orders, the *compagnonnages*, which were associated with the Templars and which aided, for instance, the master architect John Morow at Melrose Abbey. The wonder and beauty of the presbytery at Ely served as the prototype for the later dome of St Paul's Cathedral in London, and remained the supreme example of the use of the octagon in English architecture.

The medieval *compagnonnage* was divided into three parts; the Sons of Solomon, who were stonemasons, joiners and locksmiths, and received members of all religious faiths; the Sons of Maître Jacques, who included the same three trades, and attracted many other craftsmen, but admitted only Roman Catholic Companions; and the Sons of Maître Soubise, who were carpenters, tilers and plasterers, but lost some of their Companion carpenters to the Sons of Maître Jacques. Most of the centres of the three organizations were in the South of France, where the Roman tradition of craft guilds – as well as the Cathar heresy – was strongest: at Montpellier, Toulouse and the destroyed city of Béziers. They existed in no urban centre north of Paris. According to the nineteenth-century historian of the *compagnonnage*, Perdiguier, himself a Son of Solomon, the stonemasons were the most ancient of the Companions and had adopted as part of their ritual lore the legend of Hiram, builder of the Temple at Jerusalem. As for Maître Jacques, he was venerated as the sculptor of the two columns of the Temple, Jachin and Boaz; there he is said to have met Maître Soubise, at first his sworn friend, and then his jealous enemy who sent traitors to assassinate Maître Jacques at prayer in La Sainte-Beaume, at the shrine of St Mary Magdalene. Making his cane the symbol of the *compagnonnage*, his dying words were:

I deliver my soul to God, my Creator; and you, my friends, receive from me the kiss of peace. When I shall have rejoined the Supreme Being, I shall still watch over you. I desire that the last kiss which I give you, be imparted always to the Companions whom you may make, as coming from their Father; they will transmit it to those whom they make; I will watch over them as over you; tell them I shall follow them everywhere so long as they remain faithful to God and to their charge [*devoir*] and never forget . . .

Both the Cathars and the Knights Templars were accused at their trials of giving the kiss of peace on the mouth – and elsewhere – the heretical *consolamentum* which allowed the soul to join the Supreme Being. According to Perdiguier the Sons of Solomon had been the only *compagnonnage*, until seceders put themselves under the protection of Jacques de Molay, the last Grand Master of the Templars. By this means, he became Maître Jacques with his residence in the Holy Land and the cane representing the Templar lance, while his betrayal and death at the stake conformed to the legend of Hiram. Even though the comparison was forced, it confirmed the medieval connection between the Templars and the *compagnonnage* in the design and building of many of the Gothic cathedrals. And in view of the notorious independence and indiscipline of the three French groups of Companions, the Peasants' Revolt or Jacquerie of 1358 may have had something to do with their influence or name, or with their celebration of St James or Jacques, the disciple of Jesus decapitated by Herod who was the patron saint of Compostela as well as of the crusades and the Military Orders.

The *compagnonnage* and the early British, Flemish and German crafts and guilds were also the supporters of the rights of towns against their feudal overlords. In this perpetual struggle, they were usually backed by their respective kings, who granted the merchants and operatives many privileges and charters in return for taxes and loyalty to the royal court rather than to the local baron or count. This was the attitude taken by Robert the Bruce, when he appointed the most faithful supporters of the monarchy, the St Clairs of Roslin, thc hereditary Masters of the

Crafts and Guilds of Scotland. He might count on them to keep the towns of the nation true to the royal cause, not to the local clan chieftains. Such was the practice of the Capetian kings also in their treatment of the *compagnonnages*.

The French Companions and the Knights Templars also revered Zerubbabel; according to the prophet Ezekiel, Zerubbabel rebuilt the second Temple in Jerusalem with his comrades, holding a sword in one hand and a trowel in the other – the first warrior stonemason. Strangely enough, in Rosslyn Chapel by the spiral Apprentice Pillar, influenced by eastern and Byzantine models, there is a direct reference to the reconstruction of the Temple. A carved relief inscribed in Latin shows King David waking from a dream to hear the meaning of a riddle. One of his three guards was Zerubbabel, who interpreted his dream:

WINE IS STRONG
THE KING IS STRONGER
WOMEN ARE STRONGEST
BUT TRUTH CONQUERS ALL

The king was so pleased with this saying that he permitted the making of another Temple in Jerusalem and the return of the Ark of the Covenant and the sacred treasures there.

My interest in Templar architecture and round churches was later to lead me to those in England and Bornholm, an island off Denmark, as well as in Norway and Orkney and at Llanleff, a strange arched tower in Brittany. Yet this further quest was in pursuit of a provenance for the Newport Tower in Rhode Island, a stone monument believed by many to be of Viking, Scottish or Portuguese origin. For the time being, however, I was preoccupied with the shape of the three Temples of Solomon, Ezekiel and Herod, all destroyed and impossible to recreate. Impossible, that is, were it not for copies of them depicted in painting and stone, in picture and carving, in whole chapels and in every Masonic Lodge.

The design of the original Temple of Solomon remains inscrutable in spite of the detailed account of its workmanship in the Books of Kings and Chronicles. It would have been modelled on a Phoenician temple of the tenth century BC, since the master designer Hiram came from Tyre, sent to his work by King Hiram, who also provided the cedarwood for the holy structures. The shrine of Taïnat in Upper Syria between Aleppo and Antioch was built a hundred years later and supplies a rough parallel: two pillars supporting a porch before an outer chamber, leading into a dark inner chamber with an altar, the whole a

91

rectangle. The differences in Solomon's building were in its orientation to the east, the siting of the whole edifice on a platform, and the lightless Holy of Holies, containing the Ark, planned as a perfect cube.

For later French Companions and all Masons, the most important features were the twin pillars at the open entrance. While Chronicles and Kings detailed the wealth and beauty of the Temple, with its golden palm trees, brass oxen and lions, and two cherubim above the Ark, its molten sea and shovels and bowls and candlesticks all made by Hiram, his particular legacy to the Masonic movement would be the two great pillars of the Temple.

> And he set up the pillars in the porch of the temple: and he set up the right pillar, and called the name thereof Jachin: and he set up the left pillar, and called the name thereof Boaz.
> And upon the top of the pillars was lily work: so was the work of the pillars finished.

King Solomon himself declared the Temple the house of God Who would look on it with favour and give it His holy name:

> Then spake Solomon. The Lord said that he would dwell in the thick darkness.
> I have surely built thee an house to dwell in, a settled place for thee to abide in for ever . . .
> That thine eyes may be opened towards this house night and day, even toward the place of which thou has said, My name shall be there . . .

Solomon was also held to have instituted the customs and practices of the medieval masons and other crafts and guilds who had built his Temple. "Solomon confirmed the Charges that David his father had given to Masons," the earliest English Masonic document, the Cook Manuscript of 1410, declares. "And Solomon himself taught them their manners, but little differing from the manners now used." He was the Grand Master of the primal Lodge at Jerusalem, while Hiram was the Deputy Grand Master, the most accomplished Designer and Operator on Earth.

The plan of the second Temple of Zerubbabel and Ezekiel is known. The form was a great square with three gateways facing east, north and south. These led to an outer court enclosing a rectangular temple with three fortified entrances aligned to the outer gates. They took the faithful towards the inner chamber and altar, which was built in the shape of a ziggurat, the stepped pyramid of Babylon, showing the influence of the occupying power. As for the third Temple of Herod, its design only exists on contemporary Roman and Jewish coins. They show a portico supported by three or four pillars, more classical than traditional. This was the Temple where Jesus overthrew the moneylenders and whose destruction soon after His death was foretold.

The Royal Arch, so important to the Knights Templars in their buildings at Charroux and other presbyteries, and later to the Free-masons in their symbols and ceremonies, was meant to have covered the Holy of Holies, the cube of darkness within the Temple of Solomon, containing the Ark of the Covenant. There is no biblical evidence of this arch, for like early Phoenician temples the Tabernacle probably had a flat roof. The Ark was crowned only by a Mercy Seat and two winged cherubim of gold. No arches were mentioned in any description of the construction of the first Temple. Yet in Ezekiel's vision of the second Temple, arches were frequently cited as spanning the pillars round the various courts. As the Templars particularly identified with Zerubbabel's warrior masons, and as the arch was fundamental to their sacred architecture, they probably used it as a symbol in their rituals. In Templar tradition and later Masonic practice, the Royal Arch rep-resented four concepts: the arch said to have spanned the Tabernacle in the Temple of Solomon, shielding the altar and the Ark below; the arch over a hidden cellar in the Temple of Solomon, where the Ark is still preserved; the crown of the human head, under which divine intelligence is implanted by the Architect of the Universe; and the vault of the firmament, separating heaven from earth. These were the symbolic meanings of the Royal Arch to the higher degrees of the Military Orders and the later Lodges. Two versions of that holy struc-ture were finally to be revealed on the Secret Scroll.

The secret wisdom of the Jewish fraternities was held by later Masonic historians to have been absorbed by the Byzantine corporations which built the Church of the Holy Sepulchre and the Dome of the Rock. At the building of the wondrous Santa Sophia in Byzantium the Emperor Justinian was said to have exclaimed, "I have surpassed thee, O Solomon!" From there his influence passed on to the Teutonic guilds of *Steinmetzen*, which were certainly in existence by the mid-thirteenth century. The connection was demonstrated by the known use of spiral columns in the architecture of the Byzantines and the Hebrews as well as in later Masonic Lodges – and at Rosslyn, where the legend of the famed Apprentice Pillar referred to the Hiramic tradition in masonry.

This inspiration also spread to the west through the Roman building guilds who learnt of Jewish practices following the fall of Jerusalem and the final destruction of the third Temple. Diocletian may have tried to destroy Christianity, founded by a carpenter, but he was lenient to the Collegia or guilds of Rome, many of whose members were already Christians. He did martyr four aristocratic patrons of building as well as four masons and one apprentice – Claudius, Nicostratus, Simphorianus, Castorius and Simplicius. They were to become the patron saints of Lombard and Tuscan builders and later of the medieval masons of France, Germany and England. Their emblems – the saw, hammer, mallet, compasses and square, and later, the cube and the plummet, the circle and the level – can be found at Rome and Florence, Nuremberg, Antwerp and Toulouse.

These symbols and the rules of the craft were bequeathed to the mysterious *Magistri Comacini*, a guild of architects who lived on a fortified island on Lake Como at the break-up of the Roman Empire. These were held to have taught the secrets of sacred geometry and construction methods to the Italian builders of Ravenna and Venice, and through them, to the arts and trade guilds of the Middle Ages. Certainly, an edict of a Lombard king in 643 gave privileges to the Comacini and their colleagues. Their meeting-places were called *loggia*, from which the word 'lodge' is said to have derived. Their symbols included King Solomon's Knot and the endless, interwoven cord of Eternity.

Other inquiries into Masonic origins dated the knowledge of the craft as far back as Babylonian, Egyptian or Greek times. In a reference to the Tower of Babel, one early Masonic catechism gave the Answer: "We differ from the Babylonians who did presume to Build to Heaven, but we pray the blessed Trinity to let us build True, High and Square, and they shall have the praise to whom it is due . . ." Some historians believed that the Temple of Solomon was built by masons familiar with the Dionysian and Eleusinian mysteries as well as divine geometry handed down by the gods and the golden mean. To them, the Masonic mystery of the martyr Hiram was merely a reworking of the myth of the death of Orpheus, the great creator, in the Bacchic religion.

Still others looked to the Greek god Hermes, whom the Romans called Mercury, as the source of sacred geometry. The Christian Father Cyril of Alexandria had asserted the Hermetic tradition: "Have you not heard that our native Hermes of Egypt divided the world into tracts and divisions, that he measured the country with a string, made ditches and canals, made laws, named provinces, set up contracts and agreements, re-discovered the calendar of the rising of the stars, and handed down certain crops, numbers and calculations, geometry, astrology, astronomy, and music, and, finally, the whole system of grammar which he himself invented?" Hermes was the creator of the Seven Liberal Arts, of which the greatest was geometry.

At this point, the Greek god became confused with Euclid and Pythagoras in medieval Masonic thought, which was never strong on names or the chronology of great men. Another tradition, recorded by Josephus, held that the arts of astronomy and music were carved on two pillars by Adam's son Seth; this too passed into Masonic tradition – the pillars were to be recast by Hiram in the Temple of Solomon. Zoroaster, the ultimate Magus, was likewise believed to have inscribed the seven Liberal Arts on fourteen pillars, half of brass and half of baked brick. These pillars and those of the Greek god Hermes, on which all true knowledge was inscribed, were said to have been rediscovered by Hermes Trismegistus, the founder of alchemy and the Hermetic doctrine, which was so much to influence the Knights of the Order of the Temple of Solomon and, through them, the Masons. Later, fourteen pillars were to be set up in Rosslyn Chapel, surrounding the two elaborately carved pillars representing the pair from the Temple of Solomon.

Belief in the Temple as the mystic centre of the world, was inherited by the Templars from the Gnostics and St John the Divine; strengthened by this, they secretly resisted the power and authority of the Popes and Kings of Europe. The black-and-white devices of their Order, black octagonal cross against white habit, showed their Gnosticism and Manicheanism, the belief in the continuing struggle of the world of the Devil against the Divine Intelligence. They bequeathed to the Masons the black-and-white lozenges and Indented Tessels of their Lodges. And before his death, the last of the official Grand Masters, Jacques de Molay, was claimed to have "organized and instituted what afterwards came to be called the Occult, Hermetic, or Scottish Masonry."

What all these theories of the origins of Masonic belief had in common was a derivation from the mysticism of the Near East as well as from the Old and New Testaments of the Holy Bible. A perfect catalyst between the legendary and the practical was the building of the House of the Lord by King Solomon. Certainly, in the romances of the Middle Ages, Solomon and his Temple were second only to King Arthur and the Grail as a source of inspiration. "And it was precisely at that time," the leading researcher into the Temple of Solomon has written, "that the framers of the Masonic Legend were at work in developing the various aspects of the traditional history of their Craft."

Precisely at that time, too, the Knights of the Order of the Temple of Solomon guarded what was thought by pilgrims to be the King's Temple in Jerusalem, the octagonal shrine of the Dome of the Rock. Its builder, Caliph Umar, was said like the Emperor Justinian to have cried on its completion, "Behold a greater than Solomon is here." The

Templar seal of 1214 showed the Dome as the Temple of Solomon in a curious hybrid: three pillars supporting two arched doorways, crowned by two pediments under a Royal Arch or cupola, surmounted by the Order's octagonal cross. The knights also passed on to the troubadours and craft guilds of Europe much of the rabbinic and cabbalistic lore relating to King Solomon, which had come down from ancient times. Solomon was thought to be a Magus or wise man, a magician and a worker of wonders, who foresaw the destruction of his Temple by the Babylonians, and so constructed a secret vault within the walls for the burial and the preservation of the Ark of the Covenant – a sacred treasure that has been the object of innumerable quests ever since its disappearance.

The Christian Fathers Clement and Eusebius had written of King Solomon's power over demons, and Gregory of Tours and Bede wrote of the wonders of the Temple and its significance. "The House of God which King Solomon built in Jerusalem represents the Holy Universal Church, which, from the First of the Elect to the last man who shall be born at the end of the world, is built daily by the grace of her peaceful King, that is, her Redeemer." Venerated as the stepping-stone of the Prophet Muhammad on his flight to Heaven and Paradise, the Temple of Solomon was also sacred to Muslims, who built the Dome of the Rock in its place. The mysticism of the Sufis, Manicheans and Gnostics thus permeated the Christian guardians of Mount Moriah with its converted mosques and shrines, and was assimilated by the knights of the Military Order of the Temple of Solomon who believed themselves to be the keepers of the House of God on earth, built by the Great Architect of the world.

In another of their roles, the Templars were literally Master Masons. They directed the building of their formidable castles such as Castle Pilgrim and ordained the shape of their octagonal chapels and circular towers. There is some evidence that, with the Sons of Solomon, they introduced holy geometry from the Near East into the building of the Gothic masterpieces of France such as Chartres Cathedral. There, the stained-glass windows still commemorate the carpenters and the masons who built it, and the tools and emblems of their trades. As for the Templars, there is no question that their secret ritual involved a faith in a sacred architecture, a single Creator of the world, and the detailed regulation of the teams of masons who built their thousands of preceptories and churches across Europe and the Levant.

With their belief in the Sophia of sacred wisdom as well as the teachings of St John the Divine, the Templars heeded his witness in the Book of Revelation:

And I saw a new heaven and a new earth for the first heaven and the first earth were passed away and there was no more sea.

And I John saw the holy city, new Jerusalem, coming down from God out of heaven, prepared as a bride adorned for her husband.

The words were a strange echo of the Jewish lament in the medieval *Zohar Hadash* for the loss of the Temple. In that work, Matrona, the spirit of the land of Israel, might no longer meet her celestial bridegroom in the destroyed Holy of Holies:

My couch, my couch, my dwelling place . . . In thee came unto me the Lord of the World, my husband, and he would lie in my arms and all that I wished for he would give me . . . From here went forth nourishment unto all the world, and light and blessings to all! I seek for my husband but he is not here. I seek in every place . . . Thou didst swear that thou wouldst never cease to love me, saying, 'If I forget thee, O Jerusalem, let my right hand forget her cunning . . .'

A medieval document from the Paris Temple, the *Léviticon*, is particularly suggestive of the beliefs that the Knights Templars brought from the Near East. Its history and their religion were interwoven. "There is no other religion than the religion of nature, preserved in the Temples of Initiation of Egypt and of Greece." Moses had initiated the chiefs of Israel, the Levites, into these mysteries, which formed the basis for the building of the Temple of Solomon, the house of God. Taught by the Essenes, Jesus understood how far the Levites of His time had departed from the ancient rule and sacrificed Himself as a divine martyr to reinspire these mysteries. St John the Beloved Disciple stayed in the East and kept these mysteries alive, while St Paul and the other disciples set up churches that forgot them. Certain Patriarchs and wise men and even Sufis sustained the traditions and the rites until Hugues de Payens was initiated into them in Jerusalem and founded the Order of the Temple of Solomon. From that time, the Templars were the custodians and transmitters of this religion of nature.

According to this pantheistic and mystical system, no distinction was made between animal, vegetable and mineral. As the *Léviticon* declared:

God is all that exists, each part of all that exists is a part of God, but is not God. Unchanging in His essence God is changing in his parts . . . God being the Sovereign intelligence, every part that is constituted is endowed with a portion of His intelligence in proportion to its destiny . . . This is the great *all* of God, which alone has the power to form, to modify, to change, and to rule all the orders of the Intelligences according to eternal and immutable laws which are infinitely good and just.

97

Belief in the nature of the Trinity also differed from that of the Catholic Church. "God the Infinite Being is composed of three powers – the Father or Existence, the Son or Action, and the Spirit or Intelligence produced from the power of the Father and the Son." This led to faith in a single Artificer or Architect of the World. The Temple of the human body could house a spark of the divine Intelligence. The individual could communicate directly with God without the church as an intermediary. And the duty of the human Temple was charity and love.

Many of the elements of this creed were oriental in origin and resulted in charges of heresy, particularly for its espousal of a direct approach to God. At their trials, the Templars were accused in devilish terms of the veneration of the serpent of wisdom and the skull or severed head. But these were only symbols of more profound beliefs. The Templar emphasis on God as a sovereign Intelligence and Creator and on the duty of charity were to devolve to the later Masons. This I would discover at the end of my quest.

Many attempts have been made to identify existing chapels and Masonic Lodges with the ancient Temple of Solomon. All are speculative, including recent claims of correspondences at Rosslyn Chapel. There are no plans of the original Temple at Jerusalem. The Books of Chronicles and Kings are unspecific. Although at Rosslyn with its Templar and Masonic history, the Apprentice Pillar does seem to represent Boaz and the Tree of the Knowledge of Good and Evil in Eden, and the far-flanking decorated pillar, Jachin and the Tree of Life, the central undecorated pillar refers more to the tradition of the Templars, as on their seal of 1214, and to the usual pattern of Masonic Lodges with their three pillars, representing Beauty and Strength as well as Wisdom. There are dozens of small Temples of Solomon carved on the Rosslyn walls, usually with the three pillars and two arches of the Templar seal.

For the Knights Templars and modern mystics, the Temple of Solomon was the creation only of Yahweh or Jehovah, the jealous God and ruler of this earth. The human mind was the true temple of wisdom. The aim of worship and self-sacrifice was to connect the spark of divine intelligence in each person to the source of all light and creation. As a recent work on *God and the Temple* states, "Jesus was the true temple in which the fullness of the divine Being dwelt." His claim to build a new temple, supplanting the old, led to His condemnation by His Jewish contemporaries. The material Temple was never to be rebuilt anywhere in its original form. And yet I would again find a three-dimensional image of that perfect shrine on the Secret Scroll, when I was to reach its lodging place.

8

The Waning of the Crusades

"I wish to send my heart instead of my body, to acquit myself
and my vow . . . Carry my heart to the Holy Sepulchre, where
our Lord was buried."

The dying words of King Robert the Bruce

THE CRUSADES had lost their sense of direction. They were no
longer aimed at Jerusalem, but directed at the rival Rome of
Byzantium, now Constantinople. Never again would they
achieve control of the Holy City, except by the subtle diplomacy of
the German Emperor Frederick the Second. They would be offered
Jerusalem to keep them from attacking Egypt, but they would refuse
the sacred bait. The Christian mission seemed more misguided as it
became more unlikely to succeed. The lost Kingdom of Jerusalem had
been replaced by the Kingdom of Acre, which was to endure another
century. The holy war was replaced by the naval contest of the great
Italian maritime cities, Genoa, Pisa and Venice. Without their fleets,
the crusaders could not reach the Near East. The crusades had now to
concern themselves more with establishing trading beach-heads than
making godly assaults on Islam.

Having visited the Nile, I became intrigued by the two crusades
which took Damietta and the one which briefly captured Alexandria.
The Fifth Crusade of 1217 had as its object the chief port on the Nile
delta nearest to Palestine. A fort on the west bank of the river supported
a chain, which stretched to the walls of the fortified city, making the
great river impassable by boat. The crusaders landed successfully on
the west bank and repeatedly assaulted the tower, eventually capturing
it from a siege-craft, which mounted a wooden fort. The chain was cut,
a bridge of boats was built to the east bank, and Damietta was surrounded by two crusader camps – exactly the situation which I was to
find illustrated on the Secret Scroll.

In spite of Muslim counter-attacks, the crusaders invested the city
and starved it into submission after two years. The Sultan of Europe
offered to trade occupied Damietta for Jerusalem with its walls restored,
as well as the captured True Cross; but the papal legate Pelagius and
the Military Orders refused, saying that they could not defend Jerusalem

99

without controlling Transjordan, and anyway, they would rather seize Cairo, then called Babylon on their inaccurate maps. Their advance down the Nile to Mansourah, however, ended in capitulation and retreat. Cut off by floods and surrounded by the Muslim army, Pelagius had to retire and concede Damietta and declare a truce for eight years. As the Norman satirist Guillaume le Clerc wrote: "The Churchman should recite his Bible and the Psalms and leave the battlefield to the knight."

The Nile port fell more easily in 1249 to the sainted King Louis the Ninth of France. The knights waded inshore and overran the abandoned city over the next days. The Egyptian forces were withdrawn to Mansourah; but King Louis delayed his advance until the dry season, not wishing to be cut off again by floods. An initial cavalry victory led by the Knights Templars, who had also distinguished themselves on the previous crusade against Damietta, developed into a charge within the winding maze of the Muslim city, where the mounted Frankish horsemen were ambushed and destroyed. Although King Louis repelled Muslim assaults on his camp, he delayed his retreat for so long that he was compelled to surrender. The Grand Master of the Temple lost his eye and died, the others were ransomed and Damietta restored. Although King Louis proceeded to Acre and conducted four years of admirable diplomacy across the Near East, befriending in particular the Ismai'ili sect of Assassins, he could achieve little. The most interesting comment on the whole crusade from the contemporary chronicler de Joinville was a report of a French friar's visit to the Assassin leader, who believed in a Gnostic gospel of the transmigration of souls from Abel into Noah into Abraham that ended in the body of St Peter, 'when God came on earth'.

There had been Scottish participation in these and other crusades. The recruitment of a personal Scots guard by the French kings in the following centuries was held to date from the experience of King Louis the Ninth in Egypt. Robert de Bruce the elder, lord of Annandale, campaigned in the Holy Land and visited Clairvaux on his return journey, strengthening the ties between the leading Scots families, the Cistercians and the Knights Templars. Curiously enough, the chronicler Matthew Paris received the news of the defeat of the crusaders in the Nile delta from the Grand Master of the Templars in Scotland, while both the Melrose Abbey *Chronicle* and the *Holyrood Chronicle* had firsthand information of events in the Near East from Templar sources: "And be it known that on the Friday before the feast of All Saints in the above year [1266], the brothers of the Hospital, the Temple, and other houses, and the commune of Acre, to the number of seven thousand men, went out at night, and took a great spoil from the Saracens . . ." And on King Louis the Ninth's last crusade to Tunis, an Almaric de St Clair accompanied the French king.

There would be another assault on Egypt, led by King Peter the First of Cyprus, who spent two and a half years in Europe canvassing support for his enterprise; he enlisted support from Henry St Clair, the first Scottish Earl of Orkney, and other knights from that country. As the chronicler Bower stated in his eulogy of King David of Scotland, he intended to join the crusade and 'showed great and special favour and friendship to his knights and esquires, many of whom had enlisted and engaged in work of that kind'. The valour of one of them in 1365 led to a break into Alexandria through the Customs Gate, from which missiles were thrown down. In Guillaume de Machaut's words, "There was a knight from Scotland who was not killed by the boulders, as he kindled up a fire in the gateway which could not be stopped; he was killed and undone by a great stone." The knight was probably a Leslie; Alexandria was sacked and not defended; the Christians sailed away with their spoils; this was their last major success on any crusade in the Near East.

The fall of Acre in 1291 ended all hope of the Knights Templars in recapturing Jerusalem. They also lost their prime purpose, which was to defend pilgrims to the Holy Land. A valiant bastion of the beleaguered past, they resisted to the end in their great fortress on the sea. The Marshal of the Order, Peter of Sevrey, transferred the treasures and archives under the command of the next Grand Master, Tibald Gaudin, by ship to the Templar castle at Sidon. He and the remaining knights died in the final Muslim assault, in which thousands perished under collapsing masonry. When Sidon fell later to another Muslim attack, the survivors took the treasures and archives on to Tortosa and to Cyprus, before a final voyage to Venice and France.

Losing their bases in the Holy Land, the Knights Templars were forced to become some of the leading mariners of their age. The first significant maps of the Mediterranean, the Portolans, began to appear. Navigation, aided by the compass and the lateen sail rig, became more secure. Cartography developed from Ptolemaic models, Roman strip maps – one of Egypt and the Holy Land has survived – and the circular world maps of the great Arab geographers such as al-Idrisi with his accurate depiction of the Nile delta. Longer voyages over the Atlantic ocean were now coming within reach.

With their wealth, arrogance and secrecy the Knights Templars were a marked Order, once their function was lost. With the rise of the new nation states, the European monarchs would not tolerate an army within the army and a state within the state, especially as the Order now served more as an international bank than a defender of pilgrims. By the thirteenth century, the Templars had fifteen thousand lances and nine thousand manors across Europe, all of which were free of taxes and provided security for the storage and transport of bullion. The treasury of the King of France was normally kept within the vaults of the Temple in Paris; King Philip le Bel himself took refuge there when threatened by city mobs. The only cash drafts that were readily redeemable were issued by the Templars. When King Louis the Seventh had accepted a large loan from the Order, he had noted that the money must be repaid quickly, 'lest their House be defamed and destroyed'. Even the Muslims banked with the Templars, in case the fortunes of war forced them to ally themselves with the Christians. Although usury was forbidden by the Church in the Middle Ages, the Templars added to the money they held or transported by paying back an agreed sum less than the original amount, while a debtor returned more than his debt. The Paris Temple became the centre of the world's money market.

The European kings were always short of funds. They regularly turned on their bankers, Italians and Jews; they defaulted on their loans and expelled their creditors. The Templars were particularly vulnerable to such treatment. They had lost the Holy Land, their arrogance was almost royal, while their secrecy provoked slander. Something of their notorious pride can be seen in an exchange between King Henry the Third of England and the Master of the Temple in London. When the King threatened to confiscate some of the Order's lands for his treasury, because of the intolerable *hauteur* of the knights, the Master replied, "What sayest thou, O King? Far be it that thy mouth should utter so disagreeable and silly a word. So long as thou dost exercise justice, thou wilt reign, but if thou infringe it, thou wilt cease to be King." The implication was that he might be deposed by the Templars.

Pride or *superbia* was considered the worst of the sins in the Middle Ages. To this, the Templars added secret rituals and oriental diplomacy, which added to the envy and hatred of princes and people. They were seen both as the poor knights of Christendom and as rich conspirators against the state and public welfare. When King Philip of France imprisoned more than six hundred of the three thousand Templars in the country in 1307, according to Inquisition records, their interrogation and torture produced confessions that corroborated medieval superstitions, but were the result of applying force and pain. They were not the evidence of truth.

The last overt Grand Master, Jacques de Molay, was experienced in war, yet unversed in diplomacy; he fell victim to his own limitations.

Among many other French Templars, he would confess under torture to heresies and abominations. When in November, 1307, the Pope ordered the kings of Europe to arrest every Templar in their territories, only Denys of Portugal and the excommunicated Robert the Bruce of Scotland did not take the opportunity of plundering such wealth. Although the goods of the Templars were finally made over to the Hospitallers, precious little slipped out of the hands of the kings; and the Hospitallers were careful to refuse such possessions as might lead them into conflict with the secular power.

Jacques de Molay, who had ruined his sect by ordering it to surrender and confess, ended by retracting his confessions and denying all the evil he had spoken of his Order. In 1314, when he was brought out on to a scaffold in front of Notre-Dame to receive his sentence, he declared: "I confess that I am indeed guilty of the greatest infamy. But the infamy is that I have lied. I have lied in admitting the disgusting charges laid against my Order. I declare, and I must declare, that the Order is innocent. Its purity and saintliness have never been defiled. In truth, I had testified otherwise, but I did so from fear of horrible tortures." He was burned alive the following day.

So ended the Templars as a known power, the victims of the greed of kings and of their own pride and wealth. As a contemporary poet asked:

> The brethren, the Masters of the Temple,
> Who were well stocked and ample
> With gold and silver and riches,
> Where are they? How have they done?
> They had such power once that none
> Dared take from them, none was so bold . . .

Then they were betrayed by their wealth to satisfy the greed of kings, in whom the state was sovereign and indivisible.

THE FLIGHT OF THE TEMPLARS

Although King Philip's seizure and destruction of Jacques de Molay and the French Templars was as efficient an operation as Hitler's coup against Röhm and his Brownshirts, there is no record of his finding the Templar treasure in Paris or the secret archives of the Order or its fleet, which was based mainly at La Rochelle in Brittany. Much evidence and some tradition points to the removal of the treasure and most of the archives by ship, with refugee Templars taking these to Portugal and to the west and east coasts of Scotland, where they were welcomed. Acting on warnings, de Molay had already had many records recalled and burned. One of the confessions extorted from the French Templar knights and recorded by the Inquisition was the testimony of John de Châlons of Poitiers. According to his statement, Gerard de Villiers, the Preceptor of the Order under the Treasurer, Hugues de Peraud, knew in advance of the mass arrests and fled the Temple in Paris with fifty knights, whom he commanded to put to sea on eighteen Templar galleys. Another knight, he added, had fled with all the Treasurer's hoard – *cum toto thesauro fratris Hugonis de Peraudo*.

Those knights who were heading for Portugal landed near Nazare, where they proceeded to their main stronghold at Tomar. Well received particularly on account of their experience in navigation, they were incorporated into the same Order under another title, the Knights of Christ. The ships of the renamed Order sailed under the eight-pointed red cross of the Templars. The African explorer Vasco de Gama was a Knight of Christ, and Prince Henry the Navigator was to become a Grand Master.

In other European countries, the Templars merged with the Hospitallers or left their Order and went underground. In Germany, where the Teutonic Knights were carving out an empire to the east, the Templars joined their ranks and accepted a slightly different ritual. Most of the sea-borne French refugee Templars reached Scotland, however, probably with their treasury and the remaining archives from the Paris Temple. According to one French Masonic tradition, the records and wealth were taken on nine vessels to the Isle of Mey in the Firth of Forth near Rosslyn. Others held that these vessels went to Ireland and then to Mull and the Western Isles of Scotland. When the authorities burst into the Irish Templar presbyteries, they found them stripped of ornaments, while Robert the Bruce was receiving new supplies of weapons before the Battle of Bannockburn – to the cost and complaint of King Edward the Second of England.

Near Kilmartin church on Loch Awe in Argyll, recent excavations have revealed Templar graves. One tombstone shows the steps of the Temple of Solomon leading up to a foliate cross beside a crusader sword, as on the William de St Clair grave at Rosslyn. At the ruined chapel of Kilneuair to the east of Loch Awe lie the remains of an ancient circular church and a gravestone with the Templar *cross patte*; the same design is found at neighbouring Kilmichael Glassary, while near Castle Sween is the ruined chapel of Kilmory, where another Templar cross was carved alongside a sailing ship, far larger than a war galley, together with a masonic set-square – such as is found only on early graves of members of the Order. The eight other Templar tombstones that I discovered at Currie near Edinburgh and at Westkirk near Culross in Fife, however, suggest that most of the Templars who fled to Scotland sailed to the Firth of Forth rather than to the Western Isles.

At the time, the excommunicated Robert the Bruce held part of Scotland with his army, fighting against the allies and armies of the English King Edward the Second, who ordered his officers to arrest all the Templars in Scotland and keep them safe in custody. Only two were arrested, although one was the Grand Master of Scotland. They were tried in 1308 by an ecclesiastical court under the supervision of William de Lamberton, the Bishop of St Andrews and an ally of the St Clairs of Roslin as well as a supporter of the claim of Robert the Bruce to the Scottish throne. The Templar knights were prosecuted by John Solario, the papal legate to Scotland, but the verdict was not proven and the Templars were soon released after testifying that their colleagues had fled overseas. An English Templar at his interrogation declared that his brethren had fled to Scotland, where the writ of the English king was only partially enforced, and not to the Baltic to join the Teutonic Knights.

Robert the Bruce, of Norman and Scottish royal ancestry, had been excommunicated for the murder of John Comyn, who had defeated three English armies in one day near Roslin with the help of the St Clairs, but had later recognized the sovereignty of England and the Church of Rome. After this apostasy, the third Scottish patriot and guerilla leader, William Wallace, had been captured and horribly executed by the English. Robert the Bruce had himself crowned on the Throne of Scone – the false Stone of Scone had been removed to England by Edward after his victory against William Wallace at the Battle of Falkirk, in which two leading Templars had assisted him, the Master of England and the Preceptor of Scotland. Before the battle, King Edward's Welsh archers had stayed at Balantrodoch, the principal Templar base, and had marched to Falkirk under Templar command. The victory had been won by a cavalry charge led by the two Templar leaders, although both had been killed. Yet now Bruce was making his stand against the English king and his army at Bannockburn, three months after Jacques de Molay was burned at the stake.

The battle took place near Stirling Castle on St John's Day, in June, a significant date for the Military Orders. Bruce's army was outnumbered by at least three to one, six thousand men pitted against twenty thousand. His deficiency lay in mounted knights. There were some three thousand in the English army, while the Scots could muster only five hundred poorly armed cavalrymen. Accounts of the conflict are sparse and fragmentary, yet they testify to two strange events. Following a charge by mounted soldiers against the English archers from a reserve kept back by Bruce, a fresh force of horsemen appeared with banners flying once all the troops were engaged, and routed the English. While one Scottish legend has it that these were camp-followers riding ponies and waving sheets, clubs and pitchforks, such a mob could never have put the English king and five hundred of his knights to immediate flight. For the charge of this new squadron struck terror in the English, who recognized the force of their foe and probably their war banner, *Beauséant*. On the anniversary of Bannockburn on St John's Day, modern Scottish Templars still pay tribute to their predecessors, who fought in the battle and were martyred there in the struggle for the freedom of Scotland.

Three of the St Clairs fought alongside Bruce at Bannockburn. One of them was the Fighting Bishop of Dunkeld, who destroyed a sea raid by the enemy the following year in Fife. "Many of the English," the family chronicler Father Hay reported, "not getting in time enough to their boats, were cut in pieces. Others, striving to save themselves by swimming, perished in the sea. Others, who were got there, for that they were already too full, were made a prey either to the water which swallowed them up, or to the enemy, who slew them from the shore. Several of their boats sunk, as being too heavily loaded."

Another of the St Clairs who fought at Bannockburn, the Lord of Rosslyn, was one of the signatories of the Scottish Declaration of Independence at Arbroath in 1320 with its defiant statement: "So long as a hundred of us are left alive, we will never in any degree be subjected to the English. It is not for glory, riches or honour that we fight, but for liberty alone which no good man loses but with his life." And the third St Clair in Bannockburn was the Sir William who died later with other Scottish knights in a charge against the Muslims in Spain, while taking the Heart of Bruce for burial in Jerusalem. His is the Grail and Templar gravestone in Rosslyn Chapel. If refugee Templar knights did enter the service of Bruce before Bannockburn, William de St Clair would have a strong claim to having been their leader. The evidence lies carved on his tomb, which shows the burial of a Master of that Military Order.

Whoever dispersed the English knights, the victory at Bannockburn confirmed Scottish freedom and Robert the Bruce as King. The benefit to the St Clairs was immediate, the grant of more lands and a bishopric. Part of the Templar fleet had evidently sailed to the Firth of Forth from France. The extensive Templar properties stretching between Rosslyn Castle and the Seton estate near Musselburgh were centred on Balantrodoch, now known simply as Temple. Its preceptory and church had been built in the middle of the twelfth century on lands under the jurisdiction of the St Clairs as Sheriffs of Midlothian. That ruined graveyard is still full of Templar and Masonic tombstones, bearing the symbols of both rites. Although six months after his victory Robert the Bruce confirmed by charter all the possessions of the Hospitallers in Scotland, he made no mention of the Templars, any more than he referred to them at the Battle of Bannockburn. Yet curiously, two charters show a Scton as the Master of the Hospitallers, presiding over 'Temple Courts' at Balantrodoch thirty-two years after the English defeat.

Templar courts and properties continued to exist in Scotland for some two centuries, and some still exist. Although the Hospitallers were given authority over their prescribed rivals, they never ingested them. Not until 1488 did King James the Fourth of Scotland confirm the union of the Templars and the Hospitallers and the grants of the lands given to both Orders in a charter entitled *Deo et Sancto Hospitali de Jerusalem et fratribus ejusdem Milititiae Templi Solomonis*. The Knights of the Temple in Scotland remained a group hidden under the mantle of the Knights of St John, and directed from the neighbouring St Clair castle at Rosslyn, where extensive rebuilding and fortification took place, as if the family had received a sudden influx of wealth and building skills.

The Scottish Knights Templars still commemorate their Oath of Fealty, first taken three years after the Battle of Bannockburn and restated in 1991 at the festival for the martyrs of the Temple held at Torpichen Preceptory, the Lothian headquarters of the rival Hospitallers, which the Templars acknowledge as causing "the especial nature of the survival of the Order of the Temple in this our native land of Scotland in the fourteenth and fifteenth centuries." The Oath of Fealty in its modern text, but unaltered in content, explicitly asserts the continuance of the Templars by Robert the Bruce:

Inasmuch as the ancient realm of Scotland did succour and receive the brethren of the most ancient and noble Order of the Temple of Jerusalem, when many distraints were being perpetrated upon their properties, and many heinous evils upon their persons, the Chevaliers of the Order do here bear witness.

Chevaliers of the Order do undertake to preserve and defend the rights, freedoms and privileges of the ancient sovereign realm of Scotland. Further they affirm that they will maintain, at peril of their bodies, the Royal House of the realm of Scotland, by God appointed.

Wishing eventually to make his peace with the Church so that a crusade could not be declared against Scotland as it had been against the heretic Cathars of the Langue d'Oc in the South of France, Robert the Bruce required the Templars to become a secret organization, which was to give rise to the later fraternities of Masons. According to an old Masonic tradition, Bruce established the Royal Order of Scotland to reward the courage of the Templars at Bannockburn, installing the St Clairs as hereditary Grand Masters. The Sovereign Grand Master was the King of Scotland, and the office still remained a royal appointment, existing to this day in its secret power. Although the Order was not combined with the Templars, many prominent Templars became members of the Royal Order, including its Grand Master in Scotland. This would further explain the burial of Sir William de St Clair in 1330 in the Templar fashion.

Robert the Bruce was also held to have raised the Kilwinning Order of Heredom (or Sanctuary) to the status of the Royal Grand Lodge of Heredom, the prime Masonic Lodge of Scotland, located beside the ancient abbey near Kilmarnock in Ayrshire. The original Kilwinning Lodge was reputed to have been founded by David the First, a generous benefactor of the Knights Templars. Curiously, the right of sanctuary in the six hundred and more old Templar properties in Scotland was preserved, even for debtors, until the nineteenth century. The Canongate Masonic Lodge in Edinburgh also took the name of the primary Lodge at Kilwinning, and the later St Clairs of Rosslyn presided there. Yet in medieval times, as the Earl of Rosslyn has stated in his recent book on the family chapel, "The Barons of Rosslyn held their principal annual meetings at Kilwinning. The ecclesiastical fraternities – the Benedictine Order as at Dunfermline, the Cistercian Order which had a monastery at Newhall, Carlops, and others – were large employers of labour, and they had many skilled builders, architects and craftsmen under their supervision during the thirteenth and fourteenth centuries, but they were largely superseded by the Masons who were held together by their oaths and customs, and who had a profound influence upon ecclesiastical architecture throughout Europe."

The Masonic tradition was confirmed by the pretender Larminius, who assumed the post of Grand Master of the Temple in France, and excluded the new Scottish Order as *Templi Desertores*. An authority on the subject, a Mason herself, has written that "the tradition connecting Kilwinning with the Templar Grades is persistent and is perpetually cropping up . . . It is plausible, as it explains the union of the trowel and the sword, that is so conspicuous in the high grades." The Tenth Degree of present Freemasonry in Sweden still preserves the names of the nine refugee knights, the same number as those who founded the Military Order with Hugues de Payens. The Scottish preservers were said to be:

> Charles d'Aumont, Prior of Brittany
> Edward Harris, an English Templar Marshal
> Pierre de Boulogne, a clerical Templar
> Etienne Stormont, an English Grand Commander
> Adamus Dalberg, a German Grand Commander
> Philibert Thierry, a knight from Flanders
> Andreas Montigny, a knight from Auvergne
> Adalbert Matignon, a knight from France
> Wolfgang von Sassen, a German knight

This vanguard was soon followed by another seventeen surviving French Templars and one Scots knight, Alfred MacDougal. They were to establish themselves afterwards in Aberdeen.

Yet these were later Templar traditions, which will be discussed. On a mission to Pope John XXII at Avignon, the Earl of Moray made crusading vows and persuaded the Pope to address Robert the Bruce in the royal manner, accepting the fact that he was the king of Scotland. As he lay dying at Cardross, Bruce requested Sir James Douglas and William de St Clair to take his heart to the Holy Sepulchre, as he could not fulfil his own crusading vows with his stricken body. That mission led to the death of the four Scottish knights at the hands of the Muslim cavalry in 1330, the return of the hearts of Douglas to his family chapel and of Bruce to Melrose Abbey, while the skull and bones of William de St Clair were buried under the Grail tombstone at Rosslyn, which I had originally recognized.

The crusades in Spain against the Moors, and in Prussia and Lithuania by the Teutonic Knights against the pagan Slavs, were proving successful. Many Scottish knights in the fourteenth century joined the Baltic crusades at the time when the Hanseatic League was growing in power and using its fleets to enter the Atlantic and compete with Scandinavian and Scottish fleets for control of the profitable trade in furs and timber, pitch and salt and fish, which extended through Viking settlements as far as Newfoundland. Until the disaster of the Battle of Tannenberg in 1410, which would end the imperial dreams of the Teutonic Knights of expanding their power as far as Russia, many Scottish nobles joined the German Military Order in its advance towards the east. The Lord of Roslin and father of Henry St Clair, who would become the first Scottish Earl of Orkney, himself died with his companions fighting for the Teutonic Knights and their possessions.

The flight of the refugee Knights Templars to Lothian and their headquarters there at Temple and St Germains led to a huge increase in the resources of the St Clair and Seton families, both of whom had fiercely defended the cause of Robert the Bruce. Christopher, Alexander and John Seton had their intestines drawn out before being hanged, beheaded and quartered in 1306 for supporting the Bruce, while Christopher's son signed the Declaration of Arbroath and Scottish independence along with the St Clairs of Roslin before his death in 1332 at the Battle of Kinghorn. With Templar resources and navigational skills at their disposal, the Setons and the St Clairs were confirmed as the defenders of Holyrood and the King's person from their strongholds near the capital.

Born in 1345, Henry St Clair became Lord of Roslin at the age of fourteen, inheriting a claim to far northern domains through his mother Isabel, daughter of Malise, Earl of Orkney, where he was subject to the King of Norway. Henry would have royal support from the Stuart kings, who succeeded David the Second on the throne, and from the Templar refugees encountered in his youthful diplomacy in Scandinavia, where he would assert his rights over the pivotal strategic islands in the northern Atlantic trade. Moreover, the great sea-power of Venice was also switching its fleets from the lost crusading ports of the Near East towards Flanders with its wool trade and the North Sea, clashing with the Hanseatic League, until then dominant in those waters. That Italian expansion would lead Earl Henry on an odyssey back to his Viking roots.

9

Venice to the North

> Since Antonio [Zeno] had as great a desire as his brother to
> see the world and its various nations, and to make himself a
> great name, he bought a ship and directed his course that way.
>
> From *The Zeno Narrative*

THE ANNIVERSARY, after five hundred years, of the 'discovery of America' by Christopher Columbus led to intense speculation about those European voyagers who reached the New World before him. There had been many, for Viking settlements certainly spread as far as Newfoundland and probably to Vinland in New England. The significance of the four expeditions of the Genoese adventurer in the service of Spain to the West Indies was to shift Atlantic trade from the northern routes to equatorial and southern passages. Of most interest to me was the Venetian *Zeno Map* and *Narrative*, which claimed in 1558 that in the late fourteenth century Antonio and Nicolò Zeno had carried a Prince Zichmni from islands north of Scotland to Estotiland, which was later called Nova Scotia. Except for a contemporary Vitalien pirate named Wichmannus, who was certainly no prince, Zichmni could only have been the St Clair Earl of Orkney. Called Zicno in Marco Barbaro's reference in his *Libro di nozze* to the Zeno brothers' northern master, St Clair with its many abbreviated Latin spellings such as San Clo and its Norse spelling Zinkler seemed close to a written Italian rendering of that spoken name.

With its loss of trade in the Near East under the rising power of the Turkish sultans, who would capture Constantinople itself in 1453, the Venetians looked to increase their commerce to the north and the west. For two centuries, however, the Hanseatic League had controlled the overland routes from the Baltic to the Mediterranean and had even made themselves dominant in the North Sea. From their six major counters – in Lübeck, Wisby in Gotland, Bergen, Novgorod, Bruges and London at the Steelyard – the Hanseatic cities dominated the major river mouths and the sounds, straits and channels of northern Europe from Russia to Britain.

Few goods passed from east to west or north to south, except at a German price. Salt and fish had made the original fortunes of Lübeck;

to these were added Scandinavian and Atlantic timber and iron, rope and pitch, sailcloth and brimstone for gunpowder and furs. Backed by the Teutonic Knights, the Hansa like the Templars became a state within every northern state. Only Scottish ships and merchants competed seriously with the Hansa, until the arrival of Venetian fleets in convoys twice a year to Flanders for the wool trade. These foragers speculated on outflanking the German traders by themselves establishing mercantile posts and privileges in Scotland and Scandinavia. If the English Channel was closed against them, they could use the Templar escape route round Ireland to the Western Isles and Orkney, the entrepot of the whole rich North Atlantic trade. Such a strategy was part of young Henry St Clair's mission for his country, when he left Roslin in 1363 as a diplomat bound for Copenhagen. King Waldemar of Denmark had seized Gotland two years previously and had defeated King Magnus of Sweden at Helsingsborg despite the aid of a large Hanseatic fleet. He would be followed by King Haakon the Sixth of Norway, who was to marry the Danish princess Margaret, in closing the vital German counter at Bergen. The League was under serious threat.

The marriage of Haakon to Margaret provided the opportunity for the later success of Henry St Clair. Because of his Norse family connections, he was knighted and appointed as the Scottish ambassador to the wedding, and he sailed to Denmark. Most of the Scandinavian royalty and nobility would be at the ceremony. Although the bride was only ten years old, she was to become ruler of all three kingdoms, united in her person. At Copenhagen, Sir Henry St Clair had the lands left by Earl Malise in Orkney confirmed as his right, but he was not yet given the title of earl by the King of Norway. He would first have to prove that he could assert royal authority in Orkney and be a faithful servant of the Norse crown, which disliked having an overmighty subject or a rebel on its Northern Isles. Bishop William of Orkney and the Shetlands was already appropriating royal revenues. Sir Henry St Clair's uncle Thomas was sent as Baillie to collect these taxes for the Norwegian crown, while Sir Henry was said by Father Hay to have concluded a marriage to Princess Florentia, a sister of King Haakon; but if he did, she died young, probably before the age of puberty, and bore no children.

Sir Henry could help his cause and fortunes by promising to assert Norwegian control over the Orcadian Islands, where the Hansa already had two trading posts. During his stay in Copenhagen, he also endeared himself to the future ruler of all Scandinavia, the child bride Margaret. In the city, too, were the North Atlantic explorers, Paul Knutson, who had led expeditions far to the west beyond Greenland, and Ivar Baardsen, with his detailed knowledge of the Greenland monasteries, which were heated by hot springs and mainly staffed by Shetland monks. Most probably, Sir Henry St Clair also met Carlo Zeno, the Venetian admiral and diplomat, then seeking to expand his maritime city's commerce to the North Sea, along with King Peter of Cyprus, collecting support for his crusade against Alexandria. Certainly, the biography of Carlo Zeno by his grandson, Bishop Giacomo of Padua, stated that Carlo met a Scottish prince on a pilgrimage to Jerusalem and assisted the King of Cyprus in his wars. If this was Henry St Clair, he would have seen the enclosed and fortified Arsenale at Venice, where the crusaders assembled, and he would have noted the lateen rigs of the merchantmen and the first mounted cannon of the war galleys, which were to take him and other Scottish knights to sack Alexandria. On their retreat, he would have visited Acre and Jerusalem under a safe-conduct for pilgrims, previously negotiated by the Holy Roman Emperor Frederick the Second. Certainly a pilgrimage at this time gave rise to his nickname, coined by the rival first Earl of Douglas, 'Henry the Holy'.

On his return to Scotland, Sir Henry St Clair married Janet Halyburton, the daughter of the lord of Dirleton Castle, twenty miles from Rosslyn. She was to give him four sons and nine daughters. He had become powerful at court and was appointed to state offices. The Scottish queen was Euphemia Ross, his great-aunt, who had married the new King Robert Stewart, the founder of that dynasty. This close relationship with the Scottish throne disturbed the King of Norway, who removed the St Clair Baillie and appointed the rival Sir Alexander de Ard to be governor of Orkney and to uphold royal authority there. As with the Romans, Norse strategy was divide and rule. De Ard was only governor for one year, and in 1379, the Norwegian king appointed Sir Henry St Clair as the Earl of Orkney under stringent conditions. Under the deed of investiture, he had to agree:

> To serve the King of Norway with a hundred armed men.
> To defend Orkney with all his power.
> To aid the King of Norway in his wars.
> Not to build a castle on Orkney without the consent of the King.
> To uphold the rights of the islanders.
> Not to sell or pledge any of the islands.
> To welcome the King or his men on any voyage to the islands.
> Not to declare any war that might harm the islands.
> To be responsible personally for any injury to an islander.
> To answer the King's summons and give him counsel.

113

Not to break the King's peace.
To make no pact with the Bishop of Orkney.
Not to give his son the earldom as an inheritance except if the title
came from the King of Norway.
To pay one thousand gold nobles for the title.

Other clauses confirmed that his cousins, Malise Sparre and Sir Alexander de Ard, would both renounce their claims to the earldom and be held as hostages in Norway. The assent of powerful Scottish nobles would be procured to confirm Henry's title as the Earl of Orkney. No lands or rights of the King of Norway on Orkney would be touched. And any breach of any of the terms of the deed would result in loss of the earldom.

The new earl had inherited considerable resources to enforce his rights and to make himself a sea-power in the north. The Register of the Great Seal of Scotland showed Bruce and Stewart grants of land to Henry St Clair, 'our chosen defender and faithful to us', a guardian of the crown prince. In addition, he had absorbed many of the Templar lands and treasures from their headquarters at Balantrodoch near Roslin. His power and state and that of his son Henry were considerable. As the family chronicler Father Hay wrote, "There were very few but were some way bound to him." The shipbuilding skills and resources on either side of the Firth of Forth at Culross and Burntisland and other ports were also his to command, thanks to his Grand Mastership of the Scottish Guilds and Orders. He could finance and furnish a fleet.

Before asserting his own authority in Orkney and the Shetlands, Earl Henry St Clair had to protect his own Scottish possessions, which now extended from Roslin to Dysart in Fife and Newburgh in Aberdeenshire. Knowing that the Stewart kings considered his loyalties divided between his home country and the kingdom of Norway, he induced his children to make three royal marriages: his eldest son and heir Henry wed Egidia Douglas, granddaughter of King Robert the Second of Scotland; his daughter Elizabeth married Sir John Drummond, brother of the wife of the Crown Prince of Scotland; and his second son John espoused the Princess Ingeborg, the last daughter of King Waldemar of Denmark, whose elder daughter's marriage to King Haakon the Sixth had been attended by Earl Henry as a young man. He also secured from King Robert of Scotland the formal cession of any right to Orkney and the recognition of King Haakon's grant of the earldom to 'our beloved relative Henry of *Orcadie*'.

The first requisite for the new Earl of Orkney was a secure base for his knights and his fleet. He knew of the Arsenale in Venice, the

Templar sea-fortress at Acre and the Douglas castle at Tantallon, where a huge wall guarded a rocky promontory, enabling ships to sail into a defended harbour beneath the cliffs. Although his deed of investiture precluded him from building a castle, he did so with the help of masons imported from Lothian, who had already set up the massive red walls of Rosslyn Castle. He was under threat from the Bishop of Orkney in his fortified palace, and he could not assert the authority of the King of Norway without a stronghold. In point of fact, King Haakon died in 1380 and was succeeded by King Olaf, while Earl Henry was constructing his monumental fortress on the site of an old Norse emplacement in Kirkwall, which afforded sanctuary for ships dragged ashore.

Once his fortress was built, Prince Henry would deal with the contentious prelate, Bishop William of Orkney, whose palace stood on the hill above St Magnus Cathedral a quarter of a mile away. The task, however, was made unnecessary by the people of Kirkwall; burdened by the Bishop's oppressions, they killed or burned him. In 1387, the released pretender Malise Sparre also forfeited his claims to the earldom of Orkney, promising 'to restore, pay and satisfy' all injuries and offences and possessions taken from Earl Henry, although the Earl would still have to kill him four years later because of another assault on Orkney from the Shetlands, which still had to be conquered.

The death of King Olaf after a short reign confirmed Prince Henry's estimation as 'a second person next to the King'. As Earl of Orkney, he was an elector to the three kingdoms of Norway, Sweden and Denmark, and sailing across the North Sea, he confirmed King Olaf's mother Margaret as Queen of Norway and Sweden and as Regent of Denmark. She adopted as her heir a five-year-old boy, her grandnephew Erik of Pomerania, and so sustained her power during his minority. Earl Henry's presence in Scandinavia caused him to miss the Battle of Otterburn against the English, but the peace of 1389 between England and the old allies, Scotland and France, allowed him to consider extending his power to the Faroes and the Shetlands, where he now contracted to pay rent to the Baillie of the King of Norway at the Church of St Magnus in Tingwall, under penalty of losing his rents on two of the islands off Orkney. Evidently, his assertion of royal authority on Orkney had been so effective that he was now asked to do the same on the neighbouring chains of the Orcadian Isles.

Before he could begin the reduction of these far islanders, who resented paying church tithes almost as much as royal taxes, Earl Henry had to pay homage at Scone to the new Stewart King of Scotland, Robert the Third. He was truly a catalyst between all the nations of the north, allied by blood and trust to the ruling families of four kingdoms. His duty done, he collected a fleet of thirteen ships and set sail for his campaigns to the north of Orkney. On his voyage, design or chance would renew his connections with the seamen he most admired, the mariners of Venice.

A VENETIAN DYNASTY

As a child, Nicolò Zeno played in his grandfather's palace, which still stands by the canal in the Venetian quarter of Canareggio; as a man, he wrote that he had torn up most of a book written in the Shetland Isles, as well as letters sent back to Venice and sea charts, the remnants of which he was later to publish in 1558 as the *Zeno Narrative* and *Map*. His confession of his childish act of destruction was disarming. He regretted his mutilation of the records of his predecessor, the explorer Antonio Zeno:

> All these letters were written by Sir Antonio to Sir Carlo his brother. I am sorry that the book and much else on these subjects have, I do not know how, been destroyed. For I was only a child when they fell into my hands, and as I did not know what they were, I tore them in pieces, as children will do, and ruined them. It is something which I cannot now recall without the greatest sorrow. Nevertheless, in order that such an important memoir should not be lost, I have put it all in order as well as I could in this Narrative. More than its predecessors, the present age may derive pleasure from the great discoveries made in those parts where they were least expected. For our age takes a great interest in new narratives and in the discoveries, made in countries unknown before, by the high courage and great energy of our ancestors.

The *Narrative*, indeed, began with a genealogy and a description of the high courage and great energy of the Zeno line. The family was one of the twenty-four in Venice that were held to be 'long' or 'old'; it reached the height of its influence during the thirteenth and fourteenth centuries. Marino Zeno had been Captain-General of the Sea, carrying the warriors of the Fourth Crusade to the sack of Constantinople. He himself became the first Vice-Doge or Podestà there, wearing the purple shoes and stockings of the Doge of Venice; and he built a wall and a fort to protect the Venetian quarter on the Golden Horn from the rest of the city. He was also responsible for transporting the military knights on to the Holy Land, which was their proper destination. So began a long association between the Zeno family and the Military Orders, which was to last for more than three centuries.

In those early days of diplomacy, the Zeno family continued to supply the state with many Captains-General of the Sea, admirals in the fleet, colonial administrators of the many Venetian island possessions, and legates or ambassadors. One of its members, Reniero, became Doge after he defeated a Genoese admiral, whose coat of arms he adopted – four diagonal purple stripes on a silver field, which was later quartered with a lion. He was responsible for the first comprehensive Venetian maritime code. When he died in 1268, he left a vast fortune, some of which came from the spoils of Constantinople – now repossessed by the Greek emperors – spoils used to endow the family church of Crosichieri in Canareggio. During his time as Doge, the Piazza San Marco also took on its present form. The marbles and treasures of Constantinople were used to embellish it, particularly the four gilded bronze horses set above the façade of the basilica – along with many religious relics. Later the Zeno family was to endow a baptismal chapel in San Marco, ornamented by radiant mosaics commemorating the voyage of St Mark himself to Egypt and the later return of his remains to Venice.

In the centuries to come, this trading wealth and these colonial connections continued to enhance the family's standing; they produced one cardinal, four bishops, three Dukes of Crete, six Dukes of Candia, twelve procurators and dozens of ambassadors, especially to the Levant. The Venetian sea-borne empire made the Zenos influential and rich, particularly as the carriers of the pilgrims and the crusaders. Pietro Zeno, called Dracone, became Captain-General of the Christian Confederation against the Turks, while his son Carlo spent his early manhood in eastern trade and diplomacy. When war broke out between Venice and Genoa, he raised a fleet which plundered the Genoese colonies of the Levant. The war went badly in home waters, and in 1380, a fleet from Genoa captured the south-western tip of the lagoons at Chioggia and blockaded the Venetians in their city. Their ships could not break out.

To confront this crisis, Carlo Zeno's fleet sailed back with its spoils from the East and blockaded the Genoese forces in their turn. He foiled all their attempts to escape, and after six months of siege and starvation, they capitulated. A decisive factor in the battle was the use of a new mounted ship's cannon, the *petriero*. This was made of welded rods held together by six or seven rings. A breech-loader, it fired a small stone ball, which caused more fear than damage. On my visits to the Zeno archives in the Libreria Marciana, I heard of four of these original ship's cannon, recently dredged from the docks in the Arsenale and on display in the Museo Storico Navale. The admiral-in-charge Gottardo confirmed to me that these *petrieri* were the type used by Carlo Zeno

117

in his victory. They soon reached the merchant cogs of the Hansa fleet, which by 1381 were mounting these primitive cannon on their floating gun platforms.

The saviour of Venice had two brothers, the Nicolò and Antonio of the later *Zeno Narrative*. Both were naval officers and colonial officials. Nicolò's distinguished service to the state earned him the title of *Ser Dracone* or *Cavaliere*, which was also given to Carlo the Procurator. When Marco Barbaro, another Venetian patrician, wrote his account of the noble families of Venice, his entry under the Zeno name, dated 1536, recorded Nicolò as 'the rich man' and the captain of a galley in the Chioggia battle against Genoa, won by his brother Carlo. In his *Libro di nozze* Barbaro further stated that Nicolò then went on to explore the northern seas, followed by his brother Antonio. They wrote together "the voyages among the islands under the Arctic Pole and the discoveries of 1390 – by order of Zicno, King of Frislanda, he [Antonio] took himself to the continent of Estotilanda in Northern America. He dwelt fourteen years in Frislanda, four with his brother Nicolò, and ten alone."

Barbaro's assertion did not coincide with the later publication of the *Zeno Narrative*, which was based on mangled evidence; but it did correspond to the biographical details of the two brothers, as they emerged in my research. Nicolò Zeno was captain and commander of the Venetian biennial fleet to London and Flanders between the spring of 1383, when he had been ambassador to Hungary, and the June of 1388, when he was transferred to Adriatic duties. In that period and in pursuit of the Venetian push to the north, he had every opportunity to sail to Orkney and the Shetlands to assist Zicno or Earl Henry St Clair in his campaigns to assert control over those islands and destroy the domination of the Hansa in the northern Atlantic.

There was also no record of Nicolò Zeno in the archives between 1396 and August 1400, when he made a will in Venice. He had been banned from office and sent into exile on charges of corruption while serving as procurator in various Venetian colonies. If he had taken his brother Antonio with him from the Flanders convoy on his first expedition to Orkney and left him, as Barbaro wrote, with Zicno as a hostage for fourteen years, he could then have gone to rejoin him, having heard of his northern campaigns and exploits in the correspondence that came back to Canareggio. That would have allowed one or both of the Zeno brothers to survey Greenland and to navigate the northern expedition to Estotilanda between 1396 and 1398, which was the basis of the *Zeno Narrative*. The fact that there was no record kept in Venice of Antonio Zeno between 1380 and his death there just before 1403 made still more plausible Barbaro's claim of his long stay in Orkney and later voyage to North America.

The Venetian mission to the Atlantic was confirmed by the fact that Carlo Zeno himself was sent after 1396 as an ambassador to France and again to London. According to the *Zeno Narrative*, Nicolò had gone on an expedition to Greenland, and reported back to Carlo on a flourishing trade in salted fish and furs between the Norse colonies there and Iceland, the Shetlands and Scandinavia. He also described the naval power of the Scottish ruler he was serving, and the St Clair conquest of Orkney, Shetland and some of the Faroe Islands. These conquests were matters of fact. One of the proofs for the truth of most of the *Zeno Narrative*, said to be based on the letters sent back by Nicolò and Antonio to their brother Carlo from Orkney and the Shetlands, was the accurate description of obscure campaigns and wars in the islands. The Zeno family was being directed by the Venetian state in a drive for trade and influence in the North Atlantic.

The opportunity could hardly be more favourable. The Black Death had winnowed the population of Norway, perhaps killing two-thirds of its sailors and shipwrights. The area extending over all the lands near the Arctic as far as North America, called 'Norveca' on early medieval maps, was slipping from the grasp of the Norse royal house, and the colonies as far as Greenland were under threat by plague and pirate attack. So enfeebled was Norway that when Queen Margaret shifted the centre of Scandinavian power to Denmark, the whole of the area of Norse sovereignty would be called the Danish Province of Greenland, *Gronlandia Provincia*. This created the chance to found a Northern Commonwealth.

The Hanseatic League had struck back with a vengeance against Denmark and Norway, where Queen Margaret wrote to her husband from Akershus Castle in 1368 of a German blockade: "My servants are in great want of food and drink, neither they nor I receive what we need." The following year, Bergen was burned and sacked by a Hansa fleet; this was followed by the capture of Copenhagen; within another three years, Denmark and Norway had restored even greater privileges to the German merchants. Queen Margaret did not dare to assault them as her father had; but she invaded and defeated Sweden, so becoming the ruler of all Scandinavia. Thus her childhood friend, Henry St Clair, now her vassal as the Earl of Orkney, became a powerful ally in her dream of establishing a Northern Commonwealth of trade which would extend from Scandinavia through the Orcadian Isles on to the Norse colonies and bishoprics in Iceland and Greenland, and to outposts in North America.

The worst threat to trade in the Baltic and the North Sea now derived from pirates, known as the Vitalien Brethren. Chased out of Wisby by the Teutonic Knights, they attacked Bergen and seized ports in southern Norway. Queen Margaret's need to use the Earl of Orkney's fleet and his access to shipbuilding materials against the Vitalien pirates was another factor in her continuing support for his enterprises. In the National Library in Copenhagen are state documents showing the St Clair seal, second in precedence to the Queen. In 1389, indeed, when Erik of Pomerania was declared her heir to the thrones of Denmark and Norway, Henry St Clair's signature followed immediately on that of Archbishop Vinoldus of Nidaros, now Trondheim. Queen Margaret had put her trust in the power of her Earl of Orkney, and he once used a safe-conduct from King Richard the Second of England to bring three ships from London to her aid.

Such was the historical scene set at the opening of the *Zeno Narrative*. Nicolò Zeno, then serving as commander of the Flanders fleet, was said to have wanted to see more of the world in order to serve his country better and gain reputation and honour. Equipping his own vessel, he was caught in a terrible storm and shipwrecked on Frislanda, which has been identified as Fair Isle between Orkney and the Shetlands or as one of the Faroe Islands. The local people were about to kill him and the crew, which had saved the goods from the ship, when a local prince appeared with his men. "He drove away the natives, addressed our people in Latin and asked them who they were and where they came from. And when he learned that they came from Italy and that they were men of that country, he was exceedingly pleased. Promising them all that they would not be made captive, and assuring them that they had come into a place where they would be well treated and very welcome, he took them under his protection and gave his word of honour that they were safe."

The Prince had a fleet of thirteen vessels – "two only were rowed with oars, the rest were small barks and one was a ship." He had established his authority on Orkney and was attempting to extend it to the Shetlands and the Faroes, where he took his impressed Venetians. Although the *Zeno Narrative* referred to him as Zichmni and misspelt most place names, Henry St Clair was the only ruler in that area at that time with a war fleet. The subsequent account of obscure fighting in the Faroes and the Shetlands would not have been known in Venice without Nicolò writing back home about the struggles and the opportunities for trade, while asking his brother Antonio to buy another ship and sail it out to the northern seas to join him. "Since Antonio had as great a desire as his brother to see the world and its various nations, and to make himself a great name, he bought a ship and directed his course that way. After a long voyage full of many dangers, he joined Sir Nicolò at last in safety and was received by him with great gladness, as his brother not only by blood, but also in courage."

After many controversies, such were the results of my researches into the Venetian connection, which supported the tale in the *Zeno Narrative* about a colonizing voyage from Orkney to the New World at the close of the fourteenth century. Yet there were many more disbelievers to confute. New evidence had to be found in Venice and the Orcadian Isles and across the Atlantic Ocean.

10

Sailing to the West

He says that it is a very great country and, as it were,
a new world.

The Fisherman's Tale
from *The Zeno Narrative*

IN THE *ZENO NARRATIVE*, there was a Fisherman's Tale of an Ancient
Mariner, who had returned from a 'new world' and informed the
Earl of Orkney of what he might discover there. The later explorer
Amerigo Vespucci would give his Christian name to that unknown
continent by telling Lorenzo de Medici of that 'new world'. Unfortunately, the earlier Fisherman had no name and died before he could
serve as a guide for a colonizing expedition. His descriptions of a land
named Drogeo suggested a passage past Florida and through the West
Indies, where the Caribs were cannibals, and a landing on the coasts
of Mexico, where the Mayans and other peoples were resisting the
expansion of the Aztec empire, and could work in gold and silver. Such
an account in a book not published until 1558 demonstrated to many
later commentators that the author, another Nicolò Zeno, had forged
his *Narrative* after the Spanish conquest of Central America, and that
his *Map*, which was dated as drawn in 1380, was a concoction of
other later maps. In its endless rivalry with Genoa, the home city of
Christopher Columbus, Venice seemed to have manufactured a discovery of North America by the brothers of its victorious hero Carlo
Zeno nearly a century before the Genoese admiral's landfall in the
Caribbean sea.

The chief interest of the *Zeno Map* was its placement of two cities
in North America, appearing to confirm a colonizing expedition there
after 1390, the previous date given for the Zeno voyage by Marco
Barbaro. Yet there had also been significant other cartographical evidence for North American colonization by knights, who knew how to
build fortifications and wore a Templar or Engrailed Cross. The earliest
version of a map called the *Rudimentium Novitorium* was published in
the Hansa centre of Lübeck about 1475 and clearly showed 'Winland'
as an island with a fortified church to the far north-west – a location
similar to that of Estotilanda on the *Zeno Map*. Another version of that

German map derived from Augsburg five years later and marked the stronghold on a promontory as 'Vinland' – the Viking name for New England. These two maps were to bolster me greatly in my later researches into the mysterious Newport Tower on Rhode Island, for they suggested a pre-Columbian structure there.

More important was another German world map by Casper Vopell of Cologne, printed in 1545. The cartographer Vavassatore published his variant in Venice thirteen years later, the same year as the publication of the *Zeno Map*. The surviving version had belonged to a Habsburg duke and is now in the Houghton Library at Harvard University. Four crowned figures were drawn into the areas corresponding to North and Central America and Asia, all of them ruling empires or colonies of the past or the present. In Asia Orientalis, the *magus Cham Cublai* was shown on his throne – the Kublai Khan known to the Venetian explorer Marco Polo. Above Hispania Major, the crowned Aztec ruler *Mutzezuma* reigned, and Cortes was mentioned as his conqueror. Beside Florida, the Spanish king was depicted, ruling over his new colonial empire in the Caribbean. And on the region of Nova Scotia labelled Baccalearum Regio, a fourth crowned and bearded knight appeared, kneeling by his shield and wearing the surcoat of the Military Orders, testimony to some memory of a past royal or princely colony there. Above the figure was a rough square cross set on a hill. Opposite the figure, the inscription read *Agricole proseu C. di laborador*. The words suggested *agriculture* or plantations *for* the benefit of a *labouring* rite such as a monkish or Military Order on the cape.*

Moreover, the earlier and seminal Dutch globe map, the *Gemma Frisius-Mercator* of 1537, had mentioned a *Promotoriu agricule seu cabo del Labrador*, or agricultural Promontory on the cape of the Labrador. The Portuguese word for landowner was *Lavrador* and again suggested a tradition of plantations worked in that area. Indeed, João Fernandez, who made many western voyages in the middle of the fifteenth century and accompanied John Cabot on his passage to Newfoundland, was known as the 'Labrador'. This tradition was depicted on the *Frisius-Mercator* globe by three flags flying in the Baccalearum Regio of Nova Scotia, all of which contained a square cross surmounted by a foliate cross. These flags might represent Spanish possession, for Spain was awarded the northern New World in 1494 and the surviving Military Orders were still powerful in that country. Yet the resemblance to the Templar cross on its war banner was remarkable. And as the *Frisius-Mercator* globe added the words to the area, *terra per britannos inventi*

---

* See Illustrations.

123

(the land was discovered by the Britons) primary evidence of a tradition of colonization by British people in Nova Scotia existed when this original globe was made.

In this context, the *Zeno Narrative* told of an expedition to Greenland by Nicolò Zeno, who came across a trading monastery of Black Friars, since identified as St Olaf's Monastery in Gael Hamke Bay. A medieval Greenlander, Ivar Baardsen, the Steward to the Bishop of Gardar, wrote of small islands near the monastery with abundant hot water – good for bathing and the cure of many diseases. The advanced agricultural techniques of the friars included the use of a natural hot spring to irrigate a market garden that produced flowers, fruits and herbs in winter. So impressed were the Eskimos, according to the *Zeno Narrative*, that when they saw these supernatural effects, they took the friars for gods. The report of this place would have encouraged Earl Henry St Clair to include monks in his colonizing expedition, as the captions in the *Frisius-Mercator* globe and the Vopell and Vavassatore map suggest.

If Earl Henry had intended to found a colony, it would explain the inscriptions beside the figure of the crowned knight set in Nova Scotia. A tradition of an early attempt to found a military and monastic Christian empire of the West in the manner of the eastern empire of the Teutonic Knights would have reached Caspar Vopell in Cologne or Vavassatore in Venice, particularly through the *Zeno Narrative* and *Map*, telling of that expedition to America. There seems no other explanation for the figure of the crowned knight on the charts. Later, Labrador became the name of a region of Canada. It was always hard ground to farm. Recent efforts to translate the term as *La Bras d'Or* or *Labora d'or* or *gold workings* appear to be far-fetched. The first European settlers there had to labour at clearing fields and planting oak trees for roof beams and laying foundations for their buildings.

Giovanni Andrea di Vavassatore was the leading wood-engraver and cartographer of his time in Venice. He devised his map from a woodcut of a world map in twelve sheets, produced in 1545 by Caspar Vopell of Cologne, who wrongly accused him of failing to acknowledge his previous achievement. Surviving Venetian maps prior to the *Zeno Map* all show Nova Scotia as part of a *Bacallareum* or *Baccalearum* or *Bacalaos* region, a name derived from the Basque word for codfish and still preserved in Bacalieu Island off Newfoundland, then called Terra Nova. In all likelihood, Basque fishermen had been exploiting the rich cod banks off Newfoundland since the thirteenth century.

All of these early maps shared much the same crude geography. The interest of Vopell and Vavassatore's version was that their bearded and crowned knight with the abbreviated commentary round him seems to have been placed there as the symbol of a colonizing mission. Certainly, the sophistication and accuracy of the *Zeno Map*, particularly in surveying the coasts of Greenland and in identifying Nova Scotia as Estotilanda, supplanted all previous efforts to chart the Baccalearum region.

There was no question that the *Zeno Narrative* and *Map* were believed not to be forgeries by fellow Europeans for one hundred and fifty years after their appearance. A new edition of Ptolemy's *Geography* published in Venice three years after the publication of the *Zeno Map* included its findings, as did Mercator himself in his great map of 1569. Greenland was now correctly delineated, but 'Frisland' was shown as a large island as well as the Faroes, and 'Drogeo' as another small island in place of the coastline of North America drawn on the edge of the *Zeno Map*. Estotilanda, however, correctly appeared at the eastern end of Canada above Terra Corterealis, discovered by the Corte-Real brothers sailing from the Azores in the first years of the sixteenth century. Below this land, Mercator placed a monastic church building on the mouth of the St Lawrence River, apparently a reference to the city said in the *Zeno Narrative* to have been founded by a Scottish prince in the New World. Vopell and Vavassatore had already placed a Corterealis island beside their crowned and kneeling knight, who was hemmed in between two rivers, each with a settlement at their mouths, perhaps those founded by the Orkney and Scots expedition to the New World. One was also captioned as a Cape, held by the Bretons or the British, while a small native tribe lived inland.

Cartographers and explorers continued to trust in the veracity of the *Zeno Map*. Ortelius used it in his *Theatrum*, published the year after Mercator's revised globe. The leading authority on exploration of the time, Giovanni Batista Ramusio, was a Venetian who knew Nicolò Zeno and published his accounts of his ancestors' polar voyages and of his great-grandfather Caterino's adventures as an ambassador in Persia; he also used the *Zeno Map* in his influential *Travels* of 1574. Martin Frobisher himself trusted the same source in his accounts of his search for the North-west Passage, while Michael Lok used it in his map, published by the Elizabethan cartographer and writer Hakluyt in his *Divers Voyages*. John Davis also referred to it in his explorations, and Purchas believed the *Zeno Map* in his *Pilgrims*. It remained the standard authority as a description of the northern polar regions until the end of the seventeenth century. Many things in it must have been right, as many sailors were travelling those seas in a period when the French were settling Canada, and the fishing fleets of northern Europe were looting the cod fisheries off Newfoundland. So eager was the mathematician John Dee to see Queen Elizabeth of England mistress of a western

125

empire that he claimed the people of Estotilanda were descendants of colonists sent out to Avalon by King Arthur – and thus subjects of the English crown.

Standing at the entrance of the Correr Museum in Venice is a large globe made in 1693 displaying a geography of the Arctic Circle still based on the *Zeno Map*. It names the region and its discoverer:

NUOVA FRANCIA
ESTOTILANDIA
THE NEW BRETAGNE
TIERRA DE LABRADOR
discovered by Sir Antonio Zeno,
Patrician of Venice in 1390
first of the other Countries of America to be made known.

The *Zeno Narrative* confirmed how a careful survey of the coasts of Greenland was carried out after the conquest of Orkney and the Shetlands, first by Nicolò Zeno after 1396 during the time of his four years' exile from Venice, and second by the Scottish prince Zichmni or St Clair, who detached support ships to complete the survey during the two years of his voyage in search of a western colony. In fact, the *Zeno Narrative* specifically credited the prince as worthy of immortal fame for his discovery of Greenland, although it had already had Norse settlements for two centuries. The prince should have been credited with the survey of both the eastern and the western coasts, translated to charts by the surviving Zeno brother Antonio, and brought back by him to Venice, to be discovered more than a century later in the family palace in Canareggio by a descendant also called Nicolò, who was to use them as the basis for the most accurate map of the polar regions in existence.

If the charts for the *Zeno Map* did not come from the voyage of the two brothers described in the *Narrative*, it is hard to know their provenance or why a false voyage of discovery should be invented to disguise the true source. The accuracy of most of the *Map* reinforced the plausibility of most of the *Narrative*. The great error in both was the description of a voyage to the fictitious island of Icaria, which has been plausibly identified as St Kilda, formerly called Hirta or Irte, or as Kerry in Ireland. As he stated, the author Nicolò Zeno had as a child destroyed many of his ancestors' letters sent from the Shetlands to Venice. His book was based on the surviving fragments. He seemed in this instance to have confused an earlier expedition to the south-west – the inhabitants of Icaria had all the characteristics of a tribal society under an

126

Irish High King. Unfortunately, in naming the place Icaria, Nicolò Zeno fell into the fashionable trap of giving a classical name to an unknown place that sounded much the same. Icarus certainly never fell from his flight into the sea near Icaria, nor was it settled by a King Daedalus of Scotland. No island existed where its inventor showed it to be. Other mistakes on the *Map*, particularly the large size attributed to Frisland (probably the Faroes), were explicable in terms of the *Narrative*, which set much of its action there and confused the islands with a German Frisian colony, described in the eleventh century by Adam of Bremen. Yet in view of the fact that all early maps contained serious errors of geography and included fabled places or misshapen continents, much of the *Zeno Map* was an advance on the cartography of the time.

The reputation of its maker must also be considered. Nicolò Zeno was a leading Venetian author as well as a public servant. He was born in 1510, went to Constantinople with his grandfather Pietro, and then returned to Venice, living to the age of fifty-five. He was acknowledged as a historian, who was devoted to the reputation of his family. He wrote an account of the wars of Venice against the Turks in four volumes. In it, he praised the role played by his grandfather Pietro in the peace negotiations. He also wrote a book on the founding of the Venetian Republic and ancient memories of the barbarians who destroyed the Roman Empire. Another treatise dealt with the origins and customs of the Arabs. As well as his *Zeno Narrative* and *Map*, he edited an account of his great-grandfather Caterino's service to Venice as an ambassador in Persia. This literary activity did not stop him from serving his country in the family tradition. He was consul in Syria for six years, then returned to Venice to sit on the Council of Ten, holding four other posts before his retirement in 1550. His brother Ottavio was a poet and a canon of Padua. Nicolò Zeno's distinguished family, his own writing and his public service gave his word credit in Venice. He was personally known to Ramusio, the great authority of the day on voyages and discoveries, who included the *Zeno Narrative* and *Map* in his publications. His own countrymen considered him the leading geographer of his time.

The erroneous grid which Nicolò Zeno drew on the sea charts of his ancestors to make up his map has been corrected by Miller Christy, the geologist William Herbert Hobbs, Arlington Mallery and most recently by Professor Charles Hapgood, who had the benefit of a Strategic Air Command survey. As sailors in the Middle Ages could only use rough latitudes, their longitudes were conjectural, a fault compounded by the confusion of the magnetic with the true North Pole. The corrections by the four experts, however, demonstrated the surprising accuracy of the survey of the east and west coasts of Greenland by Nicolò and Antonio Zeno and their Scottish prince. In his revised edition of *Maps of the Ancient Sea Kings*, Hapgood points out that Greenland was shown rightly on the *Zeno Map* with no ice cap and with a mountainous south and north and a flat central region. A reconstructed polar projection showed many correspondences on the ground between old Venetian and modern aerial cartography of the Arctic. Even the greater Iceland of the *Zeno Map* could well have been larger, for volcanic explosions in the fourteenth century submerged whole provinces. As Hobbs declared, the Zeno brothers produced a true magnetic map of Greenland and proved themselves to have been honest and reliable explorers who were far in advance of their age.

Another world map of 1450, the 'Borgia Chart', portrayed the armed Hanseatic cogs trading in waters in the Arctic ocean. One of the ports was called Albania Magna, or Great White Man's Land: a knight in a robe with a shield and lance was drawn on it. The supreme Arab geographer, al-Idrisi, had identified an Albania between Norway and Greenland some three centuries before, but the evidence on the Borgia Chart of the Hansa following previous trade routes established by Norse and Scottish adventurers and colonizers was confirmed.

The final proof, however, of the Venetian push to the north and Earl Henry St Clair's voyage to the New World came late for me, when I read a remarkable book by Gunnar Thompson, *The Friar's Map of Ancient America, 1360 AD*. In this work Thompson claims that English Franciscan monks, led by Nicholas of Lynn and working for King Edward the Third and John of Gaunt, had travelled across the Atlantic and down to South America, in order to produce a world outline, which was then passed on to England's ally, Portugal. However that might have been, a Venetian cartographer, Albertino de Virga, had drawn a commercial world map for his city in 1414, which buttressed the truth of the Fisherman's Tale in the *Zeno Narrative* and appeared to use many of the findings of the lost charts of Antonio Zeno, which served as the basis of the *Map*, published by his descendant.

The provenance of the De Virga Map was fascinating. A German-Jewish antique collector had bought it in the Austro-Hungarian city of Sebenico in 1911, and had it dated at the University of Vienna by the expert Professor Franz von Weiser, who photographed it, but failed to recognize its importance and did not acquire it for the state archives. Later, the collector had it put up for sale in Switzerland: attracting no bids, it was withdrawn and disappeared in the holocaust of the Second World War. By good fortune, however, the reproduction and the authentication remained.

The map showed Islamic influences in its lettering and in the importance given to the size of Arabia and the Persian Gulf compared to Europe. The axis of the round earth was Mount Ararat, where the Muslim and Christian patriarch Noah was meant to have landed on the Ark after the Flood. The main trade of Venice, indeed, had been to the Muslim Near East before it tried to switch to far northern waters in a search for new channels of commerce. However, identifying it as Norveca, the De Virga map showed a triangular continent *separate* from its sovereign Norway with many promontories, which represented in order: Greenland divided by the Davis Strait from Baffin Island, with the Hudson Strait between that and Labrador; Newfoundland separated by the Gulf of St Lawrence from Cape Breton; then Nova Scotia and Cape Cod; and then the peninsula of Florida with the West Indian islands beneath. This last representation was also shown in the disputed Vinland Map of 1440, now at Yale University, the Florentine Planisphere and the 'Genoese Map' of 1457, said to have been sent to the King of Portugal and studied by Columbus before his voyage to the west.

This final revelation of a Venetian commercial map of 1414, which appeared to verify much of the *Zeno Map*, ended my study of cartography and sent me back to Orkney. I had to investigate Earl Henry St Clair's preparation for his expedition towards the sunset. He had access to the most reproduced world map of his century, that of Ranulf Higden in his *Polychronicon*. Iceland was indicated as having a people who were prophets and a king who was a priest – a tribute to missionary and monastic communities. Higden also identified Fortunate Islands as fertile as Paradise with the tall timber of a New World, the aim of northern discovery.

THE ZENO VOYAGE

After the successful campaigns against the Faroe Islands described in the *Zeno Narrative*, Henry St Clair returned to the Shetlands and built another sea-castle on 'Bres', now called Bressay. A document of 1391 in the Register of the Great Seal of Scotland confirms Earl Henry's power as the effective admiral of a Northern Commonwealth and gives details of the various holdings of the Lord of Orkney and Rosslyn, on behalf of his brothers David and Richard 'de Sancto Claro'. Among many others, the more powerful families in Scotland attest to Henry's might, including the Counts of Douglas and Dalkeith, and the Bishops of Glasgow and St Andrews. All of these travelled in honour of Henry to the castle of Rothsay to witness the deed.

Consolidating his sea-power and strength in the Orcadian Isles, St Clair became even more essential to Queen Margaret, when the Vitalien pirates arrived at Bergen in 1394 with eighteen ships and seized much of her fleet. Norse colonies in the west of Greenland had been decimated by the cooling of the climate in the fourteenth century, compounded by the Black Death and an Eskimo assault. As the Vatican records show, Henry St Clair was charged with transferring the Bishop of Orkney to Greenland and returning the Bishop of Greenland back to Kirkwall. The arrival of Nicolò Zeno to promote trade and visit his hostage brother Antonio allowed the Earl of Orkney to send the more experienced Venetian captain Nicolò with three ships to effect the transfer of the bishops, reconnoitre the north-western passage, and report on the Greenland disasters.

His first port of call was a remarkable monastery of the Preaching Friars, which used hot springs to heat the building and cook food and even grow vegetables in winter in an early greenhouse. These reports seemed fantasies to later denigrators of the truth of the *Zeno Narrative*, until a succession of modern archaeologists discovered active volcanos and hot springs in Gael Hamke Bay on the east coast of Greenland near the ruins of the monastery of Sanctus Olaus or St Olaf, miscalled San Tomaso in the *Narrative*. It was normally the first landing place for trading ships from Trondheim, which took back fish and furs from there to Norway. The existence of the Augustinian monastery with its early central heating had been affirmed in 1349 by a Greenlander, Ivar Baardsen, who was the steward of the Bishop of Greenland at Gardar on the west coast. He also wrote of the hot springs on an island nearby in Unartoq Fjord which were used for washing and for healing the sick, as well as of a Benedictine nunnery on an adjacent fjord. The surviving ruins of the medieval church at Hvalso also support the *Zeno Narrative*, as does its stone architecture with an occasional arched window of splayed stones so similar to Orkney architecture.

The voyage with the Orcadian Bishop to his new diocese would have enabled Nicolò Zeno to survey the east coast of Greenland round its southern cape to the west coast at Gardar. He might also have acquired earlier charts and directions from Norse sailors and the Augustinian monks to assist his passage. Certainly, he returned from Gardar the following year with an admirable survey of the east coast and some of the west. He also brought Bishop John of Greenland back with his three ships. According to the *Narrative*, the elder Zeno captain now died from the cold and hardship of the expedition. In fact, he returned to Venice to expire there, his time of exile completed. His brother Antonio, however, was still not allowed to return by his Scots commander, who needed his navigational skills for a greater venture. "Although he tried hard in various ways and begged and prayed most earnestly, he could never obtain permission to return to his own country." As the Earl of Orkney was "a man of great enterprise and daring," he now wanted to become "master of the sea."

By 1398, the conditions for a major voyage of north-western exploration for the St Clair fleet from Bressay and Kirkwall fell into place. The previous year, Queen Margaret had achieved a diplomatic triumph at the Treaty of Kalmar with the crowning of her ward and heir, Erik of Pomerania, as the king of all Denmark, Norway and Sweden, except for a pale around Stockholm. Henry, Earl of Orkney, had been unable to attend, owing to the need to repel the pirates from Norway and the Orcadian Isles. These had been scattered after the capture of Gotland by the Teutonic Knights, who leased that pirates' nest. The Hansa were once again in control of the Baltic. Furthermore, following the Scottish victory of Otterburn, in which Henry's brother John St Clair had played a prominent role, the Stewart King Robert the Third and the Roslin estates were no longer threatened by English attack, although Channel pirates were still sailing north on their depredations. Henry St Clair's rivals for the earldom of Orkney were all dead or lying low. He could commit his forces over the ocean.

The size of the expedition was not recorded, except that it had many vessels and men. As St Clair's purpose was to reinforce the Greenland outposts and found colonies of his own, he would have added to his sailors and armoured knights more monks for the Greenland monasteries and his own foundations, particularly for their agricultural and building skills. Associated with this voyage were three medieval churches which I wished to visit in connection with my research into Templar architecture and the relation of the condemned Order with the St Clair family at Roslin: Orphir in Orkney; St Magnus Church on Egilsay, built in the twelfth century to commemorate the murder of that Saint and Earl of Orkney; and the monastery on Eynhallow or Holy Isle. A Force Ten gale was blowing the day of my visit, casting spray over clifftops two hundred feet above the slamming waves. Such weather made the first shipwreck of the Zeno brothers in these waters appear all too likely.

The round Romanesque church of St Nicholas at Orphir stood in ruins beside its whistling graveyard on a sea estuary. Mentioned as a 'noble church' in the *Orkneyinga Saga* of 1136, the surviving arched window and barrel-vault of the apse were features of other island architecture, while a late medieval gravestone bore a Latin Engrailed Cross with a base of three steps, as on the William de St Clair Grail tombstone

131

at Rosslyn Chapel. The gale then blew away and allowed a small boat to take me to the nearby islands of Egilsay and Eynhallow. On Egilsay, I found a ruined church with a round tower and doorways of narrow thick flakes crammed against one another from the side-pillars to the archstone. This feature of thin packed stones forming a semi-circle above an entrance was also seen at Eynhallow and at the ruined Bishop's palace by St Magnus Cathedral in Kirkwall. These were rough and ready versions of the design of the original Church of the Holy Sepulchre, which I had followed to Byzantine Ravenna and Charlemagne's Aachen, to Charroux and Llanleff, then to the Eunate and Tomar of Templar times, and which I would later recognize among the twenty-five round churches of Scandinavia, particularly on the island of Bornholm off Denmark.

With the equipment and the skills which he needed to reinforce the Greenland settlements and found more of his own in the New World, Henry St Clair sailed in the May of 1398 past the Shetlands and put in at Lille Dimon in the Faroes to rest and take on board water and supplies. At this point, the *Zeno Narrative* confused this expedition with a previous reconnaissance of St Kilda and Kerry in Ireland, miscalled Icaria. This was evident in the *Narrative*'s account of the expedition arriving at hostile Icaria in July, while it was to reach Estotilanda in June. In point of fact, the fleet sailed directly from the Faroes and was scattered by a storm during the first eight days of the passage. The ships regrouped and sailed on for ten days west and south-west in rough seas with a following wind. This brought them to the New World, which they were seeking. "Some of the crew then pulled ashore and soon returned with the joyful news that they had found an excellent country and a still better harbour. So we brought our barks and our boats in to land, and we entered an excellent harbour, and we saw in the distance a great mountain that poured out smoke."

The Estotilanda which the Scottish expedition had reached has been identified as Nova Scotia. The *Zeno Narrative* told of certain features – the smoking mountain, which came from a great fire in the bottom of the hill; a spring that exuded a matter like pitch that ran into the sea; and many small and timid natives who lived in caves. A geologist found oil seepages at the coastal Stellarton mines at a place now called Asphalt, where the Coal Brook carried the greasy residues down to the sea at Pictou Harbour. There were regular fires in underground coal seams in the Stellarton region in the nineteenth century, which produced smoke from the bottom of the hills. The local Micmac tribes were small and not as warlike as the neighbouring Algonquins, and they had legends of the coming of a god called Glooscap in a wonderful granite canoe like a forest. Glooscap had taught them to fish with nets like the fisherman in the tale in the *Zeno Narrative*, and sinkers and floats for nets dating from about 1400 AD were found on the sites of Micmac coastal camps. Earl Henry's probable harbours were established at Pictou and Guysborough and Advocate Harbours, the latter near Cape d'Or.

There was no hard proof for these locations. When I paid my first visit to Nova Scotia, I was shown the old photograph of a 'pre-Columbian cannon', said to have been dredged in 1849 from the sea near the fortress of Louisburg on Cape Breton Island and still kept there. I could hardly believe my eyes, for I was looking at a primitive ship's cannon with eight rings, clad round its narrow barrel of welded iron rods to keep it from bursting, and a detachable breech with a handle for its loading with gunpowder, and with a spike at its base. Its shape and type was identical with the four *petrieri* in the Museo Storico Navale in Venice; these were the ones used by Carlo Zeno at the Battle of Chioggia, and also mounted on Hansa ships by the end of the fourteenth century, when they rapidly became obsolete because of their tendency to burst and the new technology of casting the barrels of large weapons in one piece. On another visit to Cape Breton Island, I held the separate and dangerous iron breech of this stone-throwing ship's cannon in my hand like the key to a mystery. I was told that the cannon had been concealed because of French sensibilities in Canada, where the later Samuel de Champlain remained a founder and hero, while Louisburg was held to be the first colonial stronghold there.

Another *petriero* had been discovered at the portage of nearby St Peter's, although it had unfortunately been broken up. A Victorian who saw it described it as "an archaic cannon formed of bars of iron fastened with iron bands or hoops." Curiously enough, the French had chosen Louisburg and St Peter's as the sites of their first two settlements or harbours, because these two harbours were the best on the south coast of Cape Breton Island. Prince Henry's logic would have led him to the same conclusion. There was also a Micmac tradition that grassy mounds at St Peter's were the remnants of the houses or sod huts of white men, who had colonized the area before the later coming of the French settlers.

If that type of Venetian or Hansa cannon had been abandoned or fallen overboard at the landing-place of the Orkney expedition of 1398, the other characteristics of the area described in the *Zeno Narrative* should still be there. And sure enough, coal mines reach into the sea along a thirty-mile stretch of mountainous coastline running north as far as a headland called Cape Smokey. Furthermore, four Micmac

Indian reservations still existed round the central sea loch called Le Bras d'Or. This was almost too apposite. A Venetian cannon of the right period, coastal coal mines, a smoky mountain and a large Indian presence. Above all, Cape Breton was an *island* as the *Zeno Narrative* declared it was, while Nova Scotia itself was joined to the mainland of Canada.

According to the *Narrative*, the mountain that poured out smoke was visible from near the harbour which was called Trin. Cape Smokey could be seen from the mountain crests that ran north-west from St Peter's to Louisburg. The area was still abundant in fish, sea fowl and birds' eggs, which the Scottish sailors ate until they were stuffed full. And the eight days' march of the hundred soldiers and the Venetians sent by Prince Henry to explore the island would have taken them to Cape Smokey and back again. On the way myself by the coastline to the Cape, I discovered at Point Aconi what the Scottish soldiers had also discovered, "a certain matter like pitch which ran into the sea." Oily residues from the open coal seams in the cliffs and from the underwater workings of the Princess Mine still polluted the beaches.

They were, indeed, like the black and oily waters of St Katharine's healing well near the St Clair castle of Rosslyn, which were said to be a cure for skin diseases. St Katharine herself was the patron saint of the St Clairs as well as of the Scottish Guild of Wheelwrights – she had been broken on a wheel in Alexandria, where Earl Henry had gone on his crusade. The bitumen in the black water of the healing well was meant to have saved him from the Black Death as a child, although it fouled my fingernails for days when I plunged my hand into its black grease. Yet for Earl Henry, the finding of bitumen by his soldiers would have been a good omen which brought memories of the Old World to the New.

His troops reported that the smoke from the mountain came from a great fire at the bottom of the slope. Actually the Cape is now called Smokey because clouds almost always wreath its crests. Yet there were on Cape Breton Island and in Nova Scotia natural gas and coal seams burning underground, while the Micmac Indians used slash-and-burn techniques to clear 'meadows' to attract wild game to graze there as an easier prey for their arrows. These 'meadows' among the woods and on the shorelines were to be most attractive to future European settlers. And whether the soldiers saw an underground fire or a burning 'meadow' beneath Cape Smokey, they did meet "great multitudes of people, half-wild and living in caves. These were very small of stature and very timid . . ." There were sacred Indian caves in the sea-cliffs on the coastal route to the north of Cape Breton Island, particularly near Le Bras d'Or, the modern name for the huge land-locked sea lake round which most of the Micmac still lived.

When the hundred soldiers marched back to Earl Henry at Louisburg Harbour, they found him laying plans to establish a city in this New World. Antonio Zeno wrote back to his brother, the great Admiral Carlo in Venice, about his commander's decision:

> But his people had passed through a voyage so full of hardship and began to murmur, saying that they wished to return to their own homes. The winter was not far off, and if they allowed it to set in, they would not be able to get away before the following summer. He therefore kept only the row boats and those people who were willing to stay with him, and he sent all the rest away in the ships. He appointed me against my will to be their captain. I had no choice, and so I departed and sailed twenty days to the east without sighting any land. Then I turned my course towards the south-east and reached land in five days . . .

The voyage from the Faroes to Estotilanda with storms and following winds had been sailed at an average of four knots, while the return voyage against the prevailing winds averaged three knots. Antonio Zeno could report that his Scottish master was still alive, but he did not know what Earl Henry was doing in the New World. The end of the *Narrative* included the tantalizing opening of the last recorded letter sent home by Antonio Zeno:

> The things you want to know from me about the people and their habits, the animals and the countries nearby, I have written in a separate book, which, please God, I shall bring with me. In it I have described the country, the monstrous fishes, the customs and laws of Frislanda, of Islanda, of Estlanda, of the Kingdom of Norway, of Estotilanda and Drogeo. Lastly I have written the life of our brother, Nicolò the Chevalier, with the discovery he made and all about Greenland. I have also written the life and exploits of Zichmni, a prince who deserves immortal memory as much as any man that ever lived for his great bravery and remarkable goodness. In it I have described the survey of Greenland on both sides and the city that he founded.

On the *Zeno Map*, however, two cities were marked in Estotilanda. If one was founded by Earl Henry St Clair at Louisburg Harbour or possibly at St Peter's, the other might well have been founded in New England. For there was compelling evidence that he and his men went onward to the west.

135

A KNIGHT AND A TOWER

High at the top of a hill with a commanding view over Massachusetts, the Westford Knight was first recorded in 1883 in a history of that small town. The Reverend Edwin Hodgman wrote about a broad ledge of gneiss, which cropped out near the house of William Kittredge. On the surface of the rock were grooves made by glaciers in some distant geological age. "Rude outlines of the human face have been traced upon it, and the figure is said to be the work of Indians." On their way to high school, Westford boys sometimes did a war-dance on the Indian's face to show off their daring while the girls watched their antics, forming and admiring a ring around the rock. One of the boys, Thomas Fisher, used a cold chisel to add a pipe of peace to the Indian head, later called a falcon crest, to make it look more authentic.

That was that, until an amateur archaeologist and a photographer became interested in the carving on the gneiss around the time of the Second World War, when searching for the Nordic origins of odd structures such as the Newport Tower on Rhode Island was a fashionable pastime. What they saw on the rock was a hilted sword and rather more. Michael Pearson, who still lives near Westford, photographed the shape on the gneiss, and W B Goodwin published two photographs and a line drawing of it in his *The Ruins of Greater Ireland in New England*. He interpreted the shape in the middle of the glacial rock as an eleventh century Norse sword, broken as a memorial to an exceptionally brave warrior.

Goodwin's publication came to the attention of T C Lethbridge, the controversial archaeologist for the city's Antiquarian Society in Cambridge, England. His opinions and findings were as much discounted by academic archaeologists as were those of Goodwin and his successor Frank Glynn by the professors at Harvard University and the Massachusetts Archaeological Society. Goodwin died, but Glynn was in correspondence with Lethbridge, who identified the sword hilt on the stone as the large, hand-and-a-half wheel-pommel sword of the thirteenth and fourteenth centuries. Unfortunately Goodwin had not revealed where the rock carving was located, and Glynn spent years tracking it down: when he reached it, he had to strip turf and moss from the gneiss, which was badly weathered. He discovered that the images on the stone were made through series of punch-holes and hammer blows, which could have been struck in the rock by a medieval armourer. With excitement, Glynn discovered that the punch-holes ran nearly to the top of the rock and to the side, suggesting that the funeral effigy of a helmeted knight-of-arms had been punched on to the gneiss along with the shapes of his shield and his sword to act as his memorial tomb.

Now Glynn came up with the discovery of the wintering place of the St Clair expedition that Lethbridge had suggested would be found. He discovered a carved stone, which a local farmer had unearthed at the fork of tracks to the sea near Westford. The stone showed the shape of a ship with twin sails on a single mast, eight portholes or rowlocks, an arrow with four feathers on each side of the shaft, and the letters 184. On advice from Lethbridge that the numerals signified paces, Glynn found within a radius of 184 paces three roughstone enclosures, which might have been the dry dock for small Norse ships or Lethbridge's "snug little corner where Sinclair's bothy, hut, tent or whatever, was set up." At a distance, Lethbridge identified the enclosures as similar to the stone buildings in Greenland called *Storhouses* and the ship on the rock as a Norse *knorr* or merchantman. He claimed that the Scots knew of Arabic numerals by the fourteenth century and would not have written distances in Latin numerals, although the Venetian account of the St Clair expedition to the New World asserted that its leader Henry St Clair spoke in Latin and the map was dated in Latin numerals.

The town of Westford itself split over the authenticity of the Westford Knight and the carved ship stone, which was transferred to the small museum there. Two camps emerged, one holding that four Fisher boys had chiselled the carving of an Indian tomahawk and peace pipe in the late nineteenth century, and that all the other marks were the result of natural weathering. As for the ship stone with the arrow and the number 184, it was carved early in the century to inform Indians that a fur-trading ship had arrived in Boston Harbour. The other camp insisted on the truth of both carvings as proof that the St Clair expedition had reached Westford in 1399, and had left a knight's memorial in punch-holes there. They cited the evidence of two geologists, Austin Hildreth and H.J. O'Mara, who compared the deterioration of the punch-marks with those of early gneiss gravestones and concluded that the sword and profile on the rock were probably five to eight hundred years old.

In the middle of this war of opinion, I arrived at Westford, trying to prove the truth of the *Zeno Narrative* of the early colonizing expedition of Henry St Clair to the New World nearly a century before the voyage of Columbus. Aided by James Whittall of the Early Sites Research Society, who had taken over the mantle of Frank Glynn as the leading local archaeologist, another rubbing was made as on the

137

St Clair Grail tombstone in Rosslyn Chapel. A credible shape for the effigy of the knight appeared as if by invisible ink from the weathered stone. The shield of previous chalk reconstructions by Glynn had always looked distorted and toylike, a primitive effort by an armourer, who did not know of the conventions of medieval military burial. Yet the cloth impression showed a large shield of arms set squarely below the left shoulder of the figure, with two quarterings at the top, and a ship at the base of the shield similar to the St Clair ship on the coat of arms of Prince Henry's daughter, Jean St Clair, whose effigy lay at Corstorphine Church near Edinburgh. This larger shield was balanced by an insignia on the right side of the figure that resembled a rose.

Although acid rain and erosion had severely damaged the markings since the earlier investigations of the Westford Knight, the rubbing showed a helmeted knight wearing the habit of the Military Orders with his shield and his sword engraved on the rock in the formal style of the late thirteenth or early fourteenth century. The outline of the sword had remained strong. It pointed due north and suggested a ritual burial and was shown as broken twice below the hilt. The custom of the time was to break the sword of a knight of great courage and distinction, and to bury it with his body. The effigy of the Westford Knight was some seven feet tall and depicted a powerful man, although it was not as large as the huge effigy of Sir James Douglas, who had died with the Heart of Bruce and Sir William de St Clair in Spain. The figure appeared to have been laid down in his armour and habit and outlined by punch-holes on the stone. After his body was taken to a grave, his broken sword and shield were also outlined, before their removal for burial with the knight. Then the final details were punched into the gneiss.

Yet the Westford Knight was evidence only of an *inland* expedition into New England by a crusading group in the late fourteenth century. The question was where it might have landed by sea. An answer existed in the curious stone tower, which is still preserved at Newport in Rhode Island. Unless that tower of two storeys was understood as part of the second city that Earl Henry St Clair began to build in the New World, it was hard to explain. Clearly based on the stone architecture of Northern Europe in the Middle Ages, it was constructed, like the Templar round churches, on the model of the Church of the Holy Sepulchre and the Dome of the Rock in Jerusalem. When there was an eight-pointed cross built in regular pillars within the diameter of a tower, this was the Christian model of the Temple of Solomon. The design was the octagon within the circle, eight arches within a round tower. Round churches were rare. The only one in Scotland, built in the twelfth century on the model of the Church of the Holy Sepulchre, was in Orphir in Orkney, where Henry St Clair was Earl. The arch of its one surviving window was constructed in the same fashion as those of the Newport Tower.

Moreover, the unit of measurement of the Newport Tower was not the English foot or yard, nor a Portuguese or Dutch standard. It was the Scottish ell, a cloth measure used in England until Shakespeare's time, one half of the Norse fathom and the equivalent of the Hanseatic yard – just over thirty-seven inches. The diameter of each column in the Newport Tower was exactly one Scottish ell; the diameter of the circle surrounded by the columns was exactly six Scottish ells – measurements which have been verified against the standard Scottish ell kept on a gravestone at Dornoch Abbey and at Dunkeld Market near the cathedral where a St Clair was the fighting bishop at the time of Bannockburn, and where another St Clair presided at the time of Earl Henry's voyage to North America.

The Newport Tower resembled not only Templar architecture, but Scottish architecture of the period. One feature precluded its use as the windmill that some supposed it to be. On the first floor is a fireplace made to a fourteenth century design, which would burn down any flour mill. The firelight would have shown through a small facing window to act as a beacon for ships entering the harbour from Narragansett Bay. The design was reproduced in the church at Corstorphine, where Henry St Clair's daughter Jean was buried in effigy. This also had a beacon tower, where the firelight was reflected from the second storey to guide the way for travellers by land or sea.

For that is what the Newport Tower was. A Templar Church, a lighthouse on to Narragansett Bay and a watchtower. There was more evidence to date it before the British colonization of Rhode Island. Two German maps of Vinland from the end of the fourteenth century had depicted it as an island with a fortified church. An expert on the runes, Richard Nielsen, had read marks on a stone at Spirit Pond, Maine, which appeared to state that in 1402 a Baltic ship had arrived on a trading voyage. From the Corte-Real voyages to New England, a gilded sword hilt and silver Venetian trinkets had been found in Labrador. On a whaleback ledge jutting into Machias Bay at Clark's Point, Maine, the petroglyph of a cross was found incised beside one of a European ship of the late fourteenth century with a single sail and stern rudder. A breech-loading *petriero*, now in a museum in Rhode Island, was discovered in 1921 off Narragansett Bay: it was similar to the Louisburg cannon. Moreover, Verrazano identified a Norman villa on his voyage of New England, still preserved on two of his maps dating from 1529 with later additions. The shorelines and promontories were accurate: he spent two weeks in shelter in Narragansett Bay. On the map given to King Henry the Eighth of England, the harbour at Newport was called 'Refugio'; on the Ulpius map which was finished in 1542, 'Normanvilla'.

This was not all. An old map made by William Wood after 1629 sited New Plymouth correctly in Massachusetts, but listed an Old Plymouth in Narragansett Bay. Furthermore, a text from the Public Records Office in London mentioned an existing 'round stone towre' in 1632, seven years before Newport in Rhode Island was founded. This was one of the 'Commodities' which should attract settlers to Sir Edmund Plowden's proposed colony. It would house thirty soldiers or gentlemen, who could then guard the settlers in their 'trucke and trafficke . . . with the Savages'.

The Newport Tower was later adapted for use as an extremely inefficient flour mill by Governor Benedict Arnold. Yet it had been constructed centuries before its misuse, as a church, a beacon and a fortification. It was originally covered with plaster, the remains of which lie buried in its foundations. Old windmills are solid in their structure in Orkney, while the Newport Tower is an engineering folly as a windmill. Its purpose was sacred. It corresponds almost exactly with Templar churches in Paris and Laon, the Church of the Holy Sepulchre in Cambridge in England and at Charroux in France, and the twelfth-century round church at Orphir in Orkney, from where Earl Henry St Clair sailed to found his lost colony in the New World. In 1950, the director of the National Museum in Denmark remarked on the Newport Tower, "There remain as typically Romanesque architectural details the pillars, the arches and the double splay. These medievalisms are so conspicuous that, if the tower were in Europe, dating it to the Middle Ages would probably meet with no protest."

Objections to these facts have been presented thick and fast. The primitive stone-throwing and breech-loading ship's cannon of Venetian, Hansa and Portuguese manufacture have been held not to be obsolete by the early fifteenth century, but to have been in use for another hundred years. But such conclusions defy the whole development of war technology through the ages. These early versions made with welded iron rods were too dangerous and inefficient to last for long. Once a cannon could be cast in one piece, this practice superseded all previous techniques, except in primitive forges. And the breech-loading mechanism was so perilous that it was discarded as soon as possible. Curiously enough, the two most radical and incisive researchers into early American archaeology, Arlington Mallery and James Howe, have

asserted the existence of dozens of early smelting-works along the
St Lawrence River and in Virginia which, operating in the fifteenth
century, could have produced outdated ship's cannon as well as the
many iron artifacts which have recently been discovered. If this were
so, then extensive European colonization would have taken place after
Earl Henry St Clair's death and the loss of his American strongholds.
Verrazano, indeed, did remark that the people of Connecticut and
Massachusetts were unlike other Indians. "This is the most beautiful
people and the most civilized in customs that we have found on this
navigation. They excel us in size; they are of bronze colour, some
inclining more to whiteness."

On the subject of the Westford Knight, there were few who could
cavil except at the rubbing technique. Yet as this served to expose the
Grail tombstone now in Rosslyn Chapel, which is indubitably authentic,
there is no reason to doubt the results of its use on the eroded rock
in Massachusetts. I was present at the cold processing: there was no
falsification there. As for the Newport Tower, controversy has raged
over the centuries. Claims have been made for its construction by
Vikings, Scots, Portuguese and colonial Americans. The Viking claim
has been checked by the most recent investigation, made by the Deputy
Antiquary of the Danish National Museum in Copenhagen in 1995.
Lime mortar taken from the Newport Tower was carbon-dated. After
testing at the Universities of Helsingfors and Århus the samples were
held to derive from the sixteenth and seventeenth centuries, although
they did indicate a pre-colonial structure. Little consideration was given
to the total deterioration of the original mortar as at Orphir and Eynhallow before subsequent reconstruction and repointing. The beacon
fireplace with its medieval flue on the first floor, which disproved the
identification of the original structure as a windmill, was dismissed with
unsubstantiated statements from two mill engineers that fireplaces were
to be found in other European windmills. No proof or locations were
given: in fact, such fireplaces were only installed after the structure had
ceased to be a flour mill. No consideration was given to the conclusion
of the American civil engineer Edward Adams Richardson in the *Journal
of the Surveying and Mapping Division* in 1960 that he had investigated
thoroughly the archaeological interest of the Newport Tower "with
regard to structural design and to determine possible reasons for the
window and fireplace arrangement. The design proves adequate, by
modern standards, for a particular church structure, while the windows
and fireplace form a sophisticated signalling and ship guidance system
characteristic of the fourteenth century."

Other comparisons to tower windmills in England did not mention

141

that these were *conical*, to withstand stress, rather than of upright construction. The Newport Tower was then compared to the Chesterton round and arched mill in Warwickshire, near where Governor Arnold was erroneously meant to have been born. In fact, the windmill there was originally built as an observatory, possibly by Inigo Jones, and only converted to its other and inefficient use during a drought, when the estate water-mill failed. Nobody bothered to contradict the considerable research of Gad Rausing, who pointed out that the central part of the twelfth century church at Österlars on Bornholm Island corresponded most closely with the preserved part of the Newport Tower, which seemed undoubtedly to have been planned as the central part of a larger building.

This Viking interpretation had no *Zeno Narrative* or *Map* to support its plausibility, except a voyage to Vinland in 1121 by Bishop Erik Upsi of Greenland, recorded in the *Icelandic Annals*. The Portuguese claims rested on similar grounds to the Templar links of Earl Henry St Clair. The claim was backed by carvings on the nearby Dighton Rock, which still show Templar crosses and triangles held to be evidence that the Portuguese Corte-Real family discovered Narragansett Bay. The refugee and condemned Templars had not only gone to Scotland, but to Portugal from where they had made African discoveries as the Knights of the Cross. The model for the Newport Tower would have been the Templar headquarters at Tomar in Portugal, with its elegant octagonal chapel roughly reproduced in Rhode Island. There was no evidence, however, that the Corte-Real brothers took masons and monks with them in their last ill-fated venture in the early sixteenth century. The Scottish expedition was so accompanied, and their constructions reproduced the methods and designs of Orkney architecture, derived originally from the Church of the Holy Sepulchre in Jerusalem.

After a decade of exhaustive excavation and study, James Whittall presented his final conclusions in 1997 to a Sinclair Symposium in Orkney. These seemed irrefutable. He particularly stressed that the tool marks on the dressed stones of the Newport Tower were identical to those of the medieval buildings in Orkney and the Shetlands and could be found nowhere else in New England. He had summarized his research in a previous letter.

There is no logical reason for the Newport Tower to be colonial. It is totally illogical on all the existing data even to consider the possibility. The architecture is the most telling artifact. We don't know who built the tower, but we can presume that the person had Templar connections, was familiar with Scandinavian round churches and other similar structures, knew about the Sagas and Norse contact with the New World, had the ships to sail with the manpower *to construct the tower, using the same material and in the same manner as mortared buildings were constructed in Scotland from 1200 to 1400.* Therefore, in all probability, Henry St Clair is the most likely candidate.

THE LOST COLONIES

After Earl Henry's expedition to what would be called New England, where he probably left a second fortified church and colony at Newport, he returned across the Bay of Fundy to his first colony at Louisburg. He had been two years away from Orkney, and he knew his authority there would be under threat of attack. The farming monks he had left on Cape Breton Island would have already gathered their first crops, while the seamen there should have completed the survey of the west coast of Greenland, for which the *Zeno Narrative* was to praise him. He would have to construct an ocean-going fleet from the resources of Nova Scotia; but there was timber, pine tar, and fibre for ropes in abundance. He would have brought shipwrights from Fife and Orkney with him as well as masons to construct his defences.

The abiding Micmac legend of the divine Glooscap coming over the sea and departing was similar to the Mayan myth of Quetzalcoatl, the winged white God who was identified with Cortes and assisted his conquest of the Aztec empire. But if Earl Henry's coming enhanced the Indian belief in Glooscap, it could only have been by his good behaviour. He brought no conflict, he took no slaves, he taught the arts of fishing and agriculture. The Reverend Silas Rand, who first recorded the Micmac language, also wrote down the abiding legend of Glooscap in Victorian times:

> The tradition respecting Glooscap is that he came to this country from the east – far across the great sea; that he was a divine being, though in the form of a man. He was not far from any of the Indians . . . Glooscap was the friend and teacher of the Indians. All they knew of the arts he taught them. He taught them the name of the constellations and stars; he taught them how to hunt and fish, and cure what they took; how to cultivate the ground. He was always sober, grave and good. All that the Indians knew of what was wise and good he taught them. His canoe was a granite rock.

The descriptions of Glooscap's sea transport were the most convincing evidence that Earl Henry St Clair's expedition to Cape Breton Island was remembered in Micmac legend. He was said to have crossed the ocean standing with his feet on the backs of whales – a traditional Indian term for decked ships. His vessel was variously called a stone canoe and a floating island with trees on it, very manageable and able to go like magic. This suggested a ship with two masts and cross trees, able to steer with a rudder and sail to the wind. When he did finally leave, the stranger stated that he would not return to rule over the Indians – and Earl Henry never did. As a Micmac song, also recorded in Victorian times, chanted of the going of Glooscap:

> Some say that he sailed away
> In his marvellous stone canoe,
> Afar beyond the sea,
> To the country of the East.
>
> Some that he went to the West.
> And it is said in days of old
> There were men who knew where he lived,
> And they made a pilgrimage,
> And got from him what they sought . . .

The present Micmac banner, shown at the Sinclair Symposium and presented to the people of Kirkwall, is the image of the sea-flag of the Knights Templars with its horizontal red cross, crescent moon and single star.

Earl Henry St Clair lived less than a year after his return in 1400 to Orkney. In August, King Henry the Fourth of England invaded Scotland and reached Edinburgh, where he magnanimously extended his protection of the monks of Holyrood. Marine raiders from East Anglia beat off a counter-attack and captured the Scottish commander. They then proceeded up to Orkney to challenge the new sea-power of the St Clairs. They pillaged several of the islands and made a surprise attack on Kirkwall. In his description of the family, Father Hay wrote of Earl Henry's death in Orkney: "resisting them with his forces, through his too great negligence and contempt of his own friendly forces [he was] left breathless, by blows battered so fast upon him, that no man was able to resist." An account of 1446 stated tersely that he "deit Eirle of Orchadie and for the defence of the countrie was sclane thair crowellie be his innimiis."

The slaying of the Earl of Orkney after the completion of a transatlantic mission backed by Scandinavia and Venice was deliberate. The Hansa had long co-operated with the English in their control of the lucrative North Atlantic trade. Although the Vitalien pirates had largely been defeated in the Baltic, the Hansa in 1400 had to send eleven ships with 950 men to patrol the North Sea. These would have reinforced any English attack on the Orcadian islands, from where Earl Henry St Clair now threatened to revive the languishing Norwegian empire below the Arctic. He had to be eliminated, his power broken.

Even with the death of the surveyor of Greenland and the founder of Scottish colonies in the New World, relief ships might have been sent out to the settlers, who would then have escaped the future fate of Sir Walter Raleigh's 'lost' colony at Roanoke in Virginia. Unfortunately, Henry St Clair's son, Henry, who succeeded as the Earl of Orkney, was fulfilling his hereditary duty as guardian of the Crown Prince of Scotland. When King Robert the Third had his eldest son murdered by a pro-English faction, he decided in 1406 to send the Crown Prince James to safety in France, accompanied by the new Earl of Orkney. Almost marooned on the Bass Rock near the hostile Douglas sea-fortress of Tantallon, the Earl of Orkney and the young heir to the Stewart throne were picked up by a Danzig trader, the *Maryenknyght*. In Lothian, the King's forces under Sir David Fleming, who was killed, were routed at Long Hermiston Moor by the Black Douglas and his allies. For the second time, East Anglian privateers attacked a St Clair earl of Orkney, capturing him and the Stewart heir on board off Flamborough Head. Prince James became an English prisoner for fourteen years, while Henry of Orkney was also imprisoned in Durham Castle. That same year, the marriage of Erik of Pomerania to Philippa, the daughter of Henry the Fourth of England, put an end to Queen Margaret's dream of a Northern Commonwealth to oppose the Hansa and its allies.

The finding of identical early ship's cannon at the Arsenale in Venice and at Louisburg on Cape Breton Island, the cloth impression of the Westford Knight, and fresh correspondences in measurement and building methods between the Newport Tower and Norse-Scottish medieval constructions have established the general truth of the *Zeno Narrative*. If Earl Henry St Clair had not *discovered* America any more than Columbus did, he tried to plant colonies there ninety-six years before the sailor from Genoa. The Vikings had preceded his attempt by some four centuries, but Earl Henry had continued their tradition of pushing outposts of trade and settlement across the western ocean to a New World. His effort failed with his sudden death. The Eskimos, indeed, attacked and wiped out the stricken Norse colonies in Greenland; from there in 1410, the last ship arrived in Iceland. For most of the fifteenth century, the Americas were largely free of the influence of Europe, except on the coasts and the cod banks off Newfoundland. As the defenders of the Stewart kings, the second and third St Clair earls of

Orkney would transfer their energies to their lands near Edinburgh and erect castles, a library and a chapel, that would become a wonder and a mystery. And the Stewarts would take the Orcadian Isles from them and the kings of Norway for the benefit of the crown of Scotland.

I I

A Chapel of the Grail

It came in his mind to build a house for God's service, of most
curious work, the which, that it might be done with greater glory
and splendour, he caused artificers to be brought from other
regions and foreign kingdoms, and caused daily to be abundance
of all kind of workmen present, as masons, carpenters, smiths,
barrowmen, and quarriers, with others . . .

William, the Third St Clair Earl of Orkney,
described by Father Hay

THE ST CLAIR EARLS of Orkney became the victims of their own
power and glory. Their fatal attachment would be to the reign-
ing House of Stewart. The second Earl Henry inherited a position of wealth and ambiguity. He also owed allegiance to the King of
Norway for his jurisdiction over Orkney and the Shetlands – those
strategic islands that the Stewarts wished to acquire from Norway as
they had the Western Isles. In the two decades of his power before his
death from the plague in 1420, Earl Henry never renewed his links
with the Norwegian crown, relying on his actual possession of the
Orcadian Islands. He was, after all, Admiral of Scotland with large
land-holdings in Midlothian, Fife and Aberdeenshire. His Scottish com-
mitments came before his fealty to Norway.

"He was a valiant Prince," Father Hay wrote, "well-proportioned,
of middle stature, broad bodied, fair in face, hasty and stern." He had
"all his victuals brought by sea from the north in great abundance, for
his house was free for all men, so that there was no indigent that were
his friends but received food and raiment, no tenants sore oppressed,
but had sufficient to maintain them, and, in a word, he was a pattern
of piety to all his posterity." He gifted the Abbey of Holyrood with
lands that could feed seven thousand sheep. "As for the rich vestures
that he gave for the service of God at that time . . . they were of gold
and silver, and silks." His wife Egidia Douglas was even more famous
for her generosity and nature. "She was of stature somewhat above
ordinary, but the excellency of her mind, the candour of her soul, and
the holiness of her life made her incomparably more pleasant."

From their position to the north of England, the Scottish nobles

147

found themselves embroiled in the Hundred Years' War. Their French allies called on them to harry the borders, if the English pressed forward in France, or even to cross the sea to Flanders and help resist an invasion. The second Earl Henry of Orkney was unfortunate in his encounters with the old enemy, although his brother John was to take the Scottish St Clairs back to the land from which they had sprung before the Norman Conquest. There he was to found a dynasty, and many St Clairs were to serve in the Royal Scots Guard of the French monarchy.

At the Battle of Humbleton, Earl Henry was taken prisoner. No sooner was he released than he was captured again with the Crown Prince on a sea voyage to France and held in prison for several years, although allowed two safe-conducts to proceed north and settle family business during his captivity. He also went with his brother John and his brother-in-law Lord Douglas to fight for the Dauphin before the disaster at Agincourt. He had to return to defend Scotland against furious English counter-attacks, which ended in the burning of Penrith. Between the politics of Scandinavia and France, the St Clairs were now better employed in the defence of their homeland.

When his father died of disease in 1420, the new Lord of Rosslyn, William, as a minor, could not claim the title of the Earl of Orkney. He also had to act as a hostage in England against the unpaid ransom for King James the Second of Scotland. King Erik of Norway took the opportunity to assert his sovereignty over the Orcadian Isles. Sir David Menzies of Weem was the brother-in-law of the previous Earl of Orkney and held the castle of Kirkwall, establishing a reign of terror there. Other members of the St Clair family, now usually spelt Sinclair, possessed lands and rights and jockeyed for power and privilege. The King of Norway gave royal authority to various claimants at different times, in order to assert his own mastery – to David Menzies, John Sinclair, Thomas Sinclair and even to Thomas Tulloch, the Bishop of Orkney, at last reconciled with the Norwegian crown and briefly granted 'all the Orkneys with all royal rights'.

Unfortunately, most of the St Clair documents relating to the first two Earl Henrys of Orkney, were lost at sea in a transfer to the growing Roslin library. This catastrophe, which has made more difficult all research on the Zeno voyage to North America and the family possession of the Orcadian Islands, was resolved to a degree by the good Bishop Tulloch. He helped to write one of the more important documents of the history of the islands, the *Genealogy* or *Deduction of the Earls of Orkney*, which traced the claim of young William, the third St Clair Earl of Orkney, showing his descent from Rognvald of Møre, first granted the title by the ancient Kings of Norway. Not until 1434, under strong pressure from the Scottish crown, did King Erik formally grant the earldom to William St Clair according to the oaths and promises used at his grandfather's installation. That act was the opening move in a strategy of the Stewarts to gain the Northern Isles for their country.

For fifty years, Earl William exercised his power in the north. "He was a very fair man, of great stature, broad bodied, yellow haired, straight, well proportioned, humble, courteous, and given to policy, as building of Castles, Palaces, and Churches, the planting and haining of forests, as also the parking and hedging in of trees." He lived in great state, as Father Hay testified. "He had his halls and his chambers richly hung with embroidered hangings: he builded the church walls of Roslin having rounds with fair chambers, and galleries thereon. He builded also the forework that looks to the north-east: he built the bridge under the castle and sundry office houses." And he built the supreme chapel and the new town of Roslin especially for his masons and had it made into a royal borough.

Such regal state caused some jealousy and envy in the Scottish court; but Earl William's service was too valuable to be dismissed. He was made Admiral of Scotland and sent to France with the King's sister to marry her to the Dauphin: in his time, the first of ten knights from the Sinclair family became prominent members of the Royal Scots Guard of the French kings, along with other knights from the Seton and the Stewart line. He was ordered on diplomatic missions to London to secure peace at the end of the Hundred Years' War. He supported King James the Second in a struggle with the Douglas family and was appointed Lord Chancellor of the kingdom. Yet in 1456, he fell out with the King, perhaps because the governor of Iceland and his treasure were seized while sheltering from a storm in Orkney – an incident that sabotaged the efforts of the Stewarts to come to good terms with the King of Norway. Ten years later, Earl William's eldest son was to throw Bishop William Tulloch into prison in another effort to break Scottish-Norse relationships and to end talk of a marriage between the two royal families, by which Orkney and the Shetlands would go to the young King James the Third, who had Earl William as his Regent during his minority. In fact, the King's marriage with the daughter of King Christian of Denmark was concluded, and the Northern Isles were handed over to Scotland as a pledge for the payment of the princess's dowry of sixty thousand gold florins.

This pledge was followed by the removal of the title Earl of Orkney from William St Clair. He was also required to exchange Kirkwall Castle for Ravenscraig Castle on the mainland, built to withstand artillery attacks and admirable for defending his estates in Fife. Indeed, the acquisition of this stronghold made the Lords of Roslin now the chief defenders of the Scottish crown both to the south of Edinburgh and on the Firth of Forth against land and sea attack. In exchange for his estates in Nithsdale, Earl William had already been made Earl of Caithness. And as his Scottish properties were now far more valuable than the royal domains he controlled in Orkney and the Shetlands, he was pleased to resolve the problem of his dual allegiance to two crowns in favour of Scotland.

The truth of the matter was that only the first Earl Henry St Clair of Orkney had set his mind and his resources on the dream of a Northern Commonwealth. His son and grandson had become involved with the Stewart dynasty in their struggle against the power of the Douglas family; their fortunes rose and fell with the royal line. Their loyalty to the crown, however, was total and unquestioned. When the Stewart kings arranged for the transfer of sovereignty in the Orcadian Islands to the Scottish crown, the St Clairs could not resist. Moreover, William, the third and last St Clair Earl of Orkney, was different in nature to his ancestors. To him would come the inspiration and the duty of building the finest library and chapel in the south of Scotland, a place that would commemorate for ever the long connection of his family with Gnostic and Templar wisdom.

THE SEARCH FOR THE GRAIL

Rosslyn Chapel is not so much an enigma inside a riddle inside a mystery. It is a creation inside a temple inside a revelation. Its designer, William of Orkney, was an *illuminatus*. He studied the hermetic know-ledge of the later Middle Ages. As a family biographer stated, he was "more refined and less ignorant than the contemporary herd of nobles, who suspected his studies of subjects unearthly and unholy." This is clear both in the elaborate design of the chapel and in the Rosslyn-Hay Manuscript, the most important work to survive from his library – the earliest extant work in Scottish prose, a translation from René d'Anjou's writings on Battles, the Order of Knighthood and the Government of Princes. At various times in his life, René held the title of Duke not only of Anjou, but also of Calabria and Lorraine, as well as being the King of Hungary, Naples, Sicily, Aragon, Valencia and even Jerusalem. He was a conduit to Rosslyn of oriental Gnostic and cabbalistic teach-ings, which were spreading from Medici Florence throughout Europe.

The leather binding of the oak board of the manuscript is signed by

Patricius Lowis – the Lowis father and son lived in Roslin village among the masons building the chapel, and worked as bookbinders for William St Clair. Thirty-three expensive metal stamps, possibly from Cologne, decorate the binding. Apart from the signature stamp, three other names are repeated twice – Jhesus – Maria – Johannes. The addition of the name of St John to those of Jesus and Mary is unusual, but he was venerated by the Gnostics and the Templars. The same rare link was made on the Master Mason John Morow's inscription at Melrose Abbey, rebuilt at the same time as Rosslyn Chapel – Jhesus – Mari – Sweet Sanct John. Another remarkable feature of the binding was the use of the Agnus Dei, the Lamb of God, together with the Sacred Monogram, I.H.S. In Rosslyn Chapel, the Templar Seal of the Lamb of God was also carved.

The stamps of the emblems of the Twelve Apostles were arranged in a filled set-square, with eight of the stamps repeated. St John was represented by the rare devices of the Serpent of Gnostic wisdom and the chalice or Grail, while three other Apostles were depicted by masonic tools: St Simon by the saw, St James the Lesser by the fuller's club, and St Mathias by the axe. These last three Apostles were carved with their masonic tools in the south aisle of Rosslyn Chapel, along with St Jude with his carpenter's square and St Bartholomew with his flaying-knife. St John the Evangelist was also shown holding his chalice or Grail, but without the Gnostic serpents of wisdom, already incised at the base of the Apprentice Pillar.

Other mysterious symbols were stamped on the binding of the ancient manuscript as well as being repeated in Rosslyn Chapel. There was the quatrefoil of the Four Writers of the Gospels. There was the foliated staff of Moses, also a Templar emblem. There was a rose and a rosette, sacred to the Virgin Mary and venerated by the Templars. And most oddly, there was a unique stamp of a lion standing on its hind legs and fighting a dragon – reproduced exactly on the top of a pillar in the chapel. Evidently, William St Clair used his extensive library to institute the manufacture of more books at Rosslyn as well as to find designs for the carvings in his new chapel.

Unfortunately, most of the other volumes commissioned or owned by William St Clair were destroyed in a contemporary attack on Rosslyn Castle or in later assaults. So much evidence was burned that the Bishop of Orkney had to write a testimony to the King of Norway in 1446 "respecting the GENEALOGY OF WILLIAM SANCT CLARE, EARL OF ORCHADIA" in support of his legitimate claim to Orkney. The treatise was 'translatit out of Latin into Scottis' by Dean Thomas Guild, a Cistercian monk from Newbattle Abbey close by. The Canons of

St Columba at Inchcolm and the St Clair historian Father Hay were all to bear further witness to three spoilings of the Rosslyn book collection between the fifteenth and seventeenth centuries, one of them by the Puritan soldiers of General Monk and another by the Edinburgh mob. As the Bishop of Orkney wrote, charters, evidences, instruments, account books, and other "kindis of probationis war consumit be fyre, tint and alianat in the tyme of hostilitie, and of weris of unfreindfull innimiis."

No portraits survive of the scholarly William, the third St Clair Earl of Orkney. But at Corstorphine Church nearby is the effigy of his cousin, Sir John Forrester, who rebuilt his church at the same time that Rosslyn Chapel was reconstructed. Forrester's face is eroded by time, but his embroidered sword-belt and ornate armour testify to the late display of the Middle Ages. On the shields below his tomb are the three bugles of the Forresters – they were originally the foresters of the Kings of Scotland – as well as the Engrailed Cross and St Clair ship of the Earl of Orkney. John was descended from Jean St Clair, the daughter of Henry, the Earl of Orkney who had ventured to America nearly a century before Columbus. Jean St Clair herself lies in the church beside the stone effigy of her husband, Sir John Forrester, in her embroidered coif and with a Bible in her hands.

Opposite her, a Templar gravestone is set in the wall, as is another tombstone by the Priest's Door – one of two in Scotland of priests bearing the chalice or Grail, this commemorated Robert Heriot, a chaplain of Gogar who died in 1443. The earliest Arabic *graffiti* carved in Scotland in the fifteenth century were incised opposite this Grail stone: Arabs were the leading physicians and alchemists of that age. The other tomb with a chalice, this time held in the hand of a priest, is at Saddell, an old Cistercian abbey in the Mull of Kintyre. As at Corstorphine, it reinforces the links between the cult of the Grail and the Cistercians and the Sancto Claro family of the Holy Light.

There are more overt Grails in the Rosslyn Chapel designed by William St Clair. On the boss of the second chapel from the north – facing south is the Mother and Child – the Three Dead and Living Kings are carved, or the Three Magi bearing their gifts to the infant Jesus. Beside them on a draped trestle table stand three chalices or Grails, and below them, a rose blooms in stone, the symbol of the Virgin Mary.

Such symbolism encrusts the whole chapel. Particularly frequent on the bosses are representations of small Temples of Solomon. Out of their twin pillars and towers, green plants spring and entwine. They suggest that Rosslyn Chapel as a whole is not only another Temple of

Solomon, but also the Garden of the Temple – the Garden of the Bible and of Eden. In trying to fathom the remarkable mind of the scholar William St Clair and his plan for his chapel, it is noteworthy that books in the Middle Ages were called flower gardens or *rosaria*, arbours of roses. Illuminated by pictures, often of flowers, they represented the search for wisdom and faith, as well as the cult of the Virgin Mary. One of the early physicians and philosophers, Arnold of Villanova, called his original encyclopedia, *Rosarum Philosophorum*. In medieval thought, the Third Day of Creation and the sacred drawings of architecture were symbolic. The pattern of the green leaf and the shape of the dressed stone were both in the divine mind, as was the Garden of Eden with its spiritual feminine intelligence, which would appear on the Secret Scroll.

Many Templar signs and seals are carved into Rosslyn Chapel. There are clusters of five-pointed stars, reflecting the major graces of the Virgin Mary. There are the two brothers on one horse, and the Lamb of God holding the cross on its banner. There is the head of Christ on the veil of St Veronica, as well as on the ceiling of the chapel, His hand raised in benediction. There are Masonic and Templar reliefs, also the floriated cross on the Grail tombstone of Sir William de St Clair. One further carving calls to mind the Templar heresy of worshipping the head of Baphomet – a bearded face with horns, clutching the tablet of the Word of God, brought down by Moses from Mount Sinai. Another remarkable carving of an upside-down fallen angel bound by a serpentine rope tells of Gnostic and Templar wisdom, in which Lucifer was portrayed as the angel of light and intelligence, bound by the rope of order. To complete the picture was the design of the whole interior roof, culminating in the Templar vision of the grace and Word of God.

The planning of Rosslyn Chapel took a matter of fifty years in its execution. William St Clair grew old in the process. From the initial thought to the drawing board to the architectural plans, some of which are still scratched on the walls of the crypt; from the development of the iconographical mystical theme to the placement of its emblems on the exterior and interior of the building; from the importing of materials and skilled masons to the dealings with the crafts and guilds; from mind to matter and achievement – this was the work of a long lifetime.

Rarely was the patron of a chapel so completely its planner. As Father Hay wrote of William St Clair:

> It came into his mind to build a house for God's service, of most curious work, the which, that it might be done with greater glory and splendour,

he caused artificers to be brought from other regions and foreign kingdoms
. . . And to the end the work might be the more rare; first he caused the
draughts to be drawn upon Eastland boards, and made the carpenters to
carve them according to the draughts thereon, and then gave them for
patterns to the masons, that they might thereby cut the like in stone.

The construction of that whole work as a Temple of Solomon and
a Chapel of the Holy Grail was the apotheosis of William St Clair. It
was contained and perfect in its own meaning. A cross-section of the
building reveals that it was designed on the basis of the octagon and
the hexagon and triangles contained within a circle – some of the
fundamental patterns of sacred geometry and contemporary alchemy.
A study of the shapes deployed by Giordano Bruno in his hermetic
works repeats the plan of the architecture of Rosslyn, and is another
indication of the influence of oriental and Gnostic writing on the creator
of the chapel.

The eight serpents on the base of the Apprentice Pillar are further
evidence of Gnostic teaching. As the early Christian author of the
Testimony of Truth wrote, "For the serpent was *wiser* than any of the
animals that were in Paradise . . . but the creator cursed the serpent
and called him devil," for he had given Adam and Eve the knowledge
of good and evil, as if they were divine. For this, so the Gnostics taught,
they had to be cast from Paradise in case they ate from the Tree of
Life and lived for ever. The Apprentice Pillar with its serpents and a
complementary ornate pillar on the south of the Lady Chapel represented the two trees of the Garden of Eden, those of Life and of the
Knowledge of Good and Evil. They symbolized the hermetic knowledge, the secret understanding of the cosmos, given by the serpent to
mankind.

The two pillars also represented Jachin and Boaz, the pillars of the
original Temple of Solomon, revered by the Templars and the Masons.
The serpents enshrined the Shamir, the worm of wisdom whose touch
split and shaped stone. As Deuteronomy records, confirming rabbinical
and Arabic legend, King Solomon had built his Temple without the
use of tools made of iron. This, according to Masonic tradition, was
the secret of the Shamir which the martyr Hiram, the architect of the
Temple, refused to surrender, and which remained one of the Grand
Secrets of the Higher Degrees. An old ritual testified to "the wonderful
properties of that noble insect the Shamir, which cut and shaped all
the sacred utensils and holy vessels in King Solomon's Temple . . . the
wonderful creature that could cut stones."

The pursuit of the mysteries of creation was symbolized in the

154

The Cherubim above the Ark.
From Gressman, <u>Hebräische Archäologie.</u>

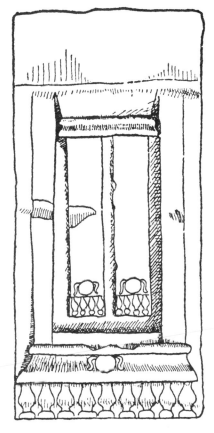

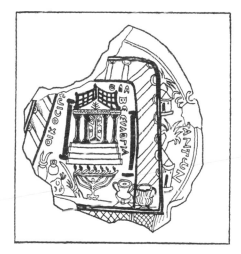

A drawing of the Temple on the glass fragment from the catacombs of Rome.

Two two detatched pillars on the façade of the temple of Melqart at Tyre, the forerunners of Jachin and Boaz in the Temple of Solomon.

From Chehab, <u>Berytus.</u>

The interior of the Dome of the Rock, Jerusalem.

The Temple of Solomon on the seal of a Templar Grand Master, 1235.

The Temple of Solomon as the Dome of the Rock crowned by a cross on the seal of a Templar Grand Master.

The temple at Jerusalem from the Kirkwall Scroll, with the River of Life flowing into it.

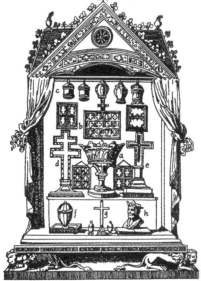

The octagonal Templar Church of the twelfth century at Eunate beside the pilgrim route to Compostela.

This engraving shows some of the most venerated relics, which were in their reliquaries in the Sainte Chapelle in Paris.

a. The Crown of Thorns
b. The swaddling clothes of Christ
  c. Relics of the Passion – His bonds,
     the sponge at the Cross, the reed and a
       phial of His blood
       d. A fragment of the True Cross
       e. The point of the Holy Lance
       f. A flask of the Virgin's milk
       g. Moses' Rod
       h. The crown of St John the Baptist's
           skull

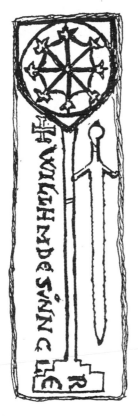

A drawing of the centre of the painted vault of the chapel of the Templar Commandery at Monsaunès near Toulouse.

The St Clair Templar Grail tombstone at Rosslyn Chapel, Scotland.

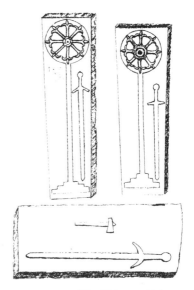

Two Templar grave slabs, Pentland, near Rosslyn, covered up.

Templar gravestones at Westkirk near Culross Abbey, Fife, with masonic symbols.

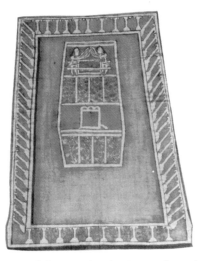

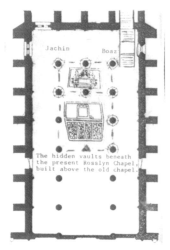

The plan of the Temple of Solomon from the Kirkwall Scroll, drawn in perspective. It corresponds in proportion with the ground plan of Rosslyn Chapel built over its hidden vaults which contain shrines and tombs. It shows the hidden Ark of the Covenant.

Ground plan of the present Rosslyn Chapel with markings of fourteen pillars. The three masonic pillars are by the altar to the east.

Jerusalem and the Temple containing the Holy of Holies. Also from the Kirkwall Scroll.

The Templar Cross wood on the Pentland hills on a straight line from the Templar headquarters at Balantrodoch through Rosslyn Chapel, pointing south-east towards Jerusalem.

The seal with the Engrailed Cross of Earl Henry St Clair of Orkney.

The view past the altar, showing the entrance to the crypt and the three pillars of the Temple to the east of Rosslyn Chapel.

The head of Christ on the starry stone ceiling of Rosslyn Chapel.

The Apprentice Pillar.

The serpents around the base of the Apprentice Pillar.

This plan of Damietta, from the Kirkwall Scroll shows the city's chain bridge and Nile bastion, which fell to the Fifth Crusade.

A modern French plan of the siege of Damietta, showing the Christian camps which surrounded it finally in 1219, as on the Kirkwall Scroll.

From a thirteenth-century manuscript, showing the final assault on the chain tower at Damietta after a year's siege.

The Mameluke Knight by the crusader camp bove Damietta, from the Kirkwall Scroll.

Rosslyn Castle.

Melchizedek offers bread and wine from an altar to Abraham, dressed as a medieval knight, after winning a victory for the King of Sodom.

A relief from Reims Cathedral.

Rosslyn Chapel.

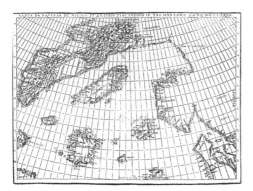

The Zeno Map, Venice, 1558.

From the Vopell and Vavassatore Map, 1545 & 1558

The Radiocarbon Dating of the central panel of the Kirkwall Scroll is most probably during the fifteenth century, when Rosslyn Chapel was constructed.

Middle Ages by the search for a new Temple and Garden of Solomon, and for a Castle and Chapel of the Grail. The medieval romance of Wolfram von Eschenbach, *Parzival*, was a further inspiration to William St Clair. He inscribed its hidden significance in stone on the chapel roof as his revelation that his shrine was also a chapel of the Grail. The roof itself was a unique structure – the only large barrel-vaulted roof built in solid stone in Scotland. It was literally a stone fallen from heaven – the *lapis exilis* of *Parzival* which was called the Grail.

The ceiling is divided into five sections stretching from east to west. In the first four segments are the flowers of Creation open in all their glory, supreme among them the rose of the Virgin Mary. In the west, the stars of the sky are clustered on high. To the south is the sun that gives light and life, then the head of Jesus Christ, and then the Holy Dove descending with the Host in its beak. Below the Dove is carved the symbol of the Grail, in the shape of the bowl of a cup or crescent moon – the emblem of Islam, the faith of Parzival's half-brother Feirefiz, the Muslim knight. Out of it pours God's grace and bounty, indicated as waves or flow. Frozen in stone with fresh algae on the Heaven behind it, this Grail seems to pour forth all the green things and wild things in wood and water carved in this chapel of the Third Day of Creation. As the mystery of this holy place unfolded from the Grail set among the stars, I heard the plea of Marlowe's Dr Faustus in my ear:

> See, see how Christ's blood streams from the firmament!
> One drop would save my soul.

Later, Niven Sinclair arranged for a groundscan of Rosslyn Chapel by the latest radar techniques developed for modern archaeology. Evidence of lower chambers revealed by this process bore out ancient drawings and medieval tales of buried St Clair knights in vaults below the chapel floor. The radar pulses also detected reflectors, which indicated metal, probably the armour of the buried knights. Particularly exciting was a large reflector under the Lady Chapel, which suggested the presence of a metallic shrine there, perhaps that of the Black Virgin, which still marks so many holy places on the pilgrim route to Compostela, a sacred way that has one of its endings in Rosslyn Chapel, where a carved scallop-shell still commemorates the past.

The problem was how to reach the vaults. The groundscan had shown two stairways leading beneath the slabs. Laboriously, one set of flagstones was lifted, rubble was cleared, and indeed, three steep stone steps were found to lead to a vault below. I was the first to squirm into this secret chamber. It was small, comprising the space between the foundations of two pillars. It was arched with stone, but access to the main vaults beyond had been sealed by a thick wall of stone masonry, perfectly shaped beneath the arch. The soggy wood from three coffins had been stacked in front of the blocking wall. Sifting through the debris below the broken coffins, I found human bones and the fragments of two skulls, two rusty Georgian coffin handles, a mason's whetstone – and a simple oak bowl, left there by a mason from his meal along with his flint for sharpening the tools of his craft. And that is what the original Grail from the Last Supper would have been – a wooden platter passed by Jesus Christ in His divine simplicity to His poor Apostles. They were working in His cause, they were fishers of men, the first builders of the edifice of the Christian Church. Such a simple workman's bowl, perhaps as old as the late Middle Ages when this chapel was designed as a Chapel of the Grail, was a Grail as good as any other, the container of God's bounty on earth.

We lifted the slabs to the second staircase, supposing they might lead down to the shrine, only to discover many feet of earth and sand beneath. The groundscan had not shown how deep were the vaults or the infill in the intervening spaces. This was a grave disappointment. We decided to call in core drillers in order to penetrate the roofs of the lower vaults. We would then lower a tube through the drill-hole and drop down an industrial endoscope. Its camera was the size of my little finger and as flexible as the head of a striking snake, and it could point at buried objects under the light of a laser beam. It could operate to a depth of ten metres and, by passing light up glass fibres integral to the instrument, transmit in colour what the camera saw on to a monitor screen above ground.

As we drilled deeper and deeper into the centre of the chapel, we struck rubble for ten feet and then the roof of the lower vault. It was three feet of solid stone. Finally, the drill bit broke through into open space. And then it jammed. There was no way of drawing it back. But after working night and day, we removed the drill and penetrated again into the lower vault and could introduce our pipe. Through it, the endoscope could drop into the chamber of the knights and the shrine, and film them there.

So we believed. Again and again we pushed the pipe down the drill-hole. Again and again, infill poured into the crevices and blocked the pipe. Again we drilled through and brought back the bit. Again we introduced the pipe, this time with the endoscope inside the tube. As it almost reached the stone roof of the vault, we could see on the monitor dust and detritus clogging up the end of the pipe, filling in our little eyehole on to the mystery that lies beneath Rosslyn.

After a week of work, we were defeated. The vaults of this Chapel of the Grail would keep their secret shrine. The St Clair knights would not be disturbed in their tombs. Perhaps that is how it should be. They had been buried beyond the reach of intruders. They would only reappear on the Day of Judgement, when the stone slabs would crack open.

THE ST CLAIRS AND THE MASONS

The secret words of Masonry were Jachin and Boaz, the twin pillars of the Temple of Solomon. This catechism from the 'Mother Kilwinning', held to be the oldest Lodge in Scotland, reaffirmed the close links between the Masons and ancient beliefs in the Temple of Solomon. Kilwinning Abbey had been built in the twelfth century at the direction of the de Morville family, who were Grand Constables of Scotland. They granted lands at Herdmanston to the Knights Templars and to the St Clairs of Rosslyn and made them Sheriffs in Lothian. They established the connection between the St Clairs and Kilwinning, where masons congregated to build the abbey. Sir David Brewster, who wrote the first *History of Free Masonry* in 1859 under the name of William Alexander Laurie, was clear on the origins of Scottish Masonry.

That Free Masonry was introduced into Scotland by those architects who built the Abbey of Kilwinning is evident, not only from those authentic documents by which the existence of the Kilwinning Lodge has been traced back as far as the end of the fifteenth century, but by other collateral arguments which amount almost to a demonstration. In every country where the temporal and spiritual jurisdiction of the Pope was acknowledged, there was a continual demand, particularly during the twelfth century, for religious structures, and consequently for operative Masons, proportionate to the piety of inhabitants and the opulence of their ecclesiastical establishment; and there was no kingdom in Europe where the zeal of the inhabitants for Popery was more ardent – the kings and nobles more liberal to the clergy – or the Church more richly endowed than in Scotland. The demand, therefore, for elegant cathedrals and ingenious artists must have been proportionately greater here than in other countries, and that demand could be supplied only from the trading associations on the Continent. When we consider, in addition to these facts, that this Society monopolized the building of all the religious edifices in Christendom, we are authorized to conclude that those numerous and elegant ruins, which still adorn various parts of Scotland, were erected by foreign Masons who introduced into this island the customs of their Order.

157

The *History of Free Masonry* further stated that during the reign of King James the Second, the office of Grand Master of the Crafts and Guilds and Orders of Scotland was granted to William St Clair, Earl of Orkney and Baron of Rosslyn. The office was made hereditary and continued until the formation of the Grand Lodge of Scotland three centuries later. The annual courts of the Grand Master for judging disputes between or within the fraternities was held at Kilwinning, site of the Mother Lodge.

The statement was correct, except that the St Clairs had been made hereditary Grand Masters by Robert the Bruce over a century earlier after the Battle of Bannockburn, when he had reorganized the artisans and Orders of Scotland on Templar principles. He had been assisted in his victory by the support of the workmen of Scotland, who made up the bulk of his infantry, by the refugee Templar knights and by three members of the St Clair family – one of them, William, was buried as a Grand Master of the Temple, as we know from his tombstone in Rosslyn Chapel.

King Robert set himself up as the Sovereign Master of all the Ancient Scottish Guilds and Orders. Beneath him, he appointed a Grand Master, as the Templars had. He made the post hereditary and vested it in the St Clair family of Rosslyn, the defenders of Scotland against English attack from the south-east. The post of Grand Master held the rank of a Prince of the Royal Order of Scotland, which explained the occasional use of a coronet on the St Clair emblems and coats of arms. The job of Grand Master was to sit as the judge of disputes between and in the guilds and Orders at an annual court at Kilwinning. His decree was final. He stood between the workmen's organizations and his Sovereign Master the King. His judgement was truly the judgement of Solomon.

Any inquiry into the way in which the rites of the Temple of Solomon entered the Masonic movement must acknowledge the fact that the Military Order of the Temple was extremely powerful in Scotland, where it held more than six hundred properties; that some of its French knights fled with their fleet and treasure to Scotland; that the Templars and the St Clair family were closely connected and helped to win the Battle of Bannockburn; and that Robert the Bruce reorganized the government of Scotland after his victory. The excommunicated Templars were forced underground, although as late as 1405 an enactment by a court in Stirling was to declare that no 'Templar' should buy or sell goods reserved to guild members. The Templars were absorbed into the new government of Scotland, either within the Royal Order under their Sovereign Master the King, or into the ancient Scottish

Orders and Guilds, under the hereditary jurisdiction of the St Clairs of Rosslyn, the neighbours and supporters of the Templar headquarters at Balantrodoch.

This inclusion of the survivors of the Order of the Temple of Solomon within the Scottish Orders and Guilds would explain the introduction of the rites and legends of the Temple into the Masonic movement. The artisans of Scotland were divided into two symbolic groups, the pillars of the realm as were Jachin and Boaz in Solomon's Temple. There were those who worked with hand or rigid materials, such as stone, iron or wood like the Masons and the Hammermen and the Shipwrights; and those who worked with soft materials, canvas, rope or leather, like the Cordiners, whose surviving medieval regalia still include a gilded human skull with cross leg-bones and a crown – the Templars, we may remember, were accused of worshipping a jewelled head. These groups of workmen now began to be organized into Lodges, each with a Master, who would report any dispute each year to the court at Kilwinning, where a St Clair would preside.

Certainly William, the third St Clair Earl of Orkney, was given or had confirmed by the King of Scotland, the post of hereditary Grand Master Mason of Scotland. By the fifteenth century, the Templars and their rites and customs had permeated the Orders and Guilds of Scotland. Their hereditary judge and catalyst, Earl William, was obliged to erect a whole new town for his masons, who were imported with their beliefs and practices from all over Europe in order to build his unique chapel. As Father Hay records:

> Because he thought the masons had not a convenient place to lodge in near the place where he builded this curious college, for the town then stood half a mile from the place where it now stands . . . therefore he made them to build the town of Roslin, that now is extant, and gave every one of them a house, and lands answerable thereunto; so that this town, all that time, by reason of the great concourse of people that had recourse unto the Prince . . . became very populous, and had in it an abundance of victuals, so that it was thought to be the chiefest town in all Lothian, except Edinburgh and Hadington. He rewarded the masons according to their degree, as to the master mason he gave forty pounds yearly, and to every one of the rest ten pounds, and accordingly did he reward the others, as the smiths and the carpenters with others.

Earl William's town was a unique creation, enabling his masons to live not in huts, but in houses with land. Soon Roslin was confirmed as a royal borough. The wandering bands of masons came to rest under the patronage of their hereditary judge.

Therefore, to the end he might not seem altogether unthankful to God for the benefices he received from him, it came in his mind to build a house for God's service, of most curious work, the which, that it might be done with greater glory and splendour, he caused artificers to be brought from other regions and foreign kingdoms, and caused daily to be abundance of all kind of workmen present, as masons, carpenters, smiths, barrowmen, and quarriers, with others; for it is remembered, that for the space of thirty-four years before, he never wanted great numbers of such workmen. The Foundation of this rare work he caused to be laid in the year of our Lord 1446 . . .

He was building a house for God's service, a Temple of Solomon. He believed in the Temple, he ruled over the masons, his was the judgement of Solomon.

At every Templar site in Scotland, Masonic graves can still be found, sometimes bearing representations of the original Temple. At ruined Dunkeld Cathedral, where two St Clairs were bishops, an octagonal tower still recalls the sacred architecture, while a fresco of the Judgement of Solomon can be dimly seen within the lower stones. Masonic tombs abound around the eroding windows of the roofless nave, as they do at Westkirk and at Culross, where the merchant's house of Sir George Bruce is particularly interesting for the painting of the Temple of Solomon on its timber walls. In this house the Guild of Hammermen used to hold the meetings of their Lodge: their symbol of the hammer is set in the garden walls, as it is set on an old Templar gravestone in Westkirk nearby. At St Andrews and Abdie, in the Douglas Chapel and at Currie and Corstorphine, at Melrose and Balantrodoch, in Kilmory and Siddall, wherever broken Templar tombstones are to be found, there are later Masonic graves bearing similar emblems nearby. The merging of the Templars into the Masons is writ on stone all across Scotland.

This is especially so in Rosslyn Chapel, where Templar insignia proliferate beside Masonic emblems. Earl William, after all, was the designer of all the luxuriant carvings in the holy place, as well as his own Master of the Works. He ordered the construction of the spiral Apprentice Pillar with its ornate fellow Earl's Pillar, the Jachin and Boaz of his new Temple of Solomon. The building of this Collegiate Church of St Matthew with stipends for a provost, six prebendaries and two choristers was an act of belief. Its purpose was worship and the teaching of the faith. Earl William also bestowed religious treasures and rare vestments on the priests as he did on other religious institutions. Rosslyn Chapel became a treasury not only in symbols and architectural detail, but also in its wealth of holy relics. Since the first

St Clair had come to Scotland as the cupbearer of Queen and St Margaret, the family had been the guardians of sacred things. And in the fall of the family, they would remain the keepers of that trust.

12

The Fall of the Sinclairs

We for ourselves and in the name of our hail brethren and
craftsmen agree and consent that William St Clair now of Roslin
for himself and his heirs purchase and obtain at ye hands of
our Sovereign Lord liberty freedom and jurisdiction upon us
and our successors *in all times coming* as patrons and judges to
us and the hail professors of our craft within this realm.

The St Clair Charter, 1628

THE DECLINE OF THE SINCLAIRS was arrested by Earl William's
grandson, Lord Henry Sinclair, who restored the family's position in the Orcadian Isles. He was also one of the more enlightened patrons of the arts in Scotland in the late fifteenth century,
commissioning and extending the family library. But, following Lord
Henry's brave death at Flodden field, his rival, Sir William of Warsetter,
was to prove the undoing of Henry's heirs as a dispute arose over the
conquest lands in Orkney and the Shetlands. In the course of this civil
war, only Sir David Sinclair and Ola Sinclair of Havera would be able
to maintain the family influence on the Orcadian Isles into the sixteenth
century, dealing with delicacy and violence between the rival claims of
Norway and Scotland.

In one of his commissions, Lord Henry requested his relative Gavin
Douglas, Bishop of Dunkeld, to make a Scottish version of the *Aeneid*.
As its prologue stated:

> At the request of ane lorde of renowne,
> Of ancestry most nobill, and illustir baroun,
> Fader of bukis, protector to science and lair,
> My special gude lord, Henry lord Sinclare,
> Quhilk with great instance, diverse tymes, sere
> Prayit me translate Virgil or Homere . . .

Lord Henry served the King of Scotland as 'Master of all our Machines
and Artillery' and sold to James the Fourth eight of the machines called
'serpentynis' for a hundred pounds, paid to his widow after both men
had died at Flodden.

This enlightened warrior made Rosslyn into a minuscule Library of

Alexandria. Not only did the family bookbinder, Patrick Lowis, work with other scribes at Rosslyn, but so too did James Gray, the writer of the earliest Scots manuscripts in the vernacular. From this period came *Wyntoun's Chronicle*, the *Lives of the Dunkeld Bishops*, the *Roist of Time*, the *Regiam Majestatem* containing *Guild Laws* and *Shipping Laws* – the hereditary interests of the Sinclairs – as well as *The Book of Troylus*, signed by the Sinclairs with the escutcheon of the Engrailed Cross, now in the Bodleian Library at Oxford. The *Rosslyn Missal*, however, had come into Lord Henry's possession as a consequence of Edward Bruce's disastrous invasion of Ireland in 1315. Written and illustrated by Irish monks in the twelfth century, it showed in the margins great dragons luxuriating over Templar crosses and sundiscs. And it bore Gnostic annotations by Lord Henry in Latin. One of his scribbles was "who wrote after the writing?" He also wrote about three sisters fleeing: "Whoever loved x^m did not choose this world." His spirit quested for heaven: "Myself is a moving part – splendidly – largely ... To you, lifting my spirit, my God." This was the direct approach to the divine.

Trying to reclaim the earldom of Caithness, Lord Henry fell foul of King James the Fourth of Scotland, but redeemed himself by arriving in support with the whole clan wearing green; they were all to die with their royal master on the battlefield. Since then, green is not worn by a Sinclair on that anniversary. Also killed at Flodden was Sir John Sinclair of Dryden near Roslin, dubbed the Queen's Knight by the poet Dunbar.

> Sir John Sinclair begouth to dance,
> For he was new come out of France:
> For any thing that he do micht,
> The ane foot gaed aye unricht,
>   And to the tother wald not gree.
> Quoth ane. Tak up the Queen's knicht:
>   A merrier dance micht na man see.

With Lord Henry's death, a civil war between the Sinclair heirs developed in the north, involving rivalry between Sinclair families in Orkney and the Shetlands, not only at Warsetter, but at Aith, Brecks Brough, Eday, Essingquoy, Evie, Havera, Houss, Hunto, Isbister, Ness, Quendale, St Ninian's, Strome, Sumburgh, Tuquoy, Ustaness and Voster. This fratricidal strife culminated in 1529 in the Battle of Summerdale, where the clan completed its bloodletting after Flodden. The tragedy of Scotland has always been that blood brothers would rather fight themselves than any intruder over the border.

The new master of Roslin, Sir Oliver Sinclair, completed the building of the chapel. His many sons further split control of the Sinclair estates in Lothian and Fife, although his handsome heir of the same name, Oliver, retained Roslin and Pentland and became the favourite of King James the Fifth and commander of the Scottish army. Father Hay called him 'the great minion' and told of his rout at Solway Moss, which signalled the impending doom of Scottish independence and the downfall of the Sinclair family.

> Oliver thought time to show his glory, and so incontinent was displayed the King's banner, and he holden up by two spears lift up upon men's shoulders, there, with sound of trumpet, was declared General Lieutenant, and all men commanded to obey him as the King's person, under the highest pains, so soon a great noise and confusion was heard. The enemy, perceiving the disorder, rushed on, the Scots fled, some passed the water, but escaping that danger, not well acquainted with the ground, fell into the slimy moss; happy was he that might get a taker. Stout Oliver was without stroke taken, flying full manfully, and so was his glory suddenly turn'd to confusion and shame.

"Oh fled Oliver!" King James cried when he heard that his dear friend had lost the battle. "Is Oliver tane? Fie fled Oliver! All is lost!" Soon afterwards he took to his bed at the age of thirty, and when he heard the news that his wife, Marie of Guise, had borne him a daughter, he said of his kingdom, "Adieu, fare well, it came with a lass, it will pass with a lass." The independent kingdom had come to the Stewarts through their marriage with a Bruce princess, and it would pass with James's child, Mary Queen of Scots. Although the Stewarts would inherit the English throne as well as that of Scotland, the twinning of the crowns would mean the lessening of Scottish liberty and the fall of the Sinclairs of Roslin from power in their country.

The Sinclairs were a devout Catholic family, bound to the crown of Scotland. Father Hay accused Oliver Sinclair and 'other minions who were pensioners to priests' of blinding James the Fifth to the Reformation, so that "he made a solemn vow to spare none that was suspected of heresy, although it were his own son." Proof lay in an extraordinary Bond and Obligation signed by Marie of Guise on the 3rd of June, 1546, when she became Regent of Scotland in the four years after the death of her husband. The Bond was given to 'Sir William Sinclar of Roslin for his personal service', and it read:

> Be it kend to all men ... Forasmeikle as the said Sir William is Bounden and obligit to us in Speciale Service and Manrent for all the days of his

life to gang and Ryde with us, and tak our sauld part with his kyn, servandis and freyndis . . . Herfor we bind and oblige us to the said Sir William. In Likewise that we sall be Leal and trew Maistres to him, his Counsill *and Secret shewn to us we sall keep Secret* – and in all mattres gif to him the best and trewest Counsell we can as we sall be requirit therto, and sall not with his Skath nor Damage but we sall stop it att our power and sall [be] Reddy att all tymes to maintain and defend him . . .

Sir William Sinclair was made Lord Justice General of Scotland and granted a royal pension of three hundred marks a year for life. This was a time of trouble with Calvinist radicals, who aimed to impose a reformation on the Catholic Church in Scotland in alliance with the Protestant English forces which had sacked Edinburgh, Melrose and Holyrood Abbey, and Rosslyn Castle itself two years before. Their purpose was to conquer Scotland before it was able to draw on the Guise family and France, posing a wider threat. Although the tombs of the Kings and Queens of Scotland were desecrated, and an eagle lectern and a solid brass font given by the Bishop of Dunkeld were stolen from Holyrood Abbey, the English raiders failed to seize the religious regalia and treasure there.

The cause of their failure was William Sinclair, whose family had endowed the abbey; he had removed the holy reliquaries and rich chalices, and refused to restore them. The Sinclairs of Roslin had been great benefactors to the monastic orders. The second St Clair Earl of Orkney had given the Abbey of Holyrood sufficient land to graze seven thousand sheep, vestments of gold and silver, and 'a number of rich, embroidered cups' or chalices 'for the more honourable celebration of divine worship'. The charters of the Cistercian abbey of Newbattle – also sacked during the English invasion – had further cause to praise his generosity, which included the gift to them of missals and of a silver cross worth fifty pounds, flanked by the figures of the Virgin Mary and temporarily stolen by the English after the Battle of Neville's Cross. Many of the treasures of the Scottish Church before the Reformation were the donation of the Sinclairs of Roslin, who felt it their duty to keep these safe.

In March, 1545, the Lords in Council ordered William Sinclair to return all jewels, vestments and ornaments of "the abbay and place of Holyrudhouse . . . put and reservit within his place." But still he would not yield them. They were part of the blessed hoard hidden in the vaults of his chapel beside the shrine, the *Secret shewn to us* in the Bond of Marie de Guise, *we sall keep secret*. These treasures probably included the piece of the True Cross in its reliquary of silver and gold and jewels, the Holy or Black Rood of Scotland, which had been guarded by St Margaret's cupbearer and the St Clair family for five centuries as Scotland's most precious holy symbol.

Although the Rood had again been seized by the English after the Scottish defeat at Neville's Cross and stood 'with Mary and John made of silver, being as yt were smoked all over' on a pillar by St Cuthbert's shrine in Durham Cathedral, the return of holy relics to Scotland had been arranged by Earl William St Clair during his diplomatic missions to the south. The Black Rood had been carried by the first St Clair in Scotland, the cupbearer to Queen Margaret Atheling, while the 'Mary and John made of silver' was a donation to Newbattle Abbey by his father. Resuming one of their hereditary duties as the guardians of the sacred things of their country, the Lords of Roslin intended this time to keep them secure against English depredations. The Reformation there had already destroyed almost all the shrines and precious relics of the old Catholic faith, and Holyrood Abbey might be highly vulnerable. Scotland was to become even more zealous in extirpating the religious treasures of the Middle Ages.

Fortunately these precious relics were not returned from Roslin. After another Scottish defeat at Pinkie Cleugh, Holyrood was again sacked. This time, the English invaders found only lead to carry away, stripping the roof of its last base metal. So complete was the destruction that Scotland's most ornate church became no more than a stone quarry for looters after the Reformation. The guardian of its religious treasures, however, Sir William Sinclair, was trusted to accompany the child Mary Queen of Scots to France, where she would be betrothed to the Dauphin, while her Guise mother tried to rule unruly Scotland in her daughter's absence.

Attacks were already being made on high Catholic officials. John Knox, a future leader of the Reformation, had seen the hand of God in the Scottish defeat at Solway Moss by the English, while he had described the putting of the Regent's Crown on the head of Marie of Guise as putting 'a saddle upon the back of an unruly cow'. In the same month as she signed her Bond to William Sinclair, a band of Fife lords broke into St Andrew's Castle and tortured Cardinal Beaton to death for condemning a leading Protestant preacher to be burned at the stake. John Knox himself joined the rebel lairds and preached from the pulpit of St Andrew's parish, before he was sent to the galleys by a French expedition, which retook the castle for Marie of Guise. By a Right of Passage in 1556, the Regent had to send her trusted William Sinclair again to France to ask for more support. During his year's absence, he was excused from his judicial duties, and Marie of Guise swore to defend the hidden treasures at Roslin.

The religious wars in Scotland intensified with the death in 1558 of the childless Catholic Queen of England, Mary Tudor, and the accession to the throne of her Protestant half-sister Elizabeth. By this time Mary Queen of Scots was married to the Dauphin; his father, King Henri, immediately had her proclaimed Queen of England and Ireland as well as of Scotland. The poet Ronsard wrote that Jupiter had decreed that she should govern England for three months, Scotland for three and France for half the year. The French and Catholic menace appeared so imminent that Scottish Protestant insurgents attacked the Border regions and temporarily took Edinburgh. Another Latin summons to 'our chosen son' William Sinclair of Rosslyn was signed by Marie of Guise a year before her death in 1560 on behalf of Francis and Mary, *deo gratia Rex et Regina Scotorum*. This ordered him to counter-attack the Border rebels, to capture and apprehend them of whatever quality and quantity they were, to destroy their fortified houses, and to punish their homicide and arson. He himself was given immunity from any criminal action he might have to take.

Known supporters of the Stewart and Catholic cause, the Sinclairs of Roslin were doomed by the Reformation, which came to pass the following year with the Scottish Parliament's institution of a Protestant confession of faith, abolishing the jurisdiction of the Pope and prohibiting the celebration of the mass under sentence of death for the third offence. These acts should have received the assent of Mary Queen of Scots, but they never did. Yet they ensured that the Reformation would succeed in Scotland, and that the Lords of Roslin would be condemned for their faith and their loyalty to the crown. Oliver Sinclair's two brothers Henry and John had already been appointed to be bishops; they officiated at the marriage of Mary Queen of Scots to Henry Stewart, Lord Darnley, at Holyrood in 1565. Oliver also became a Privy Counsellor as did Henry, who as Abbot of Kilwinning retained the family Masonic connection. Both brothers undertook diplomatic missions to France in support of the Catholic factions in the religious wars there.

With the fall of Mary Queen of Scots, and her capture by the English seven years after her mother's death, William Sinclair was arrested and the future of his estates put in jeopardy, although they were eventually restored to him. When the Ruthvens seized Mary's son, who was to become King James the Sixth of Scotland and First of England, William would redeem himself by freeing the royal hostage. Yet following the execution of Mary at the orders of Elizabeth of England at Fotheringay Castle in 1567, the Lord of Roslin incurred James's wrath for appearing at court in full armour rather than a suit of mourning. Clashing his mail, Sinclair replied: "*This* is the proper mourning for the Queen of Scotland." When later the Huntly killer of the former Regent Moray insisted on staying overnight at Ravenscraig Castle, Sinclair merely observed that he was welcome to come in, but would have been twice as welcome to have passed by.

In 1591 the presbytery of Dalkeith attacked the 'keiping images and uther monumentis of idolatry' in Rosslyn Chapel. The following year, the threat of mob attack forced the then Sir William Sinclair to demolish or hide the sacred carvings. The hundred images of the Virgin Mary and the Apostles and Saints had already been removed from their niches and hidden in the vaults, along with the shrine and the sacred treasures of the Catholic faith. The four altars dedicated to the Virgin Mary and to Saints Matthew, Andrew and Peter were pulled down. However, for two reasons, the ornate chapel, so full of idols and Green Men, was not wholly destroyed. In the first place, despite the fact that many trade organizations were leaving the Catholic faith and becoming Protestant, the Sinclairs remained the hereditary Grand Masters of the Crafts and Guilds and Masons of Scotland. The position carried weight. And, secondly, the *Secret shewn* to Marie de Guise, which she did *keep secret* – the location of the shrine below the chapel altar and the Sinclair guardianship of other Catholic treasures and relics, not only from Holyrood Abbey but from earlier Templar times – still held its power. The knowledge that Rosslyn Chapel was a holy place, revered by Masons as well as Catholics, stayed the hammers and axes of the religious radicals.

In the last years of the sixteenth century, when King James the Sixth of Scotland was preparing to become James the First of England on the death of Queen Elizabeth, the Sinclairs of Roslin appear to have become Protestants in allegiance to their sovereign, although they continued to keep their Catholic treasures hidden below the chapel. It was their continued guardianship of these treasures that gave rise to the extraordinary Schaw petition of 1600, signed by the Catholic William Schaw, Master of the King's Work and, like John Morow in the previous century, the leading Mason in Scotland. Other signatories were senior figures in the building trades. Seminal in the records of Scottish Masonry, the document requested the secret Catholic Sinclairs of Roslin to resume their role as hereditary Grand Masters of the Crafts and the Guilds and the Orders of Scotland, declaring that there had been great disorders in the past decades of the Reformation, when the function of the Sinclairs was in abeyance. The opening of the petition acknowledged the authority of the Barons of Roslin during the preceding centuries:

We deacons, masters and free men of the Masons within the realm of
Scotland with express consent and assent of William Schaw, Master of
Work to our Sovereign Lord the King – for so mickle as *from age to age* it
has been observit among us that the Lairds of Roslin has ever been patrons
and protectors of us and our privileges – like as our predecessors has obeyit
and acknowledgit them as patrons and protectors . . .

The traditional judicial position of the Lords of Roslin had been
suspended in the course of the religious conflict owing to suspicion that
they still supported the Catholic cause as well as the Stewart line. Yet
the fact that Queen Elizabeth of England was dying, and that James
the Sixth would soon be moving with his court to London, made
intolerable the prospect of more turmoils among the trade organizations
with their only judge in distant Westminster. The Sinclairs were now
apparently Protestant, and their old role was essential in Scotland. Even
so, Sir William Sinclair would be condemned to death in 1615 for
harbouring a Jesuit priest and holding a mass at his home. In the event,
only the priest was hanged, while the laird was reprieved by the King,
mindful of the long service of the family to the dynasty. He was forced
into exile in Ireland, where he was able to practise his faith in peace.
As Father Hay wrote, "the cause of his retreat was rather occasioned
by the Presbyterians, who vexed him sadly because of his religion, being
Roman Catholic."

William Schaw had other powerful Catholic allies in the Seton family,
who with the St Clairs of Roslin had been the bastions of Scottish
independence and the defenders of the Bruce and Stewart dynasties.
Schaw travelled with Lord Alexander Seton on a mission to France in
1584 to bolster the old alliance against England and Catholic influence
at court over the young King James, heir to the throne at Westminster.
He was suspected by English agents of being a Jesuit, and he was
promoted by Lord Seton to perform massive building works for the
family. Like Earl William and Lord Henry Sinclair, Alexander Seton
was described by the family historian as an *illuminatus*, "a great humanist
in prose and verse, Greek and Latin, and well versed in the mathemat-
icks and had great skill in architecture." Both he and Schaw became
friendly with James's wife, Anne of Denmark, and through her Schaw
found himself Master of the King's Works at Dunfermline and Holyrood, in which position he tried to keep the Masonic Lodges in Fife,
Lothian and Kilwinning in Catholic hands by invoking the traditional
rights of the Setons and the St Clairs of Roslin, who had merged the
Templars into the Crafts and Guilds of Scotland in the preceding
centuries.

The Schaw and later St Clair charters explicitly confirmed the traditional role of the family in medieval Scottish Masonry. Yet except for William Alexander Laurie, the first historian of the Masonic movement in Scotland, all other examiners of the movement have discounted the St Clair claims and the two Charters. They refuse to believe that most of the supporting documents were destroyed in successive fires in the library at Rosslyn Castle; from one of these, only four trunks of charters and papers were saved by a chaplain. After that fire, indeed, most of the work of rebuilding the castle was given to William Schaw. The following St Clair Charter of 1628, however, specifically stated that "the deacons, masters and freemen of the masons and hammermen of Scotland related that the lairds of Roslin had in the past been their patrons and protectors, and had had rights to this effect granted by the king's predecessors. But these grants had been lost when Rosslyn Castle was burnt, and through neglect the rights of the St Clairs had fallen out of use."

While defining the content of the St Clair Charter, which was signed by brothers in Lodges from Dundee to the north as far as Glasgow to the west, and while admitting to the probity of William Schaw, the most recent historian of *The Origins of Freemasonry*, Professor David Stevenson, has continued a long Protestant tradition in refusing to recognize the plain facts and truths of the Schaw and St Clair charters. Why were the declarations of Schaw and the leading Scottish Lodges false? If they were, the prime Masons were either misled or lying – a grave charge, indeed, never substantiated by any commentator on the two charters, which are indubitably authentic and signed by the Master of the King's Works and the foremost Masons of the time.

Even from London, James's successor, King Charles was obliged to concern himself with Scottish Freemasonry. The Protestant James Murray of Kilbaberton was now Master of Works and claimed the right to control the admission of craftsmen to royal building projects. Charles, however, supported the traditional St Clair rights summarized in the Second Charter, which he had seen and approved 'out of our princlie care to obviat any disordour in tymes comeing'. Already, Charles was aware of the conflict looming over the border between, on the one side, the Presbyterians who would sign the Covenant in 1638 and on the other, the bishops of the Church of Scotland and the old loyal Catholic families. Although the King temporized until the outbreak of the Civil War between the claims of the royal Masters of the Works and the traditional role of the St Clairs, yet when the swords were drawn, he knew he could count on the hereditary families such as the Setons and the St Clairs to resist the Covenanters and fight for the Marquis of Montrose and the royal cause and their own ruin.

The royalist general and brilliant strategist, James Graham, the first Marquis of Montrose, had known the seventh Lord John Sinclair at St Andrew's University. During the Civil War, Sinclair offered him possession of the castle of Stirling and the town of Perth out of shared disaffection with the Covenanters, although Montrose succeeded in taking Perth himself without a fight after one of his victories at Tippermuir. When he was finally defeated and had to flee, Montrose relaunched his last campaign in Orkney in the spring of 1650; there he raised a thousand men. Once again vanquished on the mainland at Carbisdale, he fled with only two of the Sinclair gentry, one from Orkney, the other from Caithness. Sir Edward Sinclair died in the wilderness; Montrose and Alexander Sinclair were captured and executed. Montrose spoke for other Stewart loyalists in his dying speech, which was for the King and against the orthodox Church, which had condemned him and excommunicated him:

> What I did in this kingdom was in obedience to the most just commands of my sovereign, and in his defence, in the day of his distress, against those who rose up against him. I acknowledge nothing, but fear God and honour the king, according to the commandments of God and the just laws of Nature and nations . . . I do but follow the light of my conscience, my rule; which is seconded by the working of the Spirit of God that is within me.

As with the Heart of Bruce and his defending champion Douglas, the heart of Montrose was preserved in an egg-shaped steel case made from the blade of his sword. This relic was later returned for state burial with the rest of his dismembered remains after the Restoration of Charles the Second, who did not forget all of his Scottish defenders.

In 1648, when the Civil War was already lost, the St Clair charters had been proclaimed by trumpet and a public reading at the market place in Edinburgh. Two years later, following the disaster of the Battle of Dunbar, the significance of Rosslyn Chapel was revealed by the strange mercy of vengeful English Puritans. True as always to the Stewarts, another Sir William Sinclair fought the English attack from the south. His body was brought back to the chapel and interred in full armour in the vaults on the day of the defeat at Dunbar, where his son and heir John was fighting. Father Hay was to see his corpse when the vaults were opened for the last time before being filled with sand and rubble and then sealed by stonemasons with ashlar blocks, as we found when we tried to discover the secret shrine and buried religious treasures and archives there.

His corpse seemed to be entire at the opening of the cave, but when they came to touch his body it fell into dust; he was laying in his armour, with a red velvet cap on his head on a flat stone: nothing was spoiled except a piece of the white furring that went round the cap, and answered to the hinder part of the head. All his predecessors were buried in the same manner in their armour.

When General Monk arrived with his troopers after the victory at Dunbar, he reduced most of Rosslyn Castle to ruins, although it had been valiantly defended by Sir William's son John, who was taken prisoner and sent to England. General Monk had his horses stabled in the chapel but refrained from purging it by fire and hammer, and made no attempt to break into the vaults. The most convincing reason for this is that the Lord Protector himself, Oliver Cromwell, had studied at the Temple in London, was a Master Mason in England, and knew that the Sinclairs were the hereditary Grand Master Masons of Scotland and that the chapel housed Masonic mysteries. Their estates were confiscated, but restored after the death of Cromwell to the heirs of the family.

The Lords of Roslin remained loyal to the Stewart and Catholic cause. The new Master, James Sinclair, followed the ways of his ancestors. "He was much taken up with building, and addicted to the priests," Father Hay noted of his stepfather: "those two inclinations spoiled his fortunes. He died a good age, and with the reputation of ane honest man, yet . . . he was too easie." And also, he was too loyal. His son was killed fighting for James the Second at the Battle of the Boyne, while John Graham of Claverhouse, Viscount Dundee, died from a single bullet after his victory at Killiecrankie, apparently wearing a Templar red cross on the linen beneath his armour. The survivors of the conflict formed a Jacobite Scots Brigade in France: two of its officers were from the Sinclair family.

The St Clairs of Lothian survived their approaching ruin by reason of their ancestral role in the Masonic movement. This was attested by a letter of the late seventeenth century, written by the Reverend George Hickes, chaplain to the first Duke of Lauderdale. He wrote of a visit to the St Clair castle:

This is a strong high tower house built by the Laird of Roslin in King James the fifth time. The Lairds of Roslin have been great architects and patrons of building for these many generations. They are obliged to receive the Mason's Word which is a secret signal masons have thro' out the world to know one another by. They alledge 'tis as old as since Babel when they could not understand one another and they conversed by signs. Others

172

would have it no older than Solomon. However it is, he that hath it will bring his brother mason to him without calling to him or your perceiveing of the sign.

The 'Glorious Revolution' and the accession to the throne of the Protestant Prince William of Orange led to another mob attack on chapel and castle. Father Hay chiefly mourned the sack of the famous library with its collection of medieval Catholic missals, many of them collected in the sixteenth century after they "had been taken by the rabble out of our monasteries in the time of the reformation." Hay himself lost "several books of note, and amongst others, the original manuscript of Adam Abel," who was a Grey Friar from the monastery at Jedburgh and composer of the *Rota Temporum*, a history of Scotland from early to Tudor times. Following this final attack, the chapel was left to nature with only its solid stone room and sealed vaults protecting the mysteries within. "But as nothing is done to keep it together," Dorothy Wordsworth was to note on a visit, "it must in the end fall."

Prior to this final sacking of Rosslyn library, the elements of the Secret Scroll were moved either to Yorkshire, as state the present Lodge records in Kirkwall, or more probably to Sinclair keeping in Orkney, where the Scroll would be rediscovered and preserved – and show how the Gnostic and hermetic knowledge of the crusading Knights Templars passed into the Ancient Scottish Masonic Rite.

13

The Subversive Masons

> I ought to have known that the greatest crime I or my familie
> could have committed, was persevering, to my own destruction,
> in serving the royal familie faithfully though obstinately, after so
> great a share of depression, and after they had been pleased to
> doom me and my familie to starve.
>
> John, Master of Sinclair,
> on the Jacobite Rebellion of 1715

THE SPOILS OF HISTORY also belong to the victors. He who wins rewrites the past to justify the present. This was particularly true in the accounts of the origins of Masonry, produced after the failure of the Catholic Jacobite rebellions of 1715 and 1745, and the ascendancy of the Hanoverian Kings through the eighteenth century. The definitive *History of the Lodge of Edinburgh (Mary's Chapel), embracing an account of the Rise and Progress of Freemasonry in Scotland*, published in 1873 and written by David Murray Lyon, one of the Grand Stewards of the Grand Lodge of Scotland, had as its patron the Prince of Wales. The work naturally denied the provenance of the Ancient Scottish Rite, which dated back to Kilwinning and Robert the Bruce. The Grand Lodges of Edinburgh and London were held by all subsequent Masonic historians of importance to date from English and Protestant practices, which developed under the Hanoverian kings, when the royal dukes provided a succession of Grand Masters and patrons of the Orders.

The early Freemasons, indeed, were held to be as the Knights Templars had been, a state within a state. They were accused with some justice not only of Jacobite sympathies in Scotland, but later of playing leading roles in the American Revolution and in radical movements in France, Germany and Italy. As with all secret societies with unorthodox rituals, their role was suspect in politics as well as business. According to that Jacobean Rosicrucian and Masonic brother, Elias Ashmole, Charles the Second "was a Member of the Fraternity," as Laurie confirmed, "and frequently honoured the Lodges with his presence." Laurie had based his account of the origins of the movement on Dr James Anderson's *Constitutions of the Freemasons* of 1723, the first history of the Scottish Rite, which referred to "the great respect with the institution of a Grand Lodge of Masons in London two years after the rebellion, of the Scottish Kings to this honourable Fraternity [appearing in] the records and traditions of the Lodges there kept up without interruption many hundred years." Whatever Dr Anderson saw, these records followed the St Clair archives in being destroyed after the Hanoverian takeover of the Masonic tradition in Britain. Anderson recorded the fear of execution felt among the brothers of the Ancient Scottish Rite in London following the failed Jacobite rebellion of 1715. "And after the rebellion was over, the few Lodges at London, finding themselves neglected by Christopher Wren, thought fit to cement under a Grand Master as the centre of union and harmony." To join that Grand Lodge of Masons in the capital was to accept English domination.

Sir Christopher Wren was himself a Grand Master Mason and had access to early documents of the craft. He had no doubt of the importance of the Knights of the Order of the Temple of Solomon and other crusaders in bringing back Islamic ideas on architecture from the Near East, which then became widespread throughout Europe. The *Old Charges* of the Masonic movement, which dated back to the early fifteenth century, also stressed the influence of the Levant, particularly medieval traditions relating to the building of the Temple of Solomon – so often confused by pilgrims with the Muslim shrine of the Dome of the Rock. According to this tradition the building of a Temple of the Lord God in Jerusalem had been begun by King David, who had made himself patron of the Masons and had showed high respect for their craft; he had even given them charge and control over their own rules, and increased their wages.

As Jerusalem was crowned by the Dome of the Rock, London was crowned by the dome of St Paul's. The son of its architect had no doubt where his father had found his inspiration. He was told of the origins of the Masons and of sacred architecture:

What we now vulgarly call *Gothick* ought properly and truly to be named the *Saracenick Architecture refined by the Christians*, which first of all began in the East, after the Fall of the *Greek* Empire, by the prodigious Success of those People that adhered to Mahomet's Doctrine, who, out of Zeal to their Religion, built Mosques, Caravanserais, and Sepulchres wherever they came.

These they contrived of a round Form, because they would not imitate the Christian Figure of a Cross, nor the old *Greek* Manner, which they thought to be idolatrous, and for that Reason all Sculpture became offensive to them.

Then they fell into a new Mode of their own Invention, tho' it might have been expected with better Sense, considering the *Arabians* wanted not Geometricians in that Age, nor the *Moors*, who translated many of the most useful old *Greek* Books. As they propagated their Religion with great Diligence, so they built Mosques in all their conquered Cities in Haste. [The Christian followers of this Near Eastern structural mode] stiled themselves Freemasons, and ranged from one Nation to another as they found Churches to be built (for very many in those Ages were everywhere in Building, through Piety or Emulation). Their Government was regular, and where they fixed near the Building in Hand, they made a Camp of Huts . . .

None of the many recent historians of Freemasonry have contradicted Wren's writings, which clearly attest to the Byzantine and Templar influence on church building as well as the Masonic movement. Certainly, many of the Scottish Lodges prior to the rebellion of the Old Pretender had been Jacobite. John, Master of Sinclair, swooped on the old family port of Burntisland in 1715 to seize a cargo of arms on a Fife ship, the *Margaret* of Leven, destined for the English and Protestant cause. This bold raid captured the imagination of fellow Masons and supporters of the Stewart cause. Celebrated as a military tactician, he was wounded eighteen times and decorated more often, serving in the Caribbean and the Condé, Egypt and Germany, Portugal, Russia and Spain. For his rebel exploits, the Master was later granted a pardon, but only for his life. He never assumed the title of Lord Sinclair. His possessions were lost. In a lament worthy of the keening of the bagpipes, he wrote of his hereditary attachment to the ancient Scottish royal family and its ingratitude. The Sinclairs were deserted:

. . . Without anie other thanks, having brought upon us considerable losses, and among others that of our all in Cromwell's time; and left in that condition, without the least relief, except what we found in our own virtue. My father was the only man of the Scots nation who had courage enough to protest in parliament against King William's title to the throne, which was lost, God knows how; and this at a time when the losses in the cause of the royall familie, and their usual gratitude, had scarce left him bread to maintain a numerous familie of eleven children, who had soon after sprung up to him, in spite of all which he had honourablie persisted in his principle. I say, these things considered, and after being treated as I was, and in that unluckie state, when objects appear to men in their true light, as at the hour of death, could I be blamed for making some bitter reflections to myself, and laughing at the extravagance and unaccountable humour of men, and the singularetie of my own case (an exile for the case of the Stewart family), when I ought to have known that the greatest crime I or my familie could have committed, was persevering, to my own destruction, in serving the royal familie faithfully though obstinately, after so great a share of depression, and after they had been pleased to doom me and my familie to starve?

The other loyal Lothian family of the Setons went down with the Sinclairs of Rosslyn. After the sticky fingers of the Protestant Sir James Sandilands had deprived the remnants of the Scottish Knights Templars of the last of their patrimony, David Seton led the true survivors of the Ancient Scottish Rite to exile in France, where he died in 1581 at the Monastery of St James at Ratisbon. Another exiled member of this branch of this distinguished royalist line, Alexander Seton, was imprisoned by the Protestant Elector of Saxony and died in 1610 "subjected to every torture that cruelty could suggest, yet his constant state never forsook him and he refused to betray his God-given knowledge." Another Alexander Seton defended Tantallon Castle during the Civil War, while George Seton, who died in exile in 1749, raised three hundred men for the Old Pretender; even though a Protestant, he considered it his birthright to defend the Stewart cause. The family church became target practice for the Lothian Militia, and was eventually turned into a carpenters' shop.

The flight to France, however, of the Jacobites resulted in a revival of the Scottish Knights Templars. A mystic and tormented figure played the role of another St John the Baptist in this resurrection. Andrew Michael, the Chevalier de Ramsay, was born in Ayr in 1686 and studied at Edinburgh, Leyden and Oxford. Elected as a Fellow of the Royal Society, he nonetheless wrote: "All my ambition is, that I should be forgotten." It was not to be. As a young man, he campaigned in Flanders with the Duke of Marlborough's victorious armies against the French forces and their supporting Jacobite contingents. Attracted to the spiritual teachings of Archbishop François de Fénelon of Cambrai, Ramsay changed sides and became Fénelon's pupil until his death. The seminary had become a hospital for the war-wounded and the starving. Charity and chivalry were foremost in Fénelon's teaching. There Ramsay met James Francis Edward Stewart, the Old Pretender, who was the same age, and who chose him as the tutor to his four-year-old-son, Prince Charles Edward Stewart, and his younger brother Henry, afterwards to be appointed by the Pope as Cardinal of York. Ramsay revived the Military Order of the Scottish Knights Templars and became Grand Master of its Grand Lodge in Paris. In 1736, he made a speech to a sympathetic group of Catholic aristocrats of the Age of Enlightenment, saying:

At the time of the crusades in Palestine many princes, lords and citizens associated themselves, and vowed to restore the Temple of the Christians in the Holy Land. They agreed upon several ancient signs and symbolic words drawn from the mysteries of the faith in order to recognize each other in bringing back the architecture of the Temple to its first institution.

The fatal religious discords which embarrassed and tore Europe in the sixteenth century caused our order to degenerate from the nobility of its origin. Many of the rites and usage that were contrary to the prejudices of the times were changed, disguised, suppressed. Thus it was that many of our brothers forgot, like the ancient Jews, the spirit of our laws and only retained the letter and the shell. The beginnings of a remedy have already been made. It is only necessary to continue until at last, everything be brought back to the original institution.

Recollecting the ancient wisdom of the Military Orders brought from Scotland to France, perhaps through the Royal Order instituted by Robert the Bruce, Ramsay went on to name Kilwinning as the primal Lodge of that period, alluding enigmatically to a high degree or caste of knightly priests and princes in a revived Order of Melchizedek, who sought to follow the example of the sacred king of Israel.

The word Freemason must therefore not be taken in a literal, gross, and material sense, as if our founders had been simple workers in stone, or merely curious geniuses who wished to perform the arts. They were not only skilful architects, desirous of consecrating their talents and goods to the construction of material temples; but also religious and warrior princes who designed to enlighten, edify, and protect the living Temples of the Most High.

Pope Clement the Twelfth soon forbade Catholics from becoming Freemasons under threat of excommunication, out of the usual fear that like the Knights Templars they might form a state within the state. Two years before the rebellion of the Young Pretender, the Chevalier Ramsay died – fortunately for him, since many of the Jacobites would meet their end in that failed adventure, except for those who fled to the United States. His legacy, however, was left to Karl Gotthelf Baron von Hund, who revived in Germany the Ancient Order of the Temple, once the defeat at Culloden and the harrying of the Highlands had extinguished all Stewart hopes. Von Hund's diary states that in 1742 he was initiated into the Order in Paris in the presence of Lord Kilmarnock – soon to be executed by the English for treason – and that he later met Prince Charles Edward Stewart, the Young Pretender. Other sources claim that von Hund was received into the Templars by another member of the Seton family, Alexander Montgomery, Earl of Eglinton.

Any of the three of them might have been the Grand Master of an exiled Royal Order dating back to Robert the Bruce. Von Hund was a Protestant as well as a Mason; nevertheless he revived this old Order, signing on twelve German princes, led by the Duke of Brunswick to join the resurrected body. This was opposed by a rival Swedish Order, which also held to the Ancient Scottish Rite of the Young Pretender as handed down to King Gustav the Third.

Whatever the truth, the Jacobite connection was maintained in northern Europe. For a second time, the early work of Nicolas de Bonneville during the French Revolution supported the Ancient Scottish Rite. For him, "the secret of the Freemasons is explained by the history of the Knights Templars." He told of secret ceremonies, including the exchange of blood by sword-point for the initiate, then used in Lodges of the Ancient Swedish Rite. The novice Mason received a white apron and gloves, the colour of the Cistercian monks and the Templars. The three pillars of Masonry were Jachin, Boaz and Mac-Benac, making up the initials J.B.M. or Jacq. Burg. Molay, the name of the martyred last Grand Master of the Order. Mac-Benac was also the pseudonym of Aumont, the Templar leader of those knights who had fled to Scotland.

Equally for de Bonneville, Hiram did not represent the designer of the Temple of Solomon in Chronicles and Kings, but 'Hugo-Initiatus-Igne-Ruptus-Atrocissimo-Molay', or 'Hugo-Initiated-Taken-by-Atrocious-Fire-Molay'. The cord round the neck of an initiate to Masonry did not so much refer to a Templar ceremony, but to the strangling of the knights in Montfaucon prison. Stretching credulity, de Bonneville turned his Templars into alchemists rather than spiritual teachers; their wealth came from changing brass into gold. Yet he excused them from the worship of the head of Baphomet, quoting Voltaire who wrote that the golden head on four feet which the Templars were said to adore was never found: "such an accusation destroyed itself."

More interesting was de Bonneville's recognition that the Templars, like the Muslims, worshipped a single God or Divine Creator and Intelligence. This led to their wrongful condemnation for denying the divinity of Jesus and spitting on the Cross. He even spoke of a secret tradition among the Templars that the great Saladin before his conquest of Jerusalem had been received into the Order by the Knight Hugo of Tiberias. The cry of 'Yah-Allah' was a recognition of an affinity with Islam, while the worship of the head may have sprung from ancient Gnostic Ophite rites involving the dragon serpents which guarded the Greek paradise, the Garden of Hesperides. Above all, the Masonic ceremony of venerating the image of a skeleton in a coffin was derived from the Templars, the skull being separate and representing the beheaded St John the Baptist.

The tradition of the Templars who had deserted to Scotland was now instituted. The first of the present forty-seven French Orders of the Temple was begun under the patronage of Philip, Duke of Orleans, before the French Revolution: in 1808, in the safer times of the Emperor Napoleon, some of the surviving aristocrats celebrated with pomp and ceremony a grand mass at the Church of St Paul and St Anthony in Paris on the anniversary of the death by fire of the last official Templar Grand Master, Jacques de Molay. By an unauthenticated charter in dubious Latin, de Molay was held to have invested as his successor Johannes Marcus Larminius of Jerusalem, who repudiated the Scottish refugee knights, but acknowledged the Knights of Christ as his true heirs. Larminius was meant to have invested other Grand Masters until the present day.

In Scotland, following the Hanoverian triumph, the Jacobites were executed or attainted or laid low or fled. Most remarkably, however, the last St Clair Lord of Roslin, William, was elected as the first Grand Master of the Grand Lodge of Scotland. Although still a Royal Archer, he had been forced to sell the remnants of his estates to General Saint-Clair, the second son of Lord Henry Sinclair; the lands ended in the hands of the Erskines and the Wedderburns, who became the Earls of Roslin. William St Clair had three sons and five daughters, who all died young except for one daughter. And so the male line of the Lords of Roslin and the Sancto Claros ended after seven centuries. William St Clair was reduced to living in a small house at the bottom of Liberton Wynd in Edinburgh, overlooking the Cowgate. As the premier archer and golfer in Scotland at the time of Sir Walter Scott as well as the first Grand Master of the Grand Lodge, his portrait, so like a mirror to me, had set me off on this long trail that led finally to Orkney.

Whatever the detractors of the St Clair Templar and Masonic inheritance could say, the Institution of the Grand Lodge of Scotland in 1736 affirmed again the ancient claims of the Roslin family to authority over the crafts and guilds of the country. They upheld the previous traditions recognized in the Schaw Charter and by the Stewart kings until the seventeenth century. St Clair, however, was praised for his magnanimity in renouncing these hereditary claims, while accepting the post of the first elected Grand Master for a single year. The document read:

I, William St Clair of Rossline, Esquire, taking to my consideration that the Masons in Scotland did, by several deeds, constitute and appoint William and Sir William St Clairs of Rossline, my ancestors, and their heirs to be their patrons, protectors, judges, or masters; and that my holding or claiming any such jurisdiction, right, or privilege, might be prejudicial to the Craft and vocation of Massonrie, whereof I am a member, and I being desirous to advance and promote the good and utility of the said Craft of Massonrie to the outmost of my power, doe therefore hereby, for me and my heirs, renounce, quit, claim, overgive, and discharge all right, claim, or pretence that I, or my heirs had, have or any ways may have, pretend to, or claim, to be patron, protector, judge or master of the Massons in Scotland, in virtue of any deed or deeds made and granted by the said Massons, or any grant or charter made by any of the Kings of Scotland . . .

Such a renunciation was practical policy for St Clair under the Hanoverian succession. There was no profit in being a Jacobite now. Curiously enough, the Order of the Knights Templars was to creep back officially into Scotland in the train of foreign wars. In 1761, the Grand Lodge of France would appoint Stephen Morin as the Grand Inspector of the New World, with the power of instituting Lodges according to the Ancient Scottish Rite. In 1769, the St Andrew's Lodge of Boston would confer a new Knights Templars degree. Certainly, the Scottish Rite would be important in the American War of Indepen dence, for the colonial Lodges of Boston at their celebrated Tea Party, and for that Master Mason following in the steps of Oliver Cromwell – General and President George Washington. Not only would he be painted, by order of the American Supreme Council 33° of the Ancient Scottish Rite, laying the foundation stone of the United States capital in his Masonic apron and regalia; he would also stamp Templar and Masonic symbols on the dollar currency, which survive to this day. On the bill, the eye enclosed in the triangle echoes the apocalyptic visions of the medieval seer Joachim de Fiore, the three Ages evolving to that of the Spirit, while the pyramid, left unfinished, suggested that the pinnacle of human wisdom and achievement had not been reached. These Masonic symbols were also millennial, for the American Revol-ution was inspired by a hope and belief in building a heaven on earth as well as a better society.

These rebellious American Lodges had derived from the Hanoverian and Protestant domination of Ireland and Scotland, which had resisted the ascendancy of a heretic faith and a foreign rule. After the Battle of the Boyne and the siege of Limerick, the Wild Geese had fled to fight for France, while tens of thousands more left for the United States. The Catholics who remained were subjugated by Penal Laws, which were resented. "Here are none but rebels," a clergyman of the Church of Ireland would write back in 1775 to the Under-secretary for the

Colonies in London on the eve of the American Revolution. "All our newspapers abound with intelligence favorable to the rebels. The king is reviled, the ministry cursed, religion trampled under foot."

The pattern was the same in the north of Scotland. The Highlanders had had to give way after Montrose's victories with Killiecrankie, Sherrifmuir and Culloden. The pacification of the clans forced them to serve their turncoat lairds in the British Army or to flee across the Atlantic. Their fierce resentment of government from London and their initial emigration would lead to their general support for the Declaration of American Independence and the Constitutional Convention, in which sat the Irishman and George Washington's Secretary for War, McHenry. Early in the struggle, the young Lieutenant Ridsdale would write back to the *Hibernian Magazine* that the troops which "kept up the spirit and life of the rebellion were totally Scotch and Irish." As Ebenezer Wild would remark in Valley Forge, St Patrick's Day would produce a noticeable change in camp, a celebration by the Irishmen born in America or settlers there, reinforced by deserters from the British lines.

Although Scottish regiments under British officers would fight their fellow countrymen in the War of Independence, as would the Loyalist Volunteers of Ireland, there would be six mutinies among Scottish troops raised for America, some of which would result in the discharge of the levies. Without doubt, the declaration of American Independence provoked strong support from Scotland and Ireland. "Here we sympathize more or less with the Americans," an Irish Member of Parliament would write from Dublin. "We are in water colour what they are in fresco."

Ireland had been conquered in the seventeenth century by Cromwell and the Puritans, then by the Protestant forces of the Prince of Orange. The country had been so beaten down that it gave little assistance to the later Jacobite rebellions in Scotland. There, the old clan system was destroyed by forts and roads and sheep, its chieftains bought by the chance to turn clan land into personal property. The American Revolution would change ancient wrongs and grudges into a battle for liberty, to be reflected in certain ways in the struggle between the independent mountain men – mainly Scots and Irish in ancestry – and the tidewater plantation owners, loyal to King George.

At a recent exhibition mounted by the Ulster Museum in Belfast, there appeared the missing link between the Scots Covenanters, who had supported the execution of Charles the First, and the Masonic Lodges which had deployed the Ancient Scottish Rite as a political method of organizing republicanism. I saw a remarkable wall chart derived from the Boyne Society, which was set up in 1690 to buttress the victory of the Protestant King William of Orange over the Catholic King James the Second on that river in Northern Ireland. It used Gnostic, Templar and medieval guild symbols from Scotland – signs which would become the teaching aids for members of those later aggressive forces, the Orange and Arch Purple and Black Orders, which would dominate Ulster in the nineteenth and twentieth centuries.

On a chart of great significance, displaying the steps to the Temple of Solomon and the tessellated black-and-white pavement below the Holy of Holies under the Arch supported by the twin biblical pillars, was painted the Serpent of Wisdom on the Tau Cross, while the Paschal Lamb holding the crusading banner stood above the Ark of the Covenant itself – the story of its recovery was told in surrounding pictures. These also included the victories by water of Moses and Gideon, Joshua and Elijah, as well as Noah's Ark, which saved all the species from the Flood. Such illustrations turned the Battle of the Boyne into an Old Testament triumph, with the mounted King William in the role of Melchizedek, the ruler of ancient Israel.*

Similar Covenanter and Presbyterian sources would become an inspiration to the colonial Lodges in Boston and elsewhere in the struggle for American independence. With the outbreak of the French Revolution, the Ulster Presbyterians would found the Society of United Irishmen which aimed to free Ireland as a democratic republic, uniting Protestant and Catholic in one island nation. Unfortunately, from the Peep O'Day Boys, the Orange Orders would also be formed in 1795 as the bully-boys of the local landowners, beginning a sectarian war of attrition against the Catholic Defenders, who were themselves organized by secret Lodges. The medieval Masonic symbols of harmony, wisdom and peace and the building of a new Temple under the Arch of heaven was to be plastered on the banners of the Orange and Purple Lodges, and the Red and the Black Hands of the province, with their close links to the Yeomanry.

In 1797, the Ulster Presbyterians rose up against British domination, but were suppressed before the brief victories of the southern Irish Catholic rebels at Wexford and the late arrival of supporting French forces and total defeat. After the Act of Union of 1800, these Scottish republican Lodges were seen paradoxically as the founders of the Orange Orders; the Boyne Society would become the 1st Loyal Orange Boyne Society, Armagh. Such Lodges were dedicated to the support of the British monarchy, which would preside over the bringing of

---

* See Illustrations.

prosperity to Ulster during the reign of Queen Victoria. The independence movement against the crown in Northern Ireland turned its coat for a silver lining.

The policy of the pacification of Ireland and the Highlands led to centuries of bitterness and abiding resistance. No Irishmen would forget the Massacre of Drogheda or the execution of 'martyrs' from the rebellion of 1797 to the Easter Rising of 1916. Wolfe Tone, a leader of the United Irishmen who killed himself before he was hanged, put to his recruits a most significant political catechism, based on Masonic initiation ceremonies:

Question: Are you straight?
Answer: I am.
Question: How straight?
Answer: As straight as a rush.
Question: Go on then.
Answer: In Truth, in Trust, in Unity, and in Liberty.
Question: What have you got in your hand?
Answer: A green bough.
Question: Where did it first grow?
Answer: In America.
Question: Where did it bud?
Answer: In France.
Question: Where are you going to plant it?
Answer: In the Crown of Ireland.

Curiously enough, the Irish Brigade at the Battle of Fontenoy in 1745 had defeated the Duke of Cumberland and the English with a ferocious charge, shouting, "Remember Limerick!" 'Butcher' Cumberland had then been recalled to Scotland where he massacred the Highlanders at Culloden; they were harried off the land and later cleared from it by Anglicized landowners. The result of British brutality was to incite the Irish and Scots to a hatred of orthodox government, and so keep alive that heretic streak in the Templar and Masonic faiths – the direct approach to the divine, and the opposition to established authority. Oddly enough, Scottish regiments serving in the Irish troubles had brought back the Templar beliefs to their home country. Known as 'Black Masonry' and propagated by the High Knights Templars of Ireland Kilwinning Lodge in Dublin, instituted in 1779, these degrees were transferred to Edinburgh, where the first Grand Assembly of Knights Templars was constituted in 1806 under an Irish charter. The complex Alexander Deuchar, who had taken over the Templar warrants and possessions in Scotland, had himself elected Grand Master for life; his patron was the Duke of Kent, then head of the Masonic Templars in England.

Whatever his ambitions, Deuchar saved the Ancient Scottish Rite. In 1799, knowing of the Masonic influence on the American Revolution, the Prime Minister William Pitt the Younger had passed the Secret Societies Acts. A year later, the compliant Grand Lodge of Scotland had prohibited the practice and the meeting of Lodges above the Third Degree, let alone the Thirty-Third or ultimate one. When the United Grand Lodge of England was formed in 1813, the Ancient Scottish Rite was effectively repudiated. The original Mary's Chapel Lodge in Edinburgh was suspended from its position at the head of the Masonic roll because of its recognition of the Templars. Yet by 1833, Deuchar accepted its mastership, to prevent the Lodge from becoming dormant.

The Erskines and the Wedderburns, who had taken over the title of the Earls of Rosslyn, also inherited the prestige of the St Clair ancient mastership of the crafts and guilds of Scotland. The second Earl of Rosslyn became Grand Master of the Grand Lodge of Scotland for two years after 1810; the fourth took the same post in 1870 and was re-elected in answer to a gigantic petition from nearly all the Scottish Lodges, which I had seen on its extensive roll in Rosslyn Castle upon my first stay there. That same Francis Robert St Clair-Erskine also held the titles of the head of the Supreme Grand Royal Arch Chapter of Scotland, along with his service as a Member of the Royal Order (instituted by Robert the Bruce), and of the Religious and Military Order of the Temple, and of the Supreme Grand Council of the Thirty-third and last Degree of the Ancient and Accepted Scottish Rite. Whatever the break in the bloodline, the St Clairs seemed to have bequeathed their Masonic heritage to the holders of the place of their birthright. Notably, the Victorian stained-glass windows put into the restored Rosslyn Chapel were of four saints in full medieval armour, two of them standing on the black-and-white Masonic pavement of the Templar banner, Maurice and Longinus with his Holy Lance of Gnostic renown.

Moreover, when the Supreme Grand Royal Arch Chapter had been instituted in 1817, the Charter of Constitution which was adopted also assumed that the Royal Arch had existed in Scotland prior to the erection of the Grand Lodge, and that it embraced in the 'Degrees of Freemasons' the jurisdiction from time immemorial vested in the Earls of Rosslyn. Once again, their claims were upheld, although the Royal Arch was said to be a continental import under Hanoverian rule. That assertion was contradicted, when I saw a coloured copy of the Secret

Scroll hanging on the wall of Rosslyn Castle and bearing on it two Royal Arches, derived from the Temple of Solomon long ago.

In 1858, the Supreme Council of English Masonry severed its alliance with the Scottish Council. The denial of the true history of the Ancient Scottish Rite was compounded by the retention or destruction of all evidence of its influence on the higher degrees of Masonry, particularly the top degrees of Melchizedek and the Royal Arch. The reactionary fear of Freemasonry in the age of the industrial and political revolutions of the nineteenth century would extend from the hierarchy of the Catholic Church through the German principalities, where the Rosicrucians and the Illuminati were persecuted, to Bourbon France and imperial Northern Italy, which condemned the Carbonari and all secret societies. Such a suspicion would instigate a thousand purges, culminating with the Nazis condemning the Freemasons along with the Jews to the concentration and death camps.

No supreme power will tolerate heretics and rebels who may use existing underground fraternities to oppose state beliefs. From the messianic Jewish rebels against Rome through the early Christian Gnostics and the Sufis to the Cathars and the Knights Templars and the Freemasons, defiance always resulted in their condemnation. No orthodoxy will put up with a sect which asserts the direct approach to the divine or a personal path to Paradise.

14

The Secret Scroll

And they brought up the ark, and the tabernacle of the congregation, and all the holy vessels that were in the tabernacle . . .

For the cherubims spread forth their wings over the place of the ark, and the cherubims covered the ark and the staves thereof above.

From *Chronicles*

WHEN I SAW PARADISE at the top of the Secret Scroll, it was fifteen foot off the floor under the ceiling of the Lodge. In faded pastel colours, a six-pointed sun and a moon with a face surrounded by seven stars shone down on the Garden of Eden: between them was an unintelligible row of six pictographs, which might be numerals or runes. In a strip of ocean under a mountain chain, an eel and a groundfish led a whale of sorts in front of four other varieties of sea creature. On the ground below were three doves or cocks and a swan, a ewe and a ram and a pair of horses, a single serpent and a maned lion, and three other beasts, which rang the changes from black cattle to a dromedary. They stood in front of a pink hermaphrodite, an Adam confused with an Eve under the shade of a Tree of Life. This strange human being with long hair and thin legs beckoned towards a solution. I was seeing the Sophia, the Gnostic principle of masculine merged with feminine, the ancient wisdom through which divine intelligence solved the problems of gender. I had been taught to value what I now saw.

That is the problem of viewing. My fellow members at the Sinclair Symposium on Orkney were also allowed a visit to the Secret Scroll. Some of them held themselves to be modern Knights Templars and historians. Yet they could not assess the evidence in front of their eyes. People may travel the world to the most distant places; but if they do not have the knowledge or the vision of experience, they will not know what they see. At the Symposium, which was devised by Niven Sinclair to prove the truth of Earl Henry's expedition to the New World at the close of the fourteenth century, only he and James Whittall spoke with

187

authority, along with the Micmac chiefs from Nova Scotia, who wanted no European intrusion upon their dominion. They were opposed by the Shetland archivist, whose attack on the veracity of the Zeno Voyage and the power of Henry, the first St Clair Earl of Orkney, was illuminated more by its heat than its light. He reminded me of Aaron Burr's opinion of history: "Truth is what is boldly presented and plausibly maintained." A jury of Kirkwall worthies was called upon to pronounce a verdict on the matter of the Zeno Voyage. The answer was Not Proven.

Some of the proof seemed to lie for me at the Kirkwall Kilwinning No. 38[2] Lodge, which housed the huge Secret Scroll, hanging at its full length, eighteen and a half by five and a half feet. Made of strong linen blackened at the edges, its wide centrepiece of a painted series of Masonic symbols culminated in the scene of original Creation; but it was flanked by two strips, said to depict the journey of the Tribes of Israel to the Promised Land. Examining the Scroll again privately, I saw at the apex of the Scroll a Paradise that I had not seen equalled across Europe and America in my long researches into the shape of the Garden of Eden from medieval to modern times. This simple style and the bisexual human guardian made the Eden of the Scroll more symbolic than representational. Most intriguing at a first viewing was the river that flowed into a Temple of Solomon on the right-hand geographical strip at the side of the Scroll. Four rivers had flowed into the original Eden under the Temple: the Tigris and the Euphrates, the Gihon and the Pison, later translated by medieval commentators as the Ganges and the Nile. On the two edges of the long hanging cloth were inscribed the paths of rivers, the Tigris and the Euphrates, the Nile and the Jansgar, which in the overwritten later script, appeared to me to be the Ganges, especially given its source not far from the Jordan river of biblical fame.

More intriguing at first glimpse was the figure of a mounted knight at the left base of the Scroll. Marked around him was a crusading camp besieging a city on one of the mouths of the Nile delta. My previous researches told me that this city could only be Damietta, taken and lost in two crusades. Further discoveries and connections awaited me. To assist me, I was given a drawn copy of the Scroll, together with an interpretation of it by the late Brother Speth of the Quattuor Coronati Lodge of London, dedicated to the four Roman Masonic martyrs. Speth identified many Templar symbols on the Scroll, while its provenance was described by another Brother Flett. Apparently, when the old Town Hall at Kirkwall was demolished about 1885, the Lodge Room there had already held the rarely used Scroll for the previous 130 years. Flett remembered meeting an ancient Brother, who said that the Scroll had been a floorcloth, which explained its repainting and lettering in its present state. A Minute in the Lodge's book of 1786 recorded that a Brother William Graeme of a Yorkshire Lodge had presented a floorcloth to the Orkney Lodge. This did not specify whether Graeme's gift was the present Scroll.

On examination, however, the Scroll was obviously divided between the centrepiece and the two sides. At the top, a rough outline of the Mediterranean coast from Egypt to Palestine had clearly been severed by the Garden of Paradise. Using the exact drawing of the Scroll and a copying machine, I put the two side strips together. These top sections joined perfectly, the rivers or roads matching each other in their courses. The other side sections appeared to have been stuck together out of order, a conclusion backed by Brother Speth's commentary. Evidently, the two strips were irrelevant to the middle of the Scroll, may have come from different places, and were part of other documents.

In my researches, I had come across a copy of a surviving Roman map of the eastern Mediterranean. The Peutinger Map, a road map of imperial times, was transcribed in the twelfth century from the fourth century original in the form of a long narrow scroll of parchment. The version of the Nile delta and coast up to Palestine was presented as a strip with ancient Caria and Lycia, now southern Turkey, running above it across a ribbon of sea. This design suggested that the edges of the Kirkwall Scroll had originally been a strip map no longer joined together as it once had been.

The right-hand margin consisted of five sections, which were well described by Brother Speth as the work of an artist who knew the Nile Delta and Sinai and the land of Canaan, where the biblical scenes were enacted. The base map showed the site of the Battle of Amalek from the Book of Exodus, a struggle won by Joshua because Moses held up his hand all day as a sign of victory from the Lord. This was the first triumph of the Tribes of Israel after crossing the Red Sea and reaching Mount Sinai, also marked on the map. Mulberry and almond trees were shown beside a River of Time and Life that was to flow into the Temple of Solomon; above it were outlined a desert, a camp, and manna falling from heaven to feed the wandering Jews, identified by the Rods of the Twelve Tribes, shaped as gravestones.

The section above showed Aaron and another priest worshipping the Golden Calf on an inverted Tau Cross – an emblem of the Ten Commandments brought down by Moses from the mountain was reserved for the centrepiece. Above was the Tomb of Sarah, the mother of the Twelve Tribes, and by her, two priests carrying the Ark of the

Covenant on staves. The place names given to this journey through the desert were garbled and recent, the mountains called Adger and Betho-hara and Pimmon and Pharis and the waters of Atriff. Except for the wilderness of Zin, the only name corresponding to the account of the Israelite conquest of the lands of the Amorites in the Book of Numbers, was Armoric. Otherwise, the naming appeared an inexact effort to reproduce an eroded script.

The third section on the River of Life was extraordinary, showing the Tomb of the High Priest Aaron, and two other priests worshipping the Serpent of Wisdom on a Tau Cross – Aaron's Rod, shown elsewhere in the centre of the Scroll, had also become a serpent, devouring all other arcane knowledge. As Brother Speth commented:

> The Serpent and Cross is a Symbol used in the degrees of Knights Temp-lars. The Cross is the Tau Cross and the Serpent is twined around. Its origin is found in Numbers XXI, 9, where it is said, "Moses made a serpent of brass, and put it upon a pole", which means a standard or something elevated on high as a signal and may be represented by a cross as well as a pole. Justin Martyr calls it a cross. In the Templar Degrees there is a symbol of Christ. This makes me believe it was a Templar who drew these maps.

The section above was believed by Brother Speth to be inserted wrongly, because Petra, an old Templar stronghold, was set above the Dead Sea. "It has been placed upside down proving that some one else instead of the original Artist put these together . . . All through this country [are] little buildings which I take for villages or where the Temp-lars' camps or hospitals were stationed." While agreeing that these strip maps of the Levant were wrongly arranged, I believed that the Templar geographer confused the Gulf of Aqaba, called on this map 'Gomer Sea' after the harlot wife of Hosea who prefigured the infidelity of Israel, with the Dead Sea and the Lake of Galilee, making the three waters into one stretch by the River of Life, flowing towards the Temple.

If these sections of the Scroll were not Templar in origin, the selec-tion of the few images were difficult to fathom. Why only choose to illustrate the worship of the Golden Calf on an inverted Tau Cross, two priests carrying the Ark of the Covenant on its staves, the tombs of Sarah and Aaron of the Serpents' Rod, two priests worshipping the fiery Serpent on another Tau Cross, and the River of Life leading the Twelve Tribes of Israel into the mouth of the Temple at Jerusalem? Of thousands of biblical illustrations, only these were selected by the artist and geographer. As my previous experiences in the Near East and in many libraries had shown me, such chosen symbols were Gnostic and Templar in their origin. They were signs of the direct approach to the divine intelligence through the ancient wisdom of the head and the mind.

The sections at the top depicted the Temple of Jerusalem, which led to recognizable places in the Holy Land running up to a reasonable definition of the coastline from Sinai to Syria. Some of the written names were Bethnay, Bethlem, Galalee and Gidia, Gilead and Gilboa and Judah, with their obvious biblical equivalents; from crusading times, I read Askalon, Gasah for Gaza, and Joppa. Many other names made little sense and argued for the wrong deciphering of a faded original. Yet the left-hand strip at the base promised another solution. On close examination, the large armoured rider above the camps surrounding the city at the mouth of the Nile delta turned out to be not a Knight Templar, but a Mameluke or Muslim janissary with a conical helmet and curved sword and long boots. He represented the defeat of the crusaders advancing up the Nile, confirming the Egyptian defence and repulse of the Christian assault towards Cairo, then called Babylon, after their long siege of the Mediterranean port.

On the Scroll, the recent lettering within the walls of Damietta appeared to read *aDamolus*, dog Latin for the city's name, or another failure of the penman to make out whatever letters had survived. The groundplan of the walls, however, identified the city as medieval Damietta, both in design and by its unique river tower across the Nile, taken with such difficulty by the Christian warriors of the Fifth Crusade. The camps on either side of the besieged stronghold also corresponded to the history of the followers of that crusade, who surrounded Damietta after crossing the Nile.*

Such knowledge of this campaign was unlikely to be known to any geographer, who did not take part in it – and the Knights Templars and the Knights Hospitallers of St John had been closely involved. I compared the tributaries of the Nile delta shown on this part of the Scroll against the extraordinary twelfth-century chart of the great Arab geographer, al-Idrisi, who had worked for the Norman King Roger the Second of Sicily, and who had displayed a similar knowledge of the many mouths of the great Egyptian river where it debouched into the sea. Again, the later lettering was confusing. Channels were given names such as the Perotamus Flood, the Ariworm, and the Armibricus Flood, which had no contemporary equivalents. Nor did the names of nearby cities signify much except for Memphis: Migula and Nophet and Sib,

---

* See Illustrations

191

Amthor and Moorphim. In Latin, Frankish or Arabic terms, the rivers could only translate as the Patamos, the al-Adiliya, the Al-Ashmun and al-Azra canals, while the towns might have been corruptions of Djemileh, Nenreh and Bahr-as-Saghir, and perhaps Mansourah of the great crusader defeat. Muslim towns, however, were carefully distinguished from Christian: the first had domes, the second had pyramid spires between two pillars, as in the Temple at Jerusalem.

Above this tactical map of a lost campaign appeared two decorative panels, woefully out of place. Without much lettering except to announce that the two rivers were the Euphrates and the Tigris flowing between groves of palms and cedars, fruit trees and mountain ranges, the panels should have been shown on a properly connected strip map as flowing from the Temple of Jerusalem, the source of the four Rivers of Life flowing from the Garden of Eden. Above them, situated by the Temple, the next panel became a good rendition of the coastline of Palestine, with the recognizable strongholds of Gaskalon for Askalon, Chinlet for the Templar castle of Athlit, Lazereth for Nazareth, Bethshemish for Bethlehem, and Samaria.

In the world maps of note of the early twelfth century which now survive, geography was presented as history and belief. Paradise and the Garden of Eden surmounted the work of Lambert of St Omer in his *Liber Floridus* and of Honorius of Mainz in his *Imago Mundi*. This was the case also with the Kirkwall Scroll: indeed, in the *Liber Floridus*, Paradise was seen as a sunburst with the four rivers of life flowing from it into Asia – the Tigris and the Euphrates, the Nile and the Ganges. The Tau Cross of the oceans divided the three continents, while the text named the Antipodes 'a temperate southern continent, unknown to the sons of Adam' – a possible reference to the Norse discovery of Vinland. Biblical names were inserted by Lambert – Judea and Galilea, Palestina and Moab and Bashan. In the *Imago Mundi* as on the margins of the Scroll, the journey of the Twelve Tribes to Israel was shown from the Book of Numbers and Joshua – the Wadi of Arnon, the Dead Sea and the River Jordan, Gilead and the Sea of Galilee, the Mounts of Lebanon and Tabor, also Midian and Jaboc, where the angels appeared to Jacob. Most interesting also were mythical and actual lands to the west, Iceland and Amazonia as well as the Island of Paradise in the east, a mountain with a spire.

The same journey of the Twelve Tribes was also depicted on the *Mappa Mundi* at Hereford Cathedral, along with the Fall from the Garden of Eden. The Israelites left the city of Ramasse on the day after the Passover, crossed the painted Red Sea and received the tablets of the law from Moses at Mount Sinai, before struggling through the wilderness to Wadi Arnon and Jordan and finally Jericho. This was the iconography of the Kirkwall Scroll. Yet its most convincing proof lay in the crusading maps of Palestine drawn by Matthew Paris, a Benedictine monk who lived at the time of the two crusades against Damietta, and provided Richard of Cornwall with a map of Palestine for his expedition there.

Strip maps by Matthew Paris have also come down to us, like those on the edges of the Scroll, outlining the crusaders' routes from London to Otranto in Apulia and to Sicily, the embarkation ports for the British contingents. His map of Palestine, drawn up about 1240, showed the sailing distance of three hundred leagues from Cyprus to Acre with its new fortifications constructed by King Louis of France after his debacle in Egypt. As on the other medieval maps, Paris identified the walled enclosure of Gog and Magog, representing the Mongol invasions now unleashed on Europe which were thought to herald the end of the world. Most significantly, Paris showed the coastline cities of Palestine extending from Acre through Castle Pilgrim, Caesarea, Jaffa and Askalon to Damietta on the Nile flowing to a city at last called Le Kaire rather than Babylon.* The Templar strip map on the Scroll showing the delta city captured by the crusaders was duplicated by a contemporary historian and geographer.

With the two top and separated sections of the Scroll placed side by side, a good working map was produced of the Nile delta and Palestine coastline, as known in the Middle Ages. The question was why a Templar strip map, probably dating from the Fifth or Seventh Crusade, had been cut in two to serve as the borders to a Masonic Scroll leading to a Gnostic scene of Paradise above dozens of Masonic and Templar emblems. Only one answer presented itself. The compilers of the Kirkwall Scroll in its final condition had wished to conceal the involvement of the Knights Templars in the Ancient Scottish Masonic Rite except to initiates of the higher degrees. This was particularly necessary after the Protestant Reformation and the take-over of Masonry by the Hanoverian Kings of England. The reason for the incomprehensible and fading place-names in a modern script was a later and recent attempt to ink in the Latin originals, where they existed. The repainting was an attempt to reproduce the outlines and contents of images which dated from the Middle Ages. Given these images, there was no evidence of Victorian forgery from the Templar revival in that period. Only a medieval provenance could explain the crusading strip map on the margins of the Scroll and the wonders of the centrepiece.

* See Illustrations.

At the bottom of the middle linen section, Masonic symbols were ranged, the beehive of industry and the trestleboard of building in accordance with the rules of the Supreme Architect of the Universe; the square and compass, the plumb, the skerrit and the pencil and the twenty-four inch gauge of the old crafts, signifying eight hours for work, eight hours for refreshment and sleep, and eight hours for the service of God. Above them on either side of a Templar tessellated pavement, stood the Warden's Pillars of Jachin and Boaz, framing two candles and an open Bible placed before the altar, encrusted with Masonic symbols and crowned by a third candlestick and a seven-pointed sun and a man surrounded by eight stars and the All-seeing Eye of divine insight.

The section above showed the Burning Bush over a single and triple Tau Cross and Aaron's Rod beside another altar astride a black-and-white mosaic pavement. On that altar, Brother Speth had decoded a Gnostic inscription concerning the Sophia, the ancient goddess of divine wisdom. This read:

> I am hath sent me
> unto you. I am that
> I am; I am the Rose
> of Sharon and the Lily
> of the valley. **Hegee**
> **as her hejah.** I am
> that I am, or I will
> bee that I will bee
> **Jaldadaiah**

In the right-hand corner was a groundplan of the walled cube of the Holy of Holies in the Temple of Solomon with its single entrance.

Next was painted a beautiful chart of Royal Arch Masonry, which suggested that High Degree existed long before its late Georgian revival. Under the arch of heaven resting on the twin pillars of the Temple was a firmament of Masonic symbols over the altar, on which was displayed the open Word of God shielded by the wings of two female Cherubims. The cross on the altar above the tessellated pavement contained the four figures of Revelation, the lion and the ox, the man and the eagle. To the left was the breastplate of Aaron, the High Priest, with its twelve squares surmounted by a Serpent signifying the Tribes of Israel. As Brother Speth noted, "the Serpent as a symbol obtained a prominent place in all the ancient initiations and religions. Among the Egyptians, it was the symbol of Divine Wisdom."

The axis of the Scroll provided an unexpected revelation, making my whole long quest worthwhile. At the base of the central section was a mandala, the design of ancient eastern sacred architecture. As in the Temple of Solomon, three doors led to an inner square, which was surrounded by two circles: the outer circle had six arched entrances. Above it were placed two Tau crosses with serpentine shafts, in the manner of Aaron's Rod. Enclosing the square within the circles were four geometric patterns of triangles with circles and stars, one of them an anchor, again entwined by a snake. But above these was the unforeseen image, fringed by triangles and crowned gravestones and the four banners of the divisions of the army of Israel. This was a painting in rough perspective of the hidden Tabernacle under the Temple of Solomon, over which the Royal Arch was said to have originally been built to hide the Ark of the Covenant.*

Seeing this, I was reminded of our previous electronic groundscans of Rosslyn Chapel and our drilling for the sacred treasures and Templar archives in the vaults beneath. When comparing the Kirkwall image later with an architectural survey of the St Clair chapel, I found that, allowing for the perspective of the Orkney version of the Temple of Solomon, both matched. The oblong shape of the holy places was the same, pointing to the east. The Orcadian pictures of the Ark within the Tabernacle with three Royal Arches supporting a buried catacomb corresponded to our siting of the vaults of the original Rosslyn building beneath the present chapel, where the shrine of the Black Virgin and the Holy Rood, the Templar treasures and archives, as well as the buried St Clair knights, were entombed under the stone floor. The existing stairs to the medieval underground crypt to the east might well have led south to a Tabernacle under the present Rosslyn altar. The signal of the Engrailed Cross pointing down from the centre of the chapel ceiling had always suggested another entrance beneath the stone flags between the pillars to the depths. The Scroll appeared to show the suspected plan of the hidden royal and Templar secrets of Rosslyn.†

Above the painting of the Temple of Solomon were what were identified by Brother Speth as the emblems of the Ancient Ark Mariners Degree, which even the Masonic historian Mackey could not interpret, given its distant history. Its interpretation, however, now became clear. At the base were three Royal Arches, this time crossed by waves. Above the first was the Pascal Lamb holding the Holy Lance with a banner of the Templar Cross – a carving also in Rosslyn Chapel. Between it and the second Royal Arch was an open book, the Word of God. Above were the

---

* See Illustrations.

† See Illustrations.

two Seraphs or Cherubims, similar to the pair above the Ark in the Temple of Solomon. Then, most significantly, appeared the Templar Serpent on the Tau Cross. The third Royal Arch at the base of this part of the Scroll not only referred to the Trinity, but supported the two tablets of the Ten Commandments, picked out in Roman numerals.

Two choirs of sea angels facing each other raised their voices in twin trios above. To their right, the Triple Tau Cross was drawn as the hilt of a sword, symbolizing in Masonic terms the Temple of Jerusalem, the key to a treasure, and the treasure itself. Above it was a sketch of the sacred cube of the Jewish Holy of Holies and of the Ka'aba at Mecca with four diamonds on its corners. To the left over the six sea angels was the crowned figure either of King David, who created the first Temple, or of Melchizedek, shown as priest and king of the waves with his hands uplifted in blessing and offering the bread and wine, as in the Cathedral of Reims – Melchizedek, the first mediator between earth and heaven from the Old Testament before the Temple of Solomon was built in Jerusalem. To his Order, Jesus was said in the New Testament to belong.*

My researches had told me that candidates of the Royal Arch in modern Masonry were also initiated into the Order of Melchizedek. The candidate for the Higher Degrees was anointed with oil and proclaimed for ever a priest according to that Order. As a medieval Knight Templar, he now had the power to speak with the Word of God as Christ did, and to understand the divine purpose. In the eighteenth century, the Lancashire Bolton Lodge No. 146 had recognized the ancient connection between the Royal Arch and the Templars, and an attached Chapter of Melchizedek had developed a Degree known as the Holy Royal Arch Knights Templar Priest. Also in Dublin in Ireland at that time, another Degree was developed and brought to Scotland, that of the Sacred Band Royal Arch Knights Templars, Priests after the Order of Melchizedek. Both Degrees had developed out of Catholic and nonconformist opposition to the dominant Church of England. As a priest and ruler who predated the orthodox Jewish temples as well as the Christian churches, Melchizedek remained an attractive emblem for a secret faith outside the ruling bodies of the state.

To the left of Melchizedek on the Secret Scroll was the seal of the medieval ship with its single mast, similar to that of the St Clairs of Orkney and their shipwrights from Fife at Culross and Burntisland. Round it was an odd inscription in dog Latin and code, Noterina Et Svltcrinea. The first word could only be deciphered as Distinguishing

* See Illustrations.

Marks or Symbols. The last word had no Latin equivalent and was an anagram of St Cler and Vina, referring to VINLAND, or ULNA, the Latin word for ARM or LENGTH or MEASUREMENT.

All of these correspondences supported the supposition that the Kirkwall Scroll was dispatched to Orkney following the final burning of Rosslyn Library.

At the top of the Ancient Ark Mariners Degree were two clasped hands coming from clouds, another Templar symbol. To the right, the heads of two sea-serpents, one bearing a crown, the other a cross. These were remarkably similar to the dragon crest of Earl Henry, the first St Clair Earl of Orkney, who had set out on an expedition to the Norse Vinland. Between them was another serpent on a cross, this time contained within a sun disc or a moon. More Gnostic and Templar symbols would be hard to find together, especially on an old Masonic document. To the right was an Ark again floating on billows rather than carried by staves. This reference was to Noah as well as to Moses, and it indicated a knowledge of the Ship of Solomon of the Grail romances, which carried the divine grace over the seas.

Such were my interpretations of the Ancient Ark Mariners Degree in the middle of the Secret Scroll. They were the fruit of a long odyssey from the Near East through the Mediterranean and Europe to the northern Atlantic and the passage to America. The final central section below the picture of Paradise was a transcendent Royal Arch. On the left, a foliate circle contained at its centre the Tau. Below was the eight-pointed Templar cross, shown twice within and without a double circle; then again the divine hand coming from a cloud, then a cock and an urn and Jacob's Ladder by the compasses and set-square. These symbols stood beside the Royal Arch, seen now as a rainbow beneath the triangle of the Trinity and above a Passion Cross on two series of steps, divided by the skull and crossbones of mortality and the open Word of God. The initials *I S H*, *In His Name*, were written over the Cross, while on the right was a blazing star containing a circle around the Triple Tau device. Along with other Masonic symbols was a drawing of the 47th problem of Euclid with the initials JNRI, *Jesus Nazarimus Rex Judorum*, Jesus of Nazareth King of the Jews, and a sword-point, representing the dangers run by the Knights Templars. Most significantly, below the steps was a large coiled Gnostic Serpent, wearing a crown, and the pick, shovel and crowbar of the three Sojourners and excavators of the Second Temple of Zerubbabel, who were held to have discovered the Ark in the Holy of Holies beneath the previous Temple of Solomon.*

---

* See Illustrations.

In the opinion of Brother Speth the Kirkwall Scroll was the work of a skilled Knight Templar whom he identified as the large mounted figure drawn beside the besieged Nile city surrounded by two crusader camps, although to my eyes, this figure represented a victorious mounted Muslim knight, such as Feirefiz in *Parzival*. During his advance from Palestine or his retreat there by land, the Templar "evidently made notes and sketches as he went his way with the army, or probably made very accurate mental notes of the country through which he was passing, and later drew short maps for future reference." Certainly, his pictures of the mouths of the Nile delta and the course of that river were accurate for that time.

As for the provenance of the Scroll, I had an answer. Given the crusading past of the St Clairs of the Engrailed Cross, and the Gnostic knowledge of William, third St Clair Earl of Orkney and the rebuilder of Rosslyn Chapel according to sacred and Templar designs, it was likely that both strip map and centrepiece came from the famous manuscript collection at Rosslyn Library before its final destruction. The St Clair family were the hereditary protectors of the Ancient Ark Mariners Guild, which built their fleet in Fife. The groundplan of Rosslyn Chapel over its original vaults corresponded to the drawing of the Temple of Solomon on the Scroll. The Templar and Masonic roles of the St Clairs of Roslin, who became the Earls of Orkney, offered the best explanation of how the Secret Scroll reached the Kirkwall Lodge. No other interpretation could explain all its ancient emblems and images and maps. Before my eyes hung a document which testified to the centuries of strange endeavour by which the Lords of Rosslyn had brought the mysteries of the Knights Templars to the Ancient Scottish Rite of the Masons. Here, too, was enlightenment about the roots of the Sancto Claro family of the Holy Light to which I belonged. Yet there was still another confirmation to come.

As I concluded my investigations, Sotheby's announced the sale of the Burdett Psalter. This illuminated Use of the Hours of the Virgin and the Office of the Dead was commissioned by Jean de Villiers, the Grand Master of the Knights Hospitaller of St John. Seriously wounded at the fall of Acre in 1291, he escaped with seven knights and this sacred text to the island of Cyprus, from where it found its way to East Anglia. Other than the Kirkwall Scroll, this treasure is one of the few surviving records of the crusades in the Holy Land. Its images confirmed my researches and my quest. The Grand Master is shown kneeling before St John the Baptist, his octagonal white cross on the shoulder of his black robe. In his left hand, St John bears the Grail platter of the Paschal Lamb, its head backed by the sun disc and bearing the

banner of the cross – emblems of Gnostic wisdom, as in Rosslyn Chapel
and on the Kirkwall Scroll.

Even more surprising was an illuminated letter S, its dragon shape
separating the ocean from heaven. This again showed the crowned King
David of the Temple or the Melchizedek of the waves of the Kirkwall
Scroll, with the Christian fish, the Greek cipher for Jesus Christ. Above
was God the Creator, holding the globe in his hands, separated into
the three parts of the Trinity by the Tau Cross, an image repeated in
another illumination of the initial D with God on his orange throne,
worshipped by a kneeling knight of St John in the inner margin. A
further image of Pentecost depicted the Holy Spirit as a white dove
descending with a golden Grail stone or host upon Mary Magdalene
and the twelve apostles, St Peter holding his key, another disciple with
a crusading sword.*

The unique Psalter was the work of the Méliacin Master, the leading
French court artist of the late thirteenth century. Along with the martyrs, St Margaret above her dragon and Saints Peter and Thomas
Becket, the prayer book particularly celebrated the revered figures of
the Military Orders: the warrior St Michael and the two Saints John
– the Baptist and the Evangelist – and St Katherine of the Sinai monastery, broken on the wheel and carrying a book and a sword. Also shown
was the one Grail saint recognized by the Papacy, Lawrence who sent
the Holy Vessel to Spain to inspire the first crusades there against the
Moors, and was later burned on the gridiron.

So the Orkney Scroll and the crusading Psalter set the seal on my
long investigation into the ancient wisdom of the Near East as it passed
through the returning crusaders into the esoteric knowledge of the
modern Masons and knightly Orders. The proofs were seen and shown.
Recognition was all. Or so I thought, but I should have known better.
For a quest never ends. As Socrates said, the more he knew, the less
he knew, and he concluded by knowing nothing.

I was called to the extinct volcanoes of the Auvergne at Le Puy-en-
Velay, one of the magnets of medieval pilgrimage in France, the Lourdes
of its day. On the ruins of a Druidic dolmen and a Roman temple of
the Emperor Augustus, the Roman and Christian Bishop Scutarius had
dedicated a church to the Virgin Mary, which later grew into the
Cathedral of Notre-Dame. Charlemagne was the first of thirteen kings
of France to come to Le Puy; St Louis visited three times and was
wrongly accredited with presenting the cathedral with the earliest Black
Virgin in France after his lost crusade in Egypt, probably recorded on

* See Illustrations.

199

the Secret Scroll. The dolmen became a sacred stone, meant to cure fever; so embarrassing was its reputation to the clergy that it was placed at the top of the steps of the west front of the cathedral, which remained unique in Europe for its series of six cupolas and its oriental influences.

What drew me to Le Puy was the twelfth-century Chapelle Saint-Clair, standing in the shadow of the shrine of the archangel Michael on his high lava needle. This octagonal building of basalt blocks bore an interior eight-sided dome crowned with slates with a semi-circular apse attached, as at the round Templar church at Orphir in Orkney, which was also small and built in the model of the Byzantine Church of the Holy Sepulchre at Jerusalem and Charlemagne's Dom at Aachen. Both were constructed in crusading times and had Romanesque round arched windows. The Saint-Clair chapel at Le Puy was built of dressed stones, particularly at the windows, while slender pillars held up sculpted architraves decorated with the scallops of the phases of the moon. Above these were mosaics of black-and-white lozenges, reminiscent of the Templar battle flag *Beauséant* and the later tessellated pavements of Masonic Lodges.

Above the Chapelle Saint-Clair soared the Chapelle Saint-Michel, seeming even more halfway to heaven than the Norman Mont Saint-Michel, another holy centre of pilgrimage. Built on the site of a Roman Temple to Mercury, the shrine to the warrior saint was decorated with Moorish doorways and arabesques. The triple arch of its entrance was inspired by Genesis and the Book of Revelation. Central was the Paschal Lamb, holding the crusading banner, flanked by two angels and worshipped by eight ancient men holding Grails. Below was Adam and other Green Men with foliage coming from their mouths as at Rosslyn Chapel, and two mermaids, representing those lost at land and at sea. The shrine had been founded by a dean of the Bishop Gotteskalk, who had made the reputation of Le Puy by using it as a gathering place for Burgundians and Germans wishing to make the pilgrimage in honour of another warrior saint, James with his cathedral at Santiago de Compostela, the inspiration of the northern Spanish kingdoms in their wars against the Moorish sultans of Andalusia.

A similar oriental influence permeated the Chapelle Saint-Clair, which was also constructed by crusaders returning from the Near East or Spain. While the cathedral cloister of Notre-Dame resembled that of the mosque at Córdoba in its red-black-and-white combinations of brick and stone, the St Clair chapel abounded with esoteric symbols in mosaic, four-pointed stars under a crescent or Royal Arch, a chequerboard of lozenges and the carved phases of the moon, and two small barley-sugar pillars at the entrance door, similar to those at Sintra in Portugal and at Rosslyn. Only one other perfect octagonal chapel still existed on the way to Compostela, the Templar Church of Santa Maria de Eunate in northern Spain. This strongly suggested a Templar origin for the Chapelle Saint-Clair, with its baptistery for a pilgrim hospital built behind it over the remains of a Roman Temple of Diana.*

The name of Saint Clair was unusual in the Auvergne. A medieval statue of a female saint of that title once stood in the papal palace at Avignon, while the celebrated Saint Clair, Bishop of Albi, appeared to have had little to do with the Viking branch of the Sancto Claros: his tomb in the red cathedral there was set under huge frescoes of Heaven and Hell, but is now gone. The rarity of the name pointed to the dedication of the chapel to Marie de Saint Clair, the wife of Hugues de Payens before he founded the Military Order of the Knights Templars. For the First Crusade was preached in Le Puy in 1095 by Pope Urban; and his Legate, the Bishop Adhémar de Monteil, who composed the prayer *Salve Regina*, drew up a force of four hundred crusaders including Viscount Héracle of the neighbouring fortress of Polignac, who along with Bishop Adhémar was to die at the siege of Antioch before the recovery of the Holy Lance. A descendant, Viscount Pons de Polignac, would leave more lands at Mas de Chantoin in 1210 to the Templars, supporting a long family bond.

A leader of the First Crusade was the powerful Raymond, Count of Toulouse, who presented the Black Virgin to the cathedral of Notre-Dame. The work of an Arab sculptor, who gave her a long face of polished ebony modelled on the Egyptian goddess Isis, this image was to be destroyed in the French Revolution. The cathedral, however, still retains a marvellous fresco of St Katherine on her wheel, being delivered by two warrior angels with flaming swords. Her monastery in Sinai was second in importance only to Jerusalem on medieval maps, while her sacred balm-well near Rosslyn once gave out black and healing oil to the St Clairs to save them from the plague.

All these factors seemed to point to a further connection between the crusading St Clairs and the sacred octagonal architecture of the Templars, which brought the esoteric wisdom of the Near East to Scotland and carried its ancient craft on to North America. The Chapelle Saint-Clair was built on Nordic and pagan remains during the twelfth century, a crusading age, at one of the main crossroads shared by knight and pilgrim alike. It stood above the way to Compostela and Islamic northern Spain, where William de St Clair had died with

---

* See Illustrations.

the Heart of Bruce; it lay also on the road to Rome and beyond to Jerusalem, where the infidel had again to be withstood. This chapel of a Templar pilgrim hospital with its oriental symbols of the moon and stars and black-and-white lozenges placed the Sancto Claros, the family of the Holy Light, firmly at the centre of the transmission of the secret knowledge of the Orient to the north. The evidence was again carved in stone and by name, as on the original Scots Grailstone, which I had found to start my quest.

15

Science and Grace

Kirkwall Scroll
The position of sampling was . . . central to base of scroll . .
RESULT
O x A – 8048 : 435 50 BP
University Of Oxford

RESEARCH LABORATORY FOR ARCHAEOLOGY
AND THE HISTORY OF ART
RADIOCARBON ACCELERATOR UNIT
REPORT ON RADIOCARBON DATING
BY ACCELERATOR MASS SPECTROMETRY

I N THE CASE of the Turin Shroud, science condemned one of the most holy of Christian relics as a medieval forgery. "Someone just got a bit of linen," Professor Edward Hall of the Oxford Radiocarbon Accelerator Unit was reported to have said, "faked it up and flogged it." In the case of the Kirkwall Scroll, the same process of archaeological dating dismissed the Scroll at the first sampling as a modern fraud. At the second sampling from a piece of linen taken from the base of the central panel, not from the spoiled edge, the Scroll was verified. It dated from the fifteenth century, most probably between 1400 and 1530. These dates coincided with the control of Orkney by the St Clair earls, and with the building of Rosslyn Chapel by the *illuminatus* Earl Henry, making the coincidence of the groundplan of Rosslyn Chapel with the sketch of the Temple of Solomon on the Scroll a historical probability.

I had been given four small pieces from the Kirkwall Scroll by Robert M. Petrie of the Criminal Investigation Department of the Northern Constabulary. Also a Mason from the Kirkwall Lodge, he trusted my techniques of research enough to provide me with these samples for further investigation. He believed in inquiry: his visiting card bore a caricature of Sherlock Holmes with his deerstalker hat and pipe. Fortunately, I had known Professor Hall since my undergraduate days at Cambridge, and later when I became a don there. He used to float hot-air balloons from his Oxfordshire garden, then pursue them through the lanes to their landing-place in his Rolls-Royce, followed by the likes of me on my Vespa or in my Minivan. Believing that my Orkney samples were worthy of serious analysis, he recommended me to the Research Laboratory, from which he had retired. I sent it two samples, taken by the CID Inspector from the edge of the Scroll.

Many months passed, and the result was disastrous. The pieces from the fringe were so spoiled by chemicals or use that the process declared them to be not more than fifty years old. I wrote back that the experiment was flawed. The Kirkwall Scroll had a certain provenance dating back to the eighteenth century. It might have been used as a floorcloth previously in a Lodge, and wear and tear might have spoiled its properties. I did not mention that the three samples from the Turin Shroud, which were tested by the same laboratory at Oxford as well as in Tucson and Zurich, were also taken only from a corner of the Shroud, not from its middle. With great prescience, however, my police investigator had removed one piece from the base of the significant central strip, located between the two side ones, attached at an unknown date. I sent this last hope of possible evidence to the Radiocarbon Accelerator Unit at Oxford.

Finally, the result arrived and is reproduced in this text. The most likely date of the centrepiece of the Scroll was the mid-fifteenth century. This was the period of the building of Rosslyn Chapel by the mystic third Earl of Orkney, Henry St Clair, who had passed the Gnostic and hermetic knowledge of the crusading Knights Templars on to the Ancient Scottish Masonic Rite. The many esoteric symbols on the long cloth, particularly the Ancient Ark Mariners Degree and the Garden of Eden with its hermaphrodite Eve, coincided with late medieval esoteric knowledge and the early science of alchemy. The commissioner and possessor of the best library in Scotland of the time, Earl Henry, would appear to have had the Scroll first painted for the Templar/Masons attached to Rosslyn, where so many of the symbols are still carved on the chapel walls.

As with the Turin Shroud, the radiocarbon dating of pieces taken from the corner and edge of the Scroll confirmed nothing, for these samples were spoiled, and others are unlikely to be forthcoming from the Vatican or the Kirkwall Lodge. The two side strips, however, stitched together on to Earl Henry's Templar/Masonic Scroll, with their map of crusades against Damietta, are surely evidence of a Templar provenance. There is no other likely explanation for these extraordinary borders with their arcane Gnostic symbols including the Serpent on the Tau Cross, the Ark of the Covenant, and indeed, an early picture of a Mameluke cavalryman. This Templar strip map was probably also in the possession of Earl Henry in his library and was later added to the edges of the centrepiece. What is most likely is that the Scroll, in whole or in parts, left Rosslyn for Yorkshire or Orkney before the repeated burnings of Rosslyn Castle after the Reformation. It is the most valuable treasure to remain from the medieval collection and wisdom of the St Clair Earls of Lothian and the Orcadian Isles.

The dating and discovery of the Kirkwall Scroll changes all Scottish Masonic history and does much to demonstrate how the fugitive Knights Templars informed the members of the Ancient Scottish Rite through their hereditary Grand Masters, the St Clairs. The Jacobean Schaw Charters are confirmed. The Earls of Rosslyn continued in their hereditary role, perhaps dating from the time of the early Scots kings and Robert the Bruce. Not all the records of the early Catholic Lodges have been destroyed by the Protestant Reformation, any more than Rosslyn Chapel was. This last remnant of late medieval understanding has survived to reach our time.

My journey had begun forty years ago, because an eighteenth-century portrait of an archer and a golfer, a St Clair of Roslin, happened to look rather like me. Yet my inquiry had been not so much for roots or ancestors or genealogy, but for what the Sancto Claros had achieved in spiritual knowledge, and how they had passed on their wisdom. My research into them led to my own enlightenment, as well as to an understanding of the great heresy – the direct contact of the individual with the Creator, to which the states and the churches were always opposed. I now understood better the Knights Templars and their legacy to the Freemasons as I saw their connection borne out by the history of my own family in Lothian and Orkney, where the Secret Scroll, the final evidence, awaited me.

Yes, we do not fully know what we do until it is done. As the monk and poet Thomas Merton wrote on 'Wisdom':

> How sweet my life would be, if I were wise!
> Wisdom is well known
> When it is no longer seen or thought of.
> Only then is understanding bearable.

Acknowledgements and Notes

I am deeply indebted to Niven Sinclair, who initiated, researched and financed many of these inquiries, culminating in the Sinclair Symposium of 1997 in Kirkwall, Orkney. In my interpretation of Rosslyn Chapel I am also grateful to its previous curator, Judith Fisken, for her sympathy and profound knowledge. Robert Brydon, the archivist of the Ancient Scottish Rite of the Knights Templars has been erudite, helpful and illuminating. And James Whittall of the Early Sites Research Society has been unremitting in his efforts to unearth the secrets of early American archaeology. The Lodge Kirkwall Kilwinning No. 38[2] has been unfailing in its guardianship of the Secret Scroll and its aid in this quest.

A TEMPLAR STONE

The rubbing of the St Clair Grail tombstone and later of the Westford Knight was made by Marianna Lines. Some of the material in this book derives from four other works of my own, particularly *The Sword and the Grail* (London, New York, 1992), *Jerusalem: The Endless Crusade* (London, New York, 1995), *The Discovery of the Grail* (London, Milan, New York, Paris, 1998) and *Le Jardin du Paradis* (Paris, 2000). In these books, further editorial notes on this text may be found. The three indispensable sources on the early history of the St Clair family are Father Richard Augustine Hay, *Genealogie of the Sainte-claires of Rosslyn* (Edinburgh, 1835), Roland William Saint-Clair, *The Saint-Clairs of the Isles* (Auckland, 1898), and L.-A. de Saint Clair, *Histoire généalogique de la famille de Saint Clair et de ses alliances (France-Écosse)* (Paris, 1869).

2. THE HIDDEN INSPIRATION

The seminal modern works on Gnosticism are by Elaine Pagels, *The Gnostic Gospels* (New York, 1979) and *Adam, Eve, and the Serpent* (New York, 1988). Also valuable is the concise survey by Benjamin Walker, *Gnosticism: Its History and Influence* (London, 1983). C.H. Moore, *The Religious Thought of the Greeks* (Cambridge, Mass., 1916) is helpful on the Orphic and Mithraic cults. As Hippolytos wrote in his *Elenchos*: "Now no one can be saved and rise up again without the Son, who is the serpent." I am also grateful to Malcolm Lee Peel for his edition of *The Epistle to Rheginos: A Valentinian Letter on the Resurrection* (London, 1969). Through Arabic sources, Gnostic cult objets reached Spain and the South of France. *Coffrets gnostiques*, boxes portraying naked initiates, were commonly found in Provence in the twelfth and thirteenth centuries, when the Cathari, the pure ones, preached their faith.

Inspirational in his treatment of divine vision is Dan Merkur: *Gnosis: An Esoteric Tradition of Mystical Visions and Unions* (State University of New York, 1993). For an understanding of insight, most useful is Michael Lieb, *The Visionary Mode: Biblical Prophecy, Hermeneutics, and Cultural Change* (Ithaca, N.Y., 1991). And illuminating on the sacred serpent is Claire Lalouette, *Sagesse sémitique: De l'Égypte ancienne à l'Islam* (Paris, 1998), while Peter Whitfield, *The Mapping of the Heavens* (London, 1995), brings out the serpentine symbolism of the ancient cosmos.

All inquiries into the crusades still begin and end with Sir Stephen Runciman's *A History of the Crusades* (3 vols., Cambridge, 1951–4). Generally useful on the subject are Zoé Oldenburg, *The Crusades* (London, 1966); Richard Barber, *The Knight and Chivalry* (London, 1970); Amin Maalouf, *The Crusades Through Arab Eyes* (London, 1984), and Hans Eberhard Mayer, *The Crusades* (Oxford, 1990). Jonathan Riley-Smith is admirable on the motives of the crusades in *The First Crusade and the Idea of Crusading* (London, 1993); also useful are his edition of *The Atlas of the Crusades* (London, 1991), L. and J. Riley-Smith, *The Crusades. Idea and Reality 1095–1294* (London, 1982), and Norman Housley, *The Later Crusades, 1274–1580: From Lyons to Alcazar* (Oxford, 1992). Particularly significant on St Bernard is *Vézelay et Saint Bernard* (Jacques d'Arès ed., Croissy-Beaubours, 1985), and *The Second Crusade and the Cistercians* (Michael Gervers ed., New York, 1992). For St Bernard's views on the crusades, see G. Constable, 'The Second Crusade as seen by Contemporaries', *Traditio*, 9 (1953) and J. Leclerq, 'L'encyclique de St Bernard en faveur de la croisade', *Revue bénédictine*, 81 (1974). Essential reading in its field is Alan MacQuarrie, *Scotland and the Crusades, 1095–1560* (Edinburgh, 1995).

Most interesting of recent works on the Knights Templars are Gérard de Sède, *Les Templiers sont parmi nous* (Paris, 1962); Louis Charpentier, *Les Mystères Templiers* (Paris, 1967); Guy Tarade, *Les Derniers Gardiens du Graal* (Paris, 1993); Michel Lamy, *Les Templiers* (Bordeaux, 1997); Patrick Rivière, *Les Templiers et leurs mystères* (rev. ed., Paris, 1997); Raimonde Reznikov, *Cathares et Templiers* (Portet-sur-Garonne, 1993); and Alain Desgris, *L'Ordre des Templiers* (Paris, 1994). The quotation on the Knights Templars by St Bernard of Clairvaux comes from his *De laude novae militiae*, contained in *Patrologia Latina*, clxxxii, pp. 923–6. Farhad Daftary puts the revisionist case in *The Assassin Legends: Myths of the Ismai'ilis* (London, 1994).

2. THE EASTERN MYSTERIES

Other than the work by Pagels cited in the text, the most illuminating work on the early Jewish interpretations of the Scriptures is *The Bible As It Was* (Cambridge, Mass., 1998) by James L. Kugel, who is particularly telling on the subjects of Eve and the Serpent and Melchizedek.

4. IDOL OR SKULL

Georges Bertin, *La Quête du Saint Graal et l'imaginaire* (Condé-sur-Noireau, 1997), is important on the cult of the Grail and the head in Normandy and Brittany. *Le Haut Livre du Graal Perlesvaus* was edited by William A. Nitze and collaborators in a definitive text and commentary, published by the University of Chicago Press in 1937. For the translations, I have also used *The High History of the Holy Graal*, translated from the old text by Sebastian Evans (London, 1910). I am indebted to Robert Sherman Loomis for his original and brilliant *Celtic Myth and Arthurian Romance* (Columbia University Press, New York, 1927). The two Freemason writers who identified a Knight Templar at Rosslyn Chapel putting a noose round the neck of a novice are C. Knight and R. Lomas, *The Second Messiah* (London, 1997); their supposition that the corpse of Jacques de Molay is on the Turin Shroud, however, is far-fetched.

Nicholas de Bonneville, *La Maçonnerie écossaise comparée avec les trois professions et le secret des Templiers du 14ème siècle* was first published in 1788 in Paris. Joseph von Hammer-Purgstall published his *Mysterium Baphometis revelatum* and his *Geschichte der Assassinen* in 1818 in Vienna, later translated as *The Mystery of Baphomet Revealed* and *The Guilt of the Templars*. Jean-Luc Aubarbier and Michel Binet, *Les Sites Templiers de France* (Editions Ouest-Frances, Rennes, 1997), wrote a most important guide. On the millennium, I am indebted to Damien Thompson, *The End of Time* (London, 1996), and Michael Grosso, *The Millennium Myth: Love and Death at the End of Time* (New York, 1995), while Keith Laidler, *The Head of God: The Lost Treasure of the Templars* (London, 1998), reached me at the conclusion of this book.

5. THE MAGDALENE

The definitive work on *Mary Magdalen* (London, 1993) was written by Susan Haskins. In the Orphic Gnostic tradition, naked members of the cult worshipped a sacred winged serpent. A bowl depicting the rite was recorded in Emma Jung, *The Grail Legend* (Boston, 1968).

6. THE TEMPLE

Alexander Horne, *King Solomon's Temple in the Masonic Tradition* (London, 1972), remains the most useful recent work on that theme. John Michell, *The Dimensions of Paradise: The Proportions and Symbolic Numbers of Ancient*

Cosmology (London, 1988), is visionary in the measurements of the New Jerusalem. St John the Divine's vision of the Holy City is described in Revelation, 21. Helen Rosenau, *The Ideal City: Its Architectural Evolution* (New York, 1972), is admirable in its scope and insight; so is John Passmore's analysis of *The Perfectibility of Man* (London, 1970) and Helen Adolf, *Visio Pacis: Holy City and Grail* (Pennsylvania State University, 1960).

L.J. Ringbom, *Graltempel und Paradies* (Stockholm, 1951), is invaluable on the connections of the Temple and the Grail Castle with oriental thought and architecture. Some of its theories were first put forward in L.E. Iselin, *Der morgenländische Ursprung der Graalslegende* (Halle, 1909). See also the stimulating work of P. Ponsoye, *L'Islam et le Graal* (Paris, 1957). R.E. Clements, *God and Temple* (Oxford, 1965), is evocative on its meaning in the Bible.

I have used the Penguin edition of *The Quest of the Holy Grail* (London, 1969). It was edited and translated by P.M. Matarosso, whose introduction is illuminating, and who quotes the works of Jean Marx, *La Légende arthurienne et le Graal* (Paris, 1952) and Albert Pauphilet, *Études sur la Queste del Saint Graal* (Paris, 1921). Matarosso's *The Redemption of Chivalry: A Study of the Queste del Saint Graal* (Geneva, 1979) is also excellent, while Etienne Gilson, in *La Théologie mystique de Saint Bernard* (Paris, 1947), stresses the mysticism and divine grace in the work. The text of *Parzival* is analysed in David Blamires, *Characterization and Individuality in Wolfram's 'Parzival'* (Cambridge University, 1966), and in Margaret F. Richey, *Studies of Wolfram von Eschenbach* (London, 1957). The translations from the original are largely mine. There is a good comparison in Linda B. Parshall, *The Art of Narration in Wolfram's Parzival and Albrecht's Jüngerer Titurel* (Cambridge University Press, 1981). The illuminating *Man and Temple* by Raphael Patai was published in 1979 in New York.

7. THE SHAPE OF THE TEMPLE

The medieval *compagnonnage* was examined by Robert Frere Gould in his exhaustive *The History of Freemasonry* (2 vols., London, 1885) in which he cites the works of the earlier French historian Perdiguier. The best work on the designs of the three Temples built in Jerusalem by Solomon, Zerubbabel and Herod remains André Parrot, *The Temple of Jerusalem*, London, 1957. J.N. Casavis, *The Greek Origin of Freemasonry* (New York, 1955), asserts the movement's Dionysian origins, while Alexander Horne, already cited, is the leading researcher into Masonic beliefs and the Temple of Solomon; *God and the Temple* has already been cited. Robert Graffin is most intriguing in *L'Art Templier des cathedrales: Celtisme et tradition universelle* (rev. ed., Chartres, 1993).

In his illuminating *La Tradition cachée des cathédrales* (Saint-Jean-de-Braye, 1990), Dr Jean-Pierre Bayard draws attention to the condemnation of the medieval *compagnonnage* in 1640 and 1645 by the French church and state in terms reminiscent of the trials of the Knights Templars: "These companions dishonour God greatly, profane all the mysteries of our religion...according to traditions of the Devil." Bayard stressed that the particular saints of the *compagnonnage* were Saints John the Baptist and the Evangelist.

8. THE WANING OF THE CRUSADES

The *Chronicle of Melrose*, which runs from 1175 to 1275 approximately, is preserved in the British Library. A copy is on display in the Commendator's House at Melrose Abbey. The testimony of Templar interrogators by the Inquisition is quoted in Heinrich Finke, *Papsttum und Untergang des Templerordens* (2 vols., Münster, 1907). In his second volume, Finke prints the list of refugee Knights Templars, given in documents in the Bibliothèque Nationale (Cod. Lat. 10919, fol. 84 and 236); according to this, Gerard de Villiers fled with forty knights, but twelve others escaped. The best assessment of the Templar escape to Scotland is to be found in Michael Baigent and Richard Leigh, *The Temple and the Lodge* (London, 1989); Baigent and Leigh discovered the Templar graves in Argyll and at Athlit, but ignored the probable arrival of part of the Templar fleet in the Firth of Forth near Balantrodoch and the Seton and St Clair lands. Also useful is Gérard Serbaneco, *Histoire de l'Ordre des Templiers* (Paris, 1970), and M. Barber, *The Trial of the Templars* (Cambridge, 1978). I am grateful for additional information given to me by the Templar researcher, Erling Haagensen of Bornholm, Denmark.

I am again indebted to Robert Brydon for first informing me of the ceremonies of the present Scottish Knights Templars, and for an account of their history as well as that of the Royal Order, the original Kilwinning Lodge and the medieval Crafts and Guilds and Orders of Scotland. A. Bothwell-Gosse, a Mason of the 18th Degree, was the authority on the *Templi Desertores* in her invaluable *The Knights Templars* (London, 1912).

9. VENICE TO THE NORTH

For the early history of the Zeno family, I am indebted to Philip M. Giraldi, *The Zen Family (1500–1550): Patrician Office Holding in Renaissance Venice* (Ph.D. thesis, London University, 1975). His bibliography is indispensable. The Zeno family once had an extensive archive, but little of its material survives. What does survive is preserved in the *Archivio Zeno* of the library of the Museo Correr. In *Venezia e la sua laguna* (vol. I, Venice, 1847), the archive of Count Pietro Zeno is described, but few of these manuscripts can now be traced. There is a list of young patricians serving on the Great Council – the *Barbarelli* – in the *Arogadori da Comun, Ballo d'Oro*, from 1414 to 1544, also recorded in the *Raccolta dei Consegi* in the Libreria Marciana. Also useful on the later Zeno family is the *Libro d'Oro*, the proof of nobility, kept from 1506 in Archivio di Stato. Marco Barbaro, in his *Libro di nozze, 1380–1568*, relates in sixty-four manuscripts the history of Venetian noble families of the sixteenth century. His account of the Zeno family is in the Libreria Marciana, (Mss Italiani, Cl. 7, No. 928, Coll. 8597, under entry 1216).

Admiral Gottardo, the head of the Museo Storico Navale in Venice, confirmed to the author that the *petriero* was used by Carlo Zen at the Battle of Chioggia and was manufactured between 1370 and 1400, after which it became obsolete. Nicolò Zeno published *Dello Scoprimento dell' Isole Frislanda, Eslanda, Engronelanda, Estotilanda, & Icaria, fatto per due fratelli Zeni, M. Nicolò il Cavaliere, & M. Antonio. Libro Uno, col disegno di dette Isole* was published in Venice in 1558, the same year as the Vavassatore engravings of the Vopell Map. It was republished for the Hakluyt Society in a bilingual version in 1873, edited with an introduction and end matter by Richard H. Major, who was convinced of the arguments for its authenticity apart from the author's obvious invention of Icaria.

The only example of the *Gemma Frisius-Mercator* globe of 1537 is in the Schlossmuseum at Zerbst in Germany, while the only example of the Vopell-Vavassatore map in good condition is in the Houghton Library at Harvard. It was drawn from English, French, Spanish and Portuguese voyages of discovery in the previous decades. Michael Bradley with Deanna Theilmann-Bean in *Holy Grail Across the Atlantic* (Ontario, 1988) have some insights into the presence of the Templars on Prince Henry St Clair's expedition to Canada.

Mercator's map of 1569 was published at Duisberg. I am grateful for details of the use of the *Zeno Map* to *A Book of Old Maps* (comp. and ed. by E.D. Fite and A. Freeman, Cambridge, Mass., 1926). Most important on the accuracy of the *Zeno Map* is Miller Christy, *The Silver Map of the World* (London, 1890). See also Rodney W. Shirley, *The Early Mapping of the World: Early Printed World Maps 1472–1700* (Vol. 9, London, 1984); W.F.Ganong, *Crucial Maps in the Early Cartography and Place-Nomenclature of the Atlantic Coast of Canada* (Toronto, 1933), and Leo Bagrow, *Giovanni Andreas di Vavassore: A Descriptive List of his Maps* (Jenkintown, 1939).

The identification of Icaria with Kerry was first made in the eighteenth century by Johann Reinhold Forster. Many other early supporters of the veracity of the *Zeno Narrative* and *Map* have agreed with him, including Alexander, Baron von Humboldt, *Examen critique de l'histoire de la géographie* (Vol.2, Paris, 1837–39); Joachim Lelewel, *Géographie du Moyen Age* (Vol.2, Brussels, 1852–57); Count Miniscalchi Erizzo, *Le scoperte antiche* (Venice, 1855); Gravier, *Découverte de l'Amérique par les Normands au Xe siècle* (Paris, 1874); Cornelio Desimoni, *I viaggi e la carta dei fratelli Zeno veneziana, 1390–1405* (Florence, 1878), and Adolf Erik Baron von Nordenskjöld (Stockholm, 1883), who proves conclusively how far in advance was the *Zeno Map* of all preceding maps of the northern seas, even that of Olafus Magnus.

Nicolò Zeno's other writing included the *Storia della guerra Veneto-Turca del 1537 in 4 libri* – see BMV, Ms. It. Cl. VII 2053 (7920). Other published works were *Dell'origine de Venetiae et antiquissime memorie dei Barbari che distrussero l'imperio de Roma* (Venice, 1558), and *Trattato dell'origine et costumi degli Arabi* (Venice, 1582). The Hakluyt Society republished the Ramusio Version of the *Zeno Narrative* and *Map*, (op. cit.), and of Caterino Zeno's *Travels in Persia* (London, 1873).

211

The likely dating of the voyages of Antonio and Nicolò Zeno with their Scottish prince to Orkney and the Shetlands, Greenland and the New World, has been the subject of much controversy. An article by A. de Mosto of 1933, 'I navigatori Nicolò e Antonio Zeno', published in Florence in *Ad Alessandro Luzio, Miscellanea di studi storici*, questioned the dating of the Zeno brothers' voyage to the northern seas, given the dates of Nicolò's other engagements as attested in the Venetian archives. His article was followed by Brian Cuthbertson, 'Voyages to North America Before John Cabot: Separating Fact from Fiction', a paper read before the Royal Nova Scotia Historical Society on 15 November, 1994. He was unaware of the brilliant refutation of Mosta by Giorgio Padoan in *Quaderni Veneti* (Ravenna, 1989). His researches and my own recent inquiries in the Libreria Marciana confirmed the dates for Antonio and Nicolò Zeno given in this text, which even Cuthbertson had to admit were borne out by the Venetian records. This revised dating of Venice's push to the north allows for the long sojourn of the Zeno brothers in the Orcadian Isles.

Professor William Herbert Hobbs, 'Zeno and the Cartography of Greenland' was published in *Imago Mundi*, and 'The Fourteenth-Century Discovery of America by Antonio Zeno' in *Scientific Monthly*, vol. 72, 1951. He substantiated the accuracy of Nicolò Zeno's first report from Greenland as did Professor E.G.R. Taylor and Sigurd Amundsen in 'Zeno Truth Obscured by Smoke', *Geographical Magazine*, vol. 49, 1977. The most important witnesses to the accuracy of the *Zeno Map* are Captain A.H. Mallery, *Lost America* (Columbus, 1954), and Charles H. Hapgood, *Map of the Ancient Sea Kings* (New York, 1966). Lauge Koch, D.McL. Johnson and Helga Larsen have corroborated the evidence of medieval Viking ecclesiastical settlements in East Greenland. Also useful were E.G.R. Taylor, *The Haven Finding Art* (London, 1956) and T. Campbell, 'Portolan Charts from the Late Thirteenth Century to 1500', in *The History of Cartography* (J. Harley and D. Woodward eds., Chicago, 1987).

The claims of Henry St Clair to the earldom of Orkney were fully documented in the 'Deduction concerning the genealogies of the Ancient Counts of Orkney, from their First Creation to the Fifteenth Century. Drawn up from the most authentic Records by Thomas, Bishop of Orkney, with the assistance of his Clergy and others', June, 1446, at Kirkwall. The quotations from Father Hay came from his *Genealogie of the Sainte-claires of Rosslyn* (op. cit.). The biography of Carlo Zeno by Bishop Giacomo of Padua was preserved in the Libreria Marciana at Venice (see Muratori, *RIS*, vol. 19). Although Carlo's meeting with the Scottish prince was ascribed to a later period in his life, the chronology of the biography was accurate and based on stories told by his grandfather without reference to due date. *The Register of the Great Seal of Scotland, ad 1306–1424* was edited in a new edition by John Maitland Thompson and printed in Edinburgh in 1984. King Robert of Scotland's Resignation of Orkney is quoted in Alexander Nisbet, *A System of Heraldry* (Edinburgh, 1816); Nisbet further claimed that Earl Henry St Clair became Duke of Oldenburg by his first marriage to a Danish princess, as well as 'knight of the Thistle, knight of the Cockle, and knight of the Golden Fleece'. *The Icelandic Annals* tell of the death of Bishop William of Orkney, 'killed or burnt by his flock'. The *Diplomatarium Norvegicum*, vol. 2, no. 515 (Oslo, 1852) documents Earl Henry St Clair's commitment to the Shetlands. Barbara E. Crawford is the authority on the situation in medieval Orkney; her article, 'William Sinclair, Earl of Orkney, and His Family: A Study in the Politics of Survival', has informed the writing of this chapter.

10. SAILING TO THE WEST

The *Rudimentium Novitorium* and the De Virga map of Venetian trade of 1414 were brought to my attention by Gunnar Thompson in his remarkable, *The Friar's Map of Ancient America, 1360 ad* (Seattle, Washington, 1996). Nicolò Zeno's frank admission that he had destroyed his ancestors' book and letters and worked from a sailing chart 'rotten with age' has been held by leading sceptics as a clever stratagem to excuse the discrepancies in his published *Narrative* and *Map*. Although his account was generally believed and used by distinguished cartographers and explorers until the nineteenth century, it was attacked by Admiral Zahrtmann in 1836 in the fifth volume of the *Journal of the Royal Geographical Society*, and by Frederick W. Lucas in 1898 in *The Annals of the Voyages of the Brothers Nicolò and Antonio Zeno in the North Atlantic About the End of the Fourteenth Century, and the Claim Founded Thereon to a Venetian Discovery of America, a Criticism and an Indictment* (London, 1898).

The first attack was ably refuted by Richard Henry Major in his introduction to his edition of the *Zeno Narrative* and *Map* for the Hakluyt Society in London in 1873, while many defenders of the general veracity of Nicolò Zeno have replied to Lucas's assault, beginning with Miller Christy in his erudite *The Silver Map of the World* (London, 1900). Other authorities are quoted in my text or notes. It is regrettable that Samuel Eliot Morrison in his influential *The European Discovery of America: The Northern Voyages, ad 500–1600* (Oxford, 1971) chose to believe F.W. Lucas and did not do any primary research on Venetian sources or conduct any archaeological research in Nova Scotia.

For the equation of Estotilanda with Markland, I am indebted to Professor E.G.R. Taylor, 'A Fourteenth-Century Riddle – and Its Solution', *Geographical Review*, Vol. 54, 1964. As she also stated in 'The Fisherman's Story,' *Geographical Magazine*, Vol. 37, 1964, 'The authenticity of the account has been challenged but on very flimsy grounds. It appears to the present writer to be quite out of the question that any author would invent a story which in its every detail reflects facts of which it is impossible that he would have been aware. Such is the story of Markland which Antonio Zeno, then in the Faroes, related in a letter to his brother Carlo in Venice . . .'

In his *Prince Henry Sinclair* (New York, 1970), Frederick J. Pohl used the discovery by the geologist William H. Hobbs of asphalt flowing into the sea in the Stellarton area of Nova Scotia to identify Earl Henry St Clair's harbours at Pictou and Guysborough. With his researches on the ground, Niven Sinclair generally supported Pohl's findings. I am grateful to James Whittall of the Early Sites Research Society for showing me Malcolm Pearson's photograph of the pre-Columbian cannon at Louisburg. The Victorian who described the second ringed cannon at St Peter's was R.G. Haliburton in *Popular Science Monthly*, May, 1885. For research on the Westford Knight and the Newport Tower I am again indebted to James Whittall. In a stimulating paper, David Trubey discusses the two camps that formed in Westford around the subject of the authenticity of the knight on the rock. The correspondence between Frank Glenn and T.C. Lethbridge is preserved in the Westford Library.

A.H. Mallery, C.E. Gardner and J. Howieson made a special interim report to the Council of the City of Newport on 20 October, 1955, stating that the Tower was not a colonial windmill or the summer house of Governor Benedict Arnold. It may have been a Viking tower or a Christian church, but undoubtedly was the oldest European building standing on the mainland of America. Edward Adams Richardson's study of the Newport Tower, *Journal of the Surveying and Mapping Division, Proceedings of the American Society of Civil Engineers*, February, 1960, commented on the fourteenth century fireplace on the first floor of the tower and on the unsuitability of the building as a windmill. In his view it was a signals station for ships entering the bay. The report of 1632 in the Public Records Office mentioning a 'rownd stone towre' is *The Commodities of the Island called Manate or Long Isle Within the Continent of Virginia;* it also refers to New England and was reproduced in Vol.2, *Collections of the New York Historical Society for 1869.* E.A. Richardson, C.S. Peirce, Frederick J. Pohl and H.R. Holand have all confirmed the design measurements as those of the Scottish ell or Rhineland-Norse yard, two of which make up a fathom (its exact length is 0.31374 metres, or 37.063 inches).

The William Wood map is contained in *A Book of Old Maps* (Emerson D. Fite and Archibald Freeman eds., Cambridge, Massachusetts, 1926). The weight in stone of the tower is over two hundred tons, requiring a sizeable colony to construct it. Philip Mears, *The Newport Tower* (Newport, 1942), added further evidence disproving the assertion that Governor Benedict Arnold built the tower as a windmill. William S. Godfrey's dig of the surrounds of tower (*Archaeology*, Summer, 1950) did not invalidate an earlier origin of the tower.

The then director of the National Museum of Denmark, Dr Johannes Brøndsted, published his remarks on the Newport Tower in *Aarbog før Nordisk Oldkyndighed og Historie*, 1950. Charles M. Boland, *They All Discovered America*, claimed that aerial survey pictures taken by the Commodity Stabilization Service in 1951 revealed evidence of a nave attached to the Newport Tower. Eric Fernie contributed an article 'The Church of St Magnus, Egilsay', to the admirable collection of essays, *St Magnus Cathedral and Orkney's Twelfth-century Renaissance* (Barbara E. Crawford ed., Aberdeen University, 1988). The *Orkneyinga Saga* recounts the martyrdom of St Magnus. The armorial experts who have identified the period of the sword hilt of the Westford Knight include those from the Armoury of the Tower of London.

My inquiries among present-day Micmac scholars confirmed my belief that the Glooscap legend antedated the arrival of Prince Henry's expedition to Cape Breton Island. However much he added to the myth, it is clear that he did not exploit the Indians as Columbus was to do. His good behaviour left a remembrance of a superior and wise being. The quotations are taken from the Reverend Silas Rand, *Legends of the Micmacs* (New York, 1894), and C.G. Leland and J.D. Prince, *Kulo'skap the Master and Other Algonkin Poems* (New York, 1902). The death of Earl Henry St Clair is described in Father Hay's *Genealogie of the Sainte-claires of Rosslyn* (op. cit.), and the 1446 Diploma of the Bishop of Orkney, also cited. Stephen Boardman, *The Early Stewart Kings: Robert II and Robert III, 1371–1406* (East Linton, Lothian, 1996), is excellent on the imprisonment of the second St Clair Earl of Orkney with the heir to the Scottish throne.

11. A CHAPEL OF THE GRAIL

In 'Notes on the Library of the Sinclairs of Rosslyn', 14 February, 1898, Professor H.J. Lawlor testifies to the St Clair manuscripts in my text. I am indebted to the Scottish Templar Archivist Robert Brydon for his analysis of the binding on the Rosslyn-Hay Manuscript, also for the copy of the extract from *Orcades seu Rerum Orcadensium* regarding the testimony in 1446 of Thomas, Bishop of Orkney and Zetland, to Eric, King of Norway.

Sir Gilbert Hay's translations of *The Buke of the Law of Armys* and *The Buke of the Ordre of Knychthude* and *The Buke of the Governance of Princes* are in manuscript in the National Library of Scotland, taken over from the old Advocates Library. So is the Roslin Missal. In the Midlothian County Library are copies of the *Registrum Ecclesie Collegiae of Midlothian* and the *Registrum S. Marie de Neubotle, Abbacie Cisterciensis, 1140–1528* (Edinburgh, 1849), which attest to the continuing connections between the St Clairs of Roslin, the Cistercian monks and the Templars. They are confirmed from the same source by the *Munimenta de Melros*, containing documents from Melrose Abbey dating between the twelfth and sixteenth centuries.

An interesting work by Dr Jean-Pierre Bayard, *La Tradition cachée des cathédrales: Du symbolisme mediéval à la réalisation architecturale* (Saint-Jean-de-Braye, France, 1990), confirms the principles of Templar and sacred architecture demonstrated also at Rosslyn Chapel. He deals fully with the circle containing the square and the octagon as seen at Neuvy-Saint-Sépulchre, Germigny-des-Prés, Laon, Metz and Rampillon, at the Temple in London and La Vera Cruz de Segovia, and in the fortified churches of Saintes-Maries-de-la-Mer and Simorre near Auch.

12. THE FALL OF THE SINCLAIRS

Essential reading on the St Clair Earls of Orkney are two articles by Barbara E. Crawford, 'The Fifteenth-Century Genealogy of the Earls of Orkney and its Reflection on the Contemporary Political and Cultural Situation in the Earldom', Vol.10, *Medieval Scandinavia*, 1976, and 'William Sinclair, Earl of Orkney, and His Family: A Study in the Politics of Survival'.

Gavin Douglas called Lord Henry Sinclair 'Fader of bukis . . .' Father Hay is always indispensable on the history of the St Clair family. Some idea of the riches of the Sinclair family in the fifteenth century can be found in the Inventory of the Goods of Alexander Southerland, mcccclvi, reprinted by Father Hay, which records his gift of a chalice to the new College Church of Roslin. The Black Rood and the Newbattle Silver Cross in Durham Cathedral are variously described in *Antiquities of the Abbey and Cathedral Church of Durham* and *Rites of Durham* published by the Surtees Society.

In the National Library of Scotland are preserved the Bond of Mary of Guise of 3 June, 1546; the Acts of the Lords in Council on Public Affairs of 21 March, 1545; the Right of Passage from Marie of Guise to Sir William St Clair of 14 June, 1556; her Commission to him of 20 January, 1559; and the arrest warrant of William and Oliver Sinclair of 1 September, 1567. The account of the benefactions of Henry, Earl of Orkney, is taken from R.W. Saint-Clair, *The Saint-Clairs of the Isles* (op. cit.), and from Thomas Hearne, *The Antiquities of Great Britain* (London, 1735). Important on the period is *The Renaissance and Reformation in Scotland* (Ian Cowan and Duncan Shaw eds., Edinburgh, 1983), and David Stevenson, *The Origins of Freemasonry: Scotland's Century, 1590–1710* (Cambridge, 1988). The Schaw petition of 1600 and the Masonic petition of 1630 and the St Clair renunciation of 1736 are reprinted and analysed in David Murray Lyon, *History of the Lodge of Edinburgh* (Edinburgh, 1873), and Robert Frere Gould, *The History of Freemasonry* (2 vols., London, 1885). Although both historians admitted the authenticity of the documents, they were hostile to St Clair claims to the hereditary Grand Mastership, favouring Protestant belief in the Hanoverian Succession, which was opposed to the St Clairs' covert support of the Stewarts and Catholicism.

The earlier and seminal book by William Alexander Laurie, *The History of Free Masonry and The Grand Lodge of Scotland* (Edinburgh, 1850), fully supported the St Clair position as hereditary Grand Masters over the period in question. The final mob attack on Rosslyn Chapel and Castle took place on 11 December, 1688, during the Protestant 'Glorious Revolution', and was recorded by Father Hay in his history of the St Clairs of Rosslyn (op. cit.); Dorothy Wordsworth visited the ruined chapel with the poet William Wordsworth on 17 September, 1803, and wrote of its melancholy and exquisite beauty in her diary.

13. THE SUBVERSIVE MASONS

David Murray Lyon's work on Freemasonry and that of William Alexander Laurie have already been cited. *Parentalia, or Memoirs of the Family of the Wrens; but Chiefly of Sir Christopher Wren* was compiled by his son Christopher and published in London in 1750. The downfall of the St Clairs as a result of their loyalty to the Stewarts is described in the memoirs of John, Master of St Clair, quoted in Charles Mackie, *Historical Description of the Chapel and Castle of Roslin and the Caverns of Hawthornden* (Edinburgh, 1830). Robert Brydon writes well on 'The German Tradition, the Scottish Knights and the Mystery of the Holy Grail', *The Scottish Knights Templars*, Winter, 1984/5. Peter Partner, *The Murdered Magicians: The Templars and Their Myth* (Oxford, 1982), shows how the rebirth of Templarism took place in Germany, where egalitarian Freemasonry was resisted by an elitist society, and where a demand existed for a version of the Masonic craft acceptable to conservative taste. The work of Nicolas de Bonneville has already been cited. There is excellent information on the Scots and French Templar and Masonic connections, and on the influence of Masonry on the American Revolution, in Michael Baigent and Richard Lee, *The Temple and the Lodge* (London, 1989). The chart of the Boyne Society is described in the record of *The 1798 Rebellion in Ireland: A Bicentenary Exhibition*, 3 April–31 August, 1998, compiled and edited by W.A. Maguire, for the Ulster Museum, Belfast. Also important is C.S. Kilpatrick, 'The Period 1690–1911', in *History of the Royal Arch Purple Order* (Belfast, 1993).

14. THE SECRET SCROLL

I must express again my gratitude to the Brothers of Lodge Kirkwall Kilwinning No. 38[2] for their co-operation in this inquiry. I have delivered a lecture to them on my historical findings regarding their Scroll, and have provided them with details, so that they may produce a definitive commentary on the Scroll. As I am not a Mason, their choice must determine the content of their document. They have also made copyright all their reproductions of the Scroll and of their commentary, and their permission must be sought to view the Scroll, which will continue to hang in the Kirkwall Lodge.

The commentator on the Kirkwall Scroll, Brother G.W. Speth, also described the Templar connection with the legend of Hiram and its transfer from the Near East, in his *Builders' Rites and Ceremonies: The Folk Lore of Masonry* (Ars Quatuor Coronatorum Pamphlet, London, 1951). For additional information on the place of Melchizedek in British Lodges, I have used Arthur Edward Waite, *The Hidden Church of the Holy Graal* (London, 1909); Bernard E. Jones, *Freemason's Book of the Royal Arch* (London, 1957); and with reservations, John J. Robinson, *Born in Blood – The Lost Secrets of Freemasonry* (London, 1990). Also significant is the reference in the Dumfries No. 4 Manuscript of 1710: 'No lodge or corum of masons shall give the Royal Secret to any suddenly but upon great deliberation.' A.G. Mackey produced *The History of Freemasonry* (new ed., Avenel, New Jersey, 1996); see also his *Encyclopedia of Freemasonry* (rev. ed., 2 vols., Chicago, 1946).

Extraordinary and compelling is Evelyn Edson, *Mapping Time and Space: How Medieval Mapmakers Viewed Their World* (British Library, 1997). The freshness and vision of this pioneer work enabled me to interpret the Kirkwall Scroll.

15. SCIENCE AND GRACE

I am most indebted to R.E.M. Hedges and D.C. Owen at the Research Laboratory for Archaeology and the History of Art with its Radiocarbon Accelerator Unit; the poem on wisdom is by Father Thomas Merton.